Thinking in Thin Air

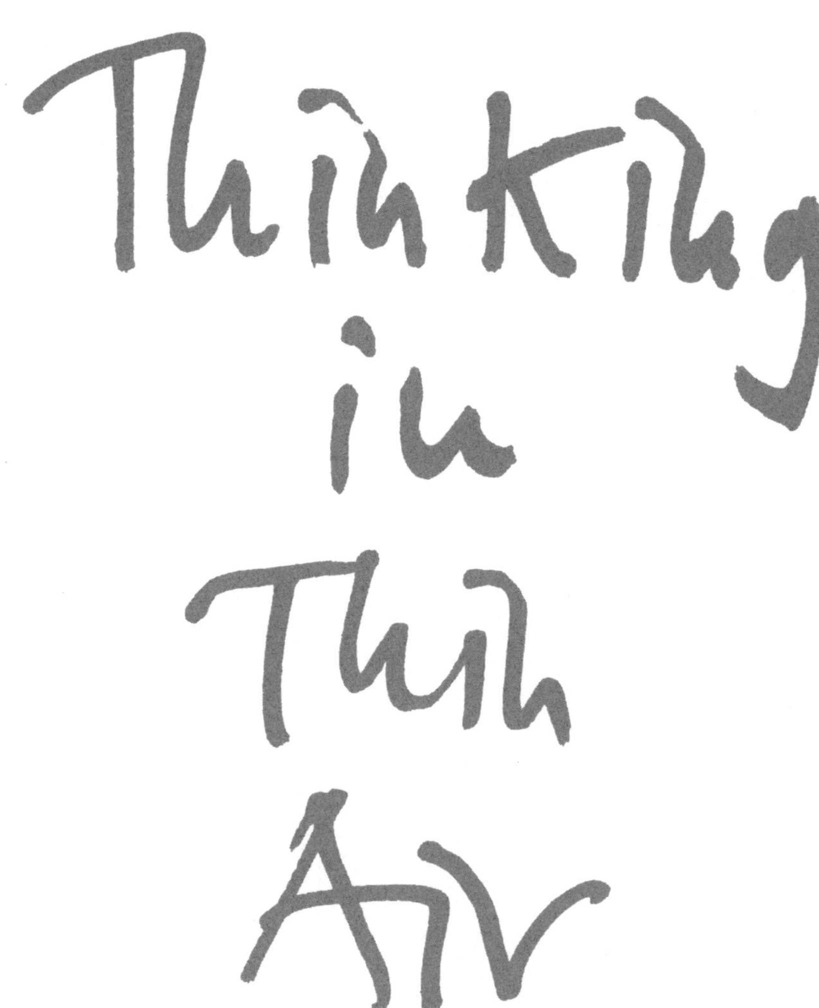

Anthology of a Decade: Engadin Art Talks
Edited by Finn Canonica

Lars Müller Publishers

Cristina Bechtler, Founder
About Engadin Art Talks

Where does the blue of the sky end? Since the Enlightenment, scientific and artistic research and discovery have always, in practice, been accompanied and driven by subjective wishes, hopes, expectations and promises.

In the Engadin mountain village of Zuoz, high in the Swiss Alps, thought leaders and disruptive minds gather every winter for the E.A.T. / Engadin Art Talks–a platform recognized internationally for bringing together leading artists, architects, writers, scientists and innovative thinkers from across the globe. Our mission is to enable meetings and concentrated exchange between creative minds of the most varied disciplines and an international audience. The talks create a platform for exchange, innovation and inspiration amid the distinctive, stimulating and stunning beauty of the Engadin: a place of inspiration for artists such as the Giacometti family, Segantini, and Nietzsche, as well as many artists nowadays. Over the past ten years more than 150 speakers have presented their ideas and visions in relation to a challenging, annually changing, socially relevant subject. The events continue to inspire and surprise.

The Engadin Art Talks were initiated by myself together with Hans Ulrich Obrist of the Serpentine Galleries and art historian Philip Ursprung of the ETH Zürich. My infinite gratitude goes to the curators Hans Ulrich Obrist, Philip Ursprung, Bice Curiger, Director of the Fondation Vincent van Gogh and Daniel Baumann, Director of the Kunsthalle Zurich, for their guidance, enthusiasm and friendship. A big thank you equally to all the speakers for their contributions, commitment and time.

Finn Canonica, Editor
About this book

Suddenly the constellation is right. Thoughts and images are in tension with each other. A seemingly eclectic ensemble of ideas, figures and forms results in something new for the listener. This coupling of figures of thought across different disciplines is the essence of the E.A.T./Engadin Art Talks. One could almost say: E.A.T. is not an event, but a process. This book also follows this principle. Its variety of topics, and the contributions from different cultural circles and epochs, reflect the border-breaking interests of the annual event in the Engadin mountains. Seen in this way, this is a publication not so much about E.A.T. as it is in the spirit of the event. One can start at any point in the book; there is no "correct" way through this collection of texts and images. Rather, the emphasis is on the recognition of underground elective affinities.

Engadin Art Talks
Location

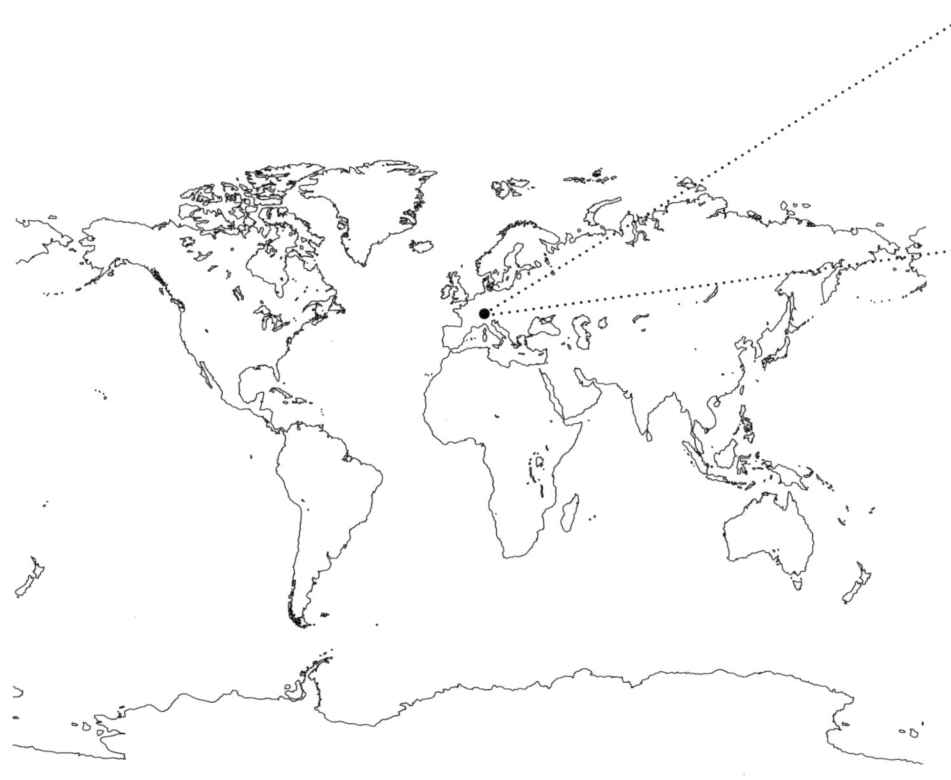

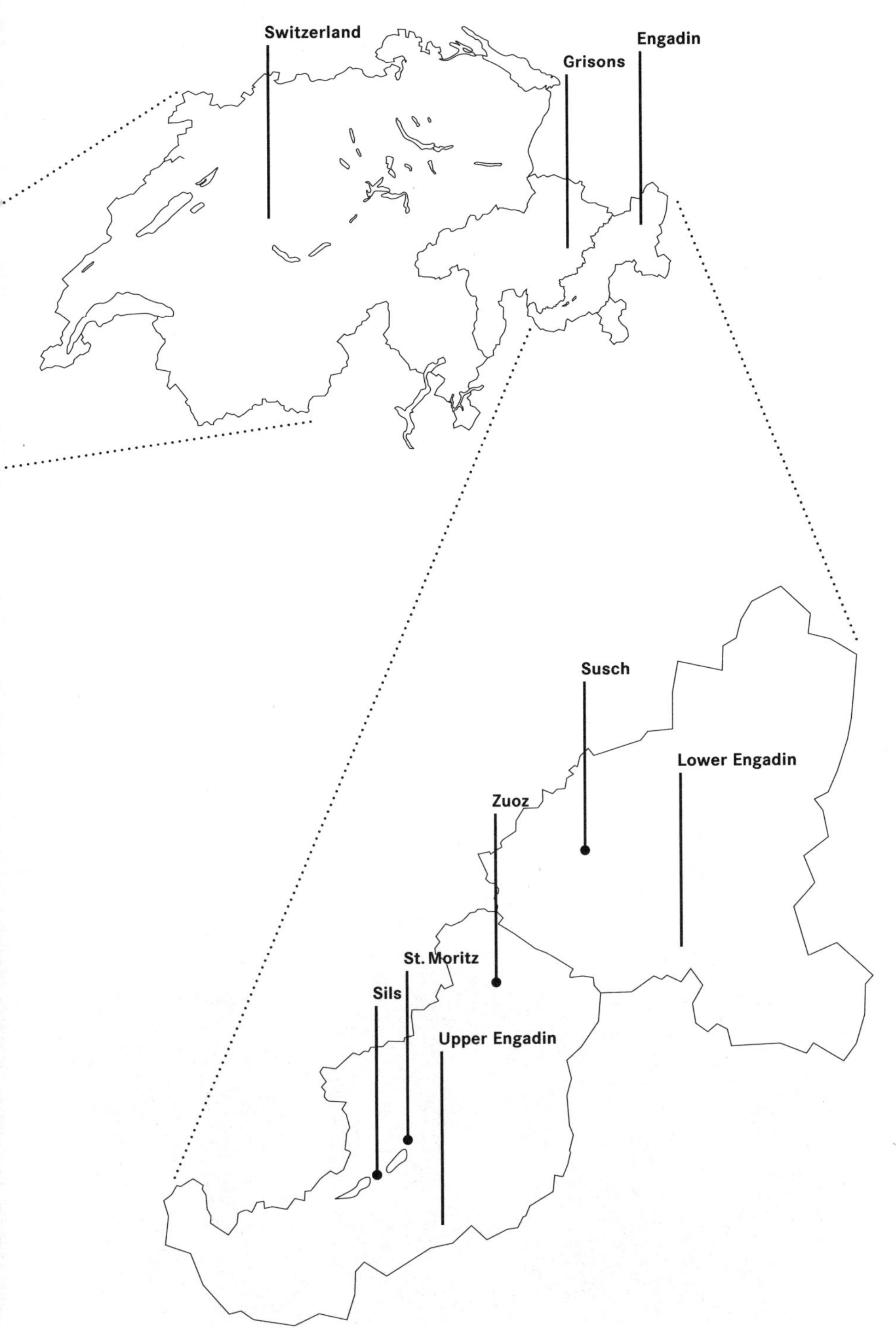

Switzerland
Grisons
Engadin
Susch
Lower Engadin
Zuoz
St. Moritz
Sils
Upper Engadin

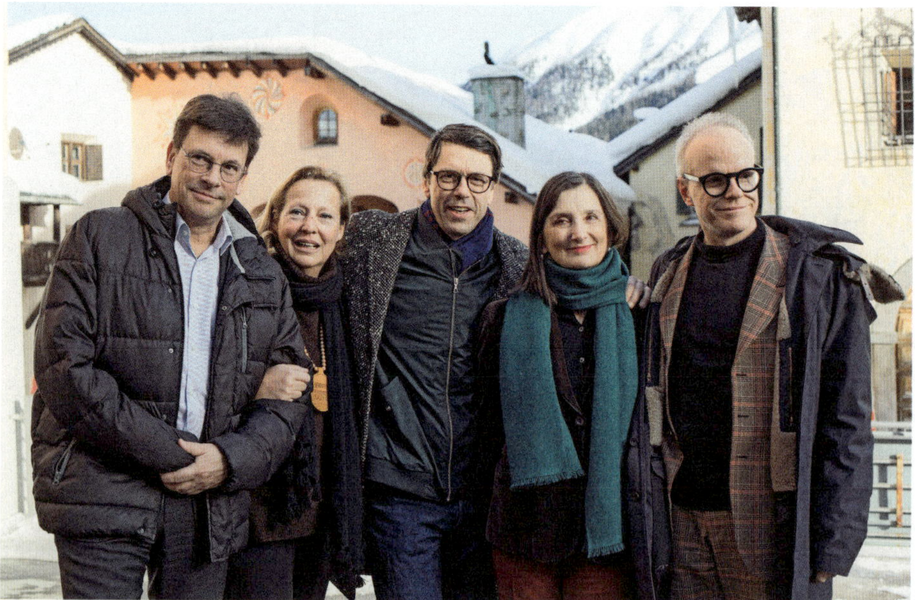

The curators and the founder: Philip Ursprung, Cristina Bechtler, Daniel Baumann, Bice Curiger, Hans Ulrich Obrist

PHILIP URSPRUNG is a professor of art history and architecture in the Department of Architecture at the ETH Zurich. Ursprung earned his PhD in art history at Freie Universität Berlin after studying in Geneva, Vienna, and Berlin.

CRISTINA BECHTLER is a Swiss art collector and publicist, and the founder and director of Ink Tree Editions, a publishing house that publishes art books.

DANIEL BAUMANN is currently the curator and director of the Kunsthalle Zurich. He was the recipient of the Swiss Award for Best Curator (2006) and Special Advisor for Frieze (2009/10). In previous years he was the curator of Adolf Wölfli Foundation at the Kunstmuseum Bern and the *Carnegie International* in Pittsburgh (2013). Baumann was a contributing writer for *Exhibition #1*. He is is an art historian, curator and writer for *Kunst-Bulletin, Parkett* and *Spike Art Quarterly.*

BICE CURIGER is a Swiss art historian, curator, critic and co-founder of *Parkett.* In 2011 she became the first solo female curator of the Venice Biennale. She is currently the Artistic Director of the Fondation Vincent Van Gogh Arles. For twenty years she was a curator at the Kunsthaus Zürich and she has published numerous texts and books on artists such as Meret Oppenheim, Sigmar Polke, Katharina Fritsch, Pipilotti Rist, Peter Fischli and David Weiss.

HANS ULRICH OBRIST is Artistic Director of the Serpentine Galleries, London. Prior to this, he was the curator of the Musée d'Art Moderne de la Ville, Paris. Since his first show *World Soup (The Kitchen Show)* in 1991 he has curated more than 250 shows. Obrist's recent publications include *Do It: The Compendium, Think Like Clouds, Ai Weiwei Speaks, Ways of Curating* and new volumes of his *Conversation Series.*

2010   THE CRYSTAL CHAIN
          Doug Aitken, Bechtler Stiftung, Cerith Wyn Evans,
          Simone Forti, Bijoy Jain, Kasper König, Josiah McElheny,
          Philippe Rahm, Camilo Restrepo, Hans-Jörg Ruch,
          Beatrix Ruf, Nina von Albertini

2011   MAPPING THE ALPS
          Nairy Baghramian, Andrea Deplazes, Hamish Fulton,
          Nikolaus Hirsch, Sarah Morris, Gianni Pettena, Walid Raad,
          Ritu Sarin, Kai Schlenter, Tenzing Sonam, Philip Ursprung,
          Jan von Brevern, Lawrence Weiner, Peter Zumthor

2012   VISIONS FOR THE ALPS
          Vito Acconci, Ron Arad, Raqs Media Collective, Hans Danuser,
          Christophe Frédéric Girot, Jefferson Hack, Arthur Loretz,
          Paulo Sergio Niemeyer, Mai-Thu Perret, Tobias Rehberger,
          François Roche, Rolf Sachs, Urban-Think-Tank, Philip Ursprung

2013   GHOSTS & THE UNCANNY
          Iso Camartin, Kurt Derungs, Dan Graham, Zvi Hecker,
          Christian Holstad, Bethan Huws, Hubert Klumpner,
          Tim Krohn, Jonathan Ledgard, Tobias Madison, Ernesto Neto,
          Katrin Sigurdardóttir, Michael Steiner, Not Vital

2016   TRACES & FRAGMENTS
          Alfredo Brillembourg, Matthias Brunner, Sylvie Fleury,
          Giorgio Griffa, Joseph Grigely, Christian Jankowski,
          Koo Jeong A, Kasper König, Ibrahim Mahama, Elli Mosayebi,
          Albert Oehlen, Rachel Rose, Michael Schindhelm,
          Julian Schnabel, Pascale Marthine Tayou, Eyal Weizman,
          Nina Zschocke

2017   SNOW & DESERT
          Subhankar Banerjee, Julian Charrière, Manuel Herz,
          Francis Kéré, Christine Levy, Heinz Mack, Eileen Myles, Emily
          Scott, Hito Steyerl, Oscar Tuazon, Not Vital,
          Rüdiger Wehner

2018   SIDE COUNTRY SIDE
          Aric Chen, Kashef Chowdhury, Claudia Comte, Bice Curiger,
          Rem Koolhaas, Niklas Maak, Mai-Thu Perret, Adrian Villar Rojas,
          Emily Segal, Pacôme Thiellement, Philip Ursprung

2019   GRACE & GRAVITY
          Cecilia Bengolea, Francesco Bonami, Elizabeth Diller,
          Ravit Helled, Lena Henke, Thomas Hirschhorn,
          Joanna Leśnierowska, Isabel Nolan, Smiljan Radic,
          Tomás Saraceno, Heji Shin, Juergen Teller

2020   SILENT—LISTEN
          Virgil Abloh, Ziba Ardalan, Tatiana Bilbao, David Claerbout,
          Emanuele Coccia, Charles Gaines, Cyrill Gutsch, Jeppe Hein,
          Charlotte Jarvis, Erling Kagge, Jeanette Kuo, Isabel Mundry,
          Emeka Ogboh, Ben Okri, Rolf Sachs, Marianna Simnett,
          Wolf Singer, Chris Watson

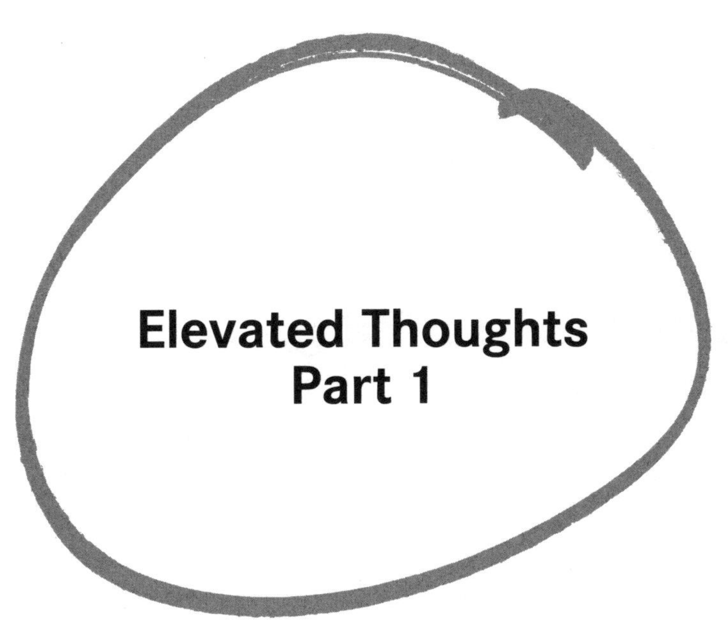

Elevated Thoughts
Part 1

Markus Breitschmid

"Architektur der Berge":
Bruno Taut

"Architektur der Berge" is the title of the second chapter of Bruno Taut's head-turning *Alpine Architecture,* the manifesto-like tract published in 1919. All but one of the drawings printed here come from that chapter. The use of the untranslated German title is owed to the double-meaning inherent in the wording of "Architektur der Berge"–a double-meaning that would make the translation far less straightforward than one would like it to be. However, this is not a loss. The dual meaning introduces from the outset a hallmark characteristic inherent in all of Bruno Taut's œuvre. At the one pole, "Architektur der Berge" refers to the architectonic of mountains in a structural-tectonic-formal sense, maybe not so much about its actual geological formation, but more about extending the magnitude in both space and time. Physical matter gets dissolved. At the end of that trajectory stand cosmological aspirations. At the other pole, "Architektur der Berge" refers to actual structures, buildings as it were, that will inhabit mountains.

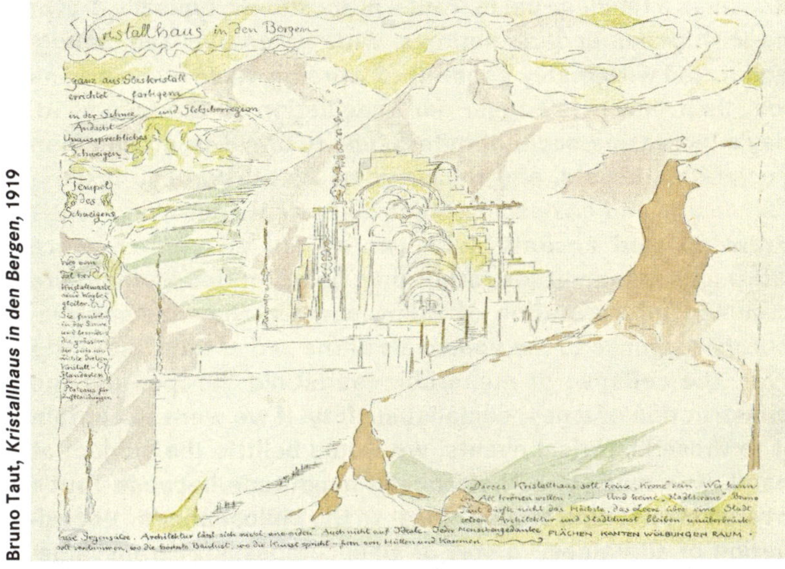

Bruno Taut, *Kristallhaus in den Bergen,* 1919

Taut's drawings are defined by the enormous distance between these two poles, yet both are organically part of an all-encompassing notion of building. One pole is dedicated to building a metaphysical home between the "here" and the "there," the other pole stands for the desire of building an actual home proper made out of materials such as glass, steel, or concrete. This distance exists in all representations of Taut's work, for example, in his most famous building, the famed

Glass House for the *Werkbund Exhibition* in Cologne in 1914, and it has an even more overwhelming presence in his theoretical body of work. What we witness is the simultaneous presence of a matter-of-fact objectivity (the embrace of the newest and most advanced technical possibilities) and a quixotic otherworldliness (the projecting of fantastic spatial temperament in its widest imaginable sense). Without these concurrent qualities in mind, Taut's drawings remain largely inaccessible, despite their beauty of composition and coloration. The ideational wealth of the drawings would be lost.

The extreme range is also the justification as to why it is of value to keep looking at these drawings today. Presenting these drawings here one full century after their publication is not simply the presentation of a noteworthy historical artifact. Rather, it is exactly the enormity between the rigid built fact of buildings and the concurrent promise for the extension of our possibilities inherent in these structures that gives these drawings a timeless value. Taut's propositions, typically drawn up with pencil and, sometimes, with watercolor and usually annotated with highly condensed wording, have by no means lost their power to trigger our imagination. In the face of today's increasing societal heterogeneity in which no common social ideal exists, and therefore no institution can issue a convincing and coalescing order that orients our lives, Taut's drawings and accompanying words are of a much more Nietzschean magnitude rather than being limited by the more common interpretation of them, namely, the then-contemporary response to the upheavals of the end of the First World War, the collapse of monarchic-feudal old Europe, and the construction of a new socialist society. If we were to contain it to those historical events, we would belittle the subject at hand. It is more of a Nietzschean magnitude because Taut's overall proposition stands closer to the philosopher's "Reevaluation of all Values," a sort of all-encompassing "transvaluation," and thus exceeds by far the scope of war and political revolution. The Latin dictum on the cover page of *Alpine Architecture* addresses this scope head-on: "Aedificare necesse est, vivre non est necesse" (Building is necessary, life is not necessary). Of course, for the benefit of the reintroduction of Taut's drawings in this volume, it serve as a happy coincidence that Friedrich Nietzsche—who spent summers in the Alpine settlement of Sils-Maria and conceived his *Zarathustra* while pacing the Engadin Valley-housed *Zarathustra,* the metaphorical inceptor of that grandest of transvaluations, high up on a mountain peak, presumably in a nearby Alpine mountain. In any case, what the philosopher conceived is, too, an act of building. Therefore when Taut, the architect, fabricated his drawings, he fully embraced the fact that his work ought to embody a sort of reevaluation of all values as well. Only such work could carry existential significance for humankind.

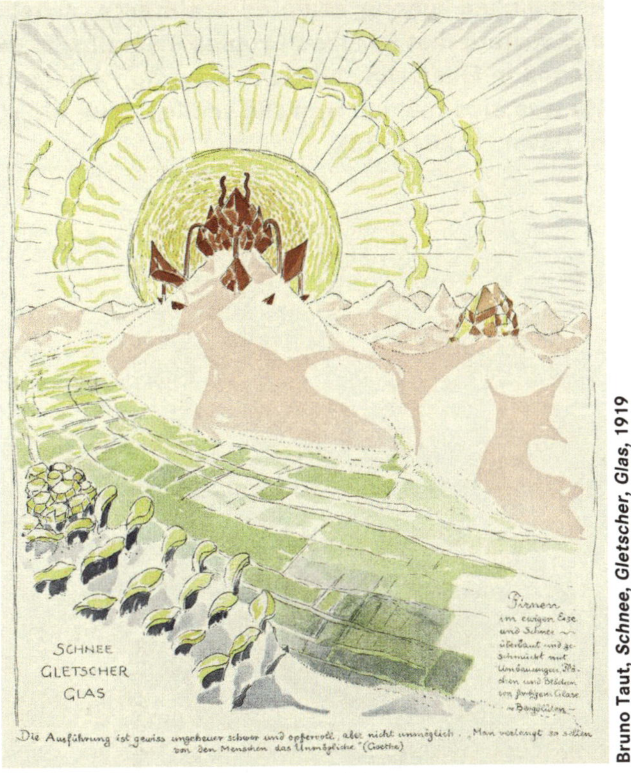

Bruno Taut, *Schnee, Gletscher, Glas,* 1919

Alpine Architecture was the work of the German architect Bruno Taut (1880–1938), who was responsible for several groundbreaking buildings such as the Träger-Verkaufskontor pavilion in Berlin (1910), the Monument des Eisens in Leipzig (1913), and the aforementioned Glass House. Taut was also the architect of several large housing developments, including the famed Hufeisensiedlung (1925–1933) and Onkel Toms Hütte (1926–1931), both of which are located in Berlin and are listed as UNESCO World Heritage sites. Taut's involvement with larger public and social questions is even more apparent, however, in his prolific theoretical œuvre. Besides *Alpine*

Architecture, Taut published *Architecture Program* (1918), in many ways the ideational precursor to Walter Gropius's Bauhaus program; *Die Stadtkrone* (The City Crown, 1919); *Die Auflösung der Stadt* (The Dissolution of the City, 1920)—produced in conjunction with *Alpine Architecture;* and *Der Weltbaumeister* (The World Building Master, 1920). Taut spearheaded the *Gläserne Kette* (1919–1920), alternatively translated as either *Glass Chain* or *Crystal Chain,* a correspondence established among selected architects, artists, engineers, and writers that included Gropius, Paul Gosch, Wenzel Hablik, Hermann Finsterlin and Hans Scharoun among their number. He was also the editor of the seminal journal *Frühlicht* (Light of Dawn, 1920–1923).

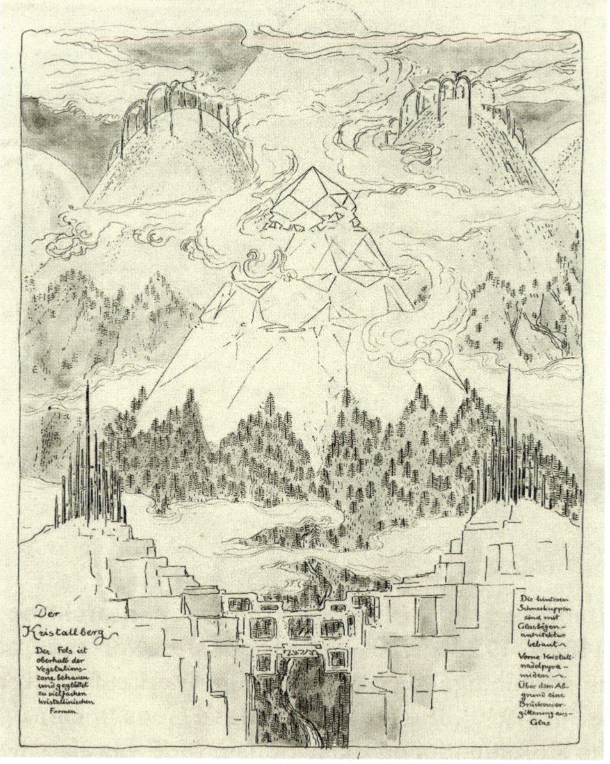

Bruno Taut, *Der Kristallberg,* 1919

It is helpful to view the drawings of *Alpine Architecture* in the context of these other undertakings. Looked at in unison, each work gains from the others. *Alpine Architecture* was conceptualized in 1917, fabricated in spring and summer of 1918, and published by Folkwang Publishers in Hagen-Germany in 1919. To label *Alpine Architecture* a treatise creates difficulties for any traditional conception of the genre. Its formal presentation is as radical as its content. It consists of thirty annotated drawings (twenty-two monochromatic and eight colored plates of 39.5 cm by 33.5 cm, a title page, and a table of contents page, which depict a tour of the fundamental act of building at all scales—from "Kristallhaus" (Crystal House), to "Architektur der Berge" (Mountain Architecture), to "Der Alpenbau" (Buildings of the Alps), to "Erdrindenbau" (Terrestrial Building). In its fifth and final part, "Sternbau" (Interstellar Building), the work addresses interstellar space and the beyond with such notions as "the nameless" and "the great nothing."

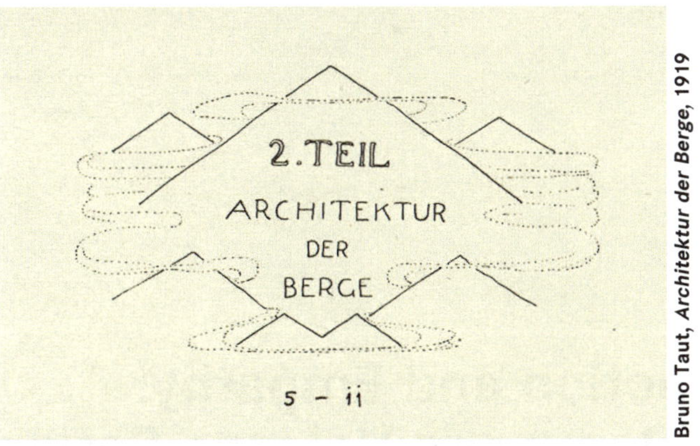

Bruno Taut, Architektur der Berge, 1919

Taut's drawings are also difficult to decipher if one does not consider the annotations. The depictions are often curiously unconcrete. Indeed, from an architectural point of view, the drawings lack the plasticity of actual spatial configurations. For this reason, the annotations are of great importance for understanding the work. Annotations used in the drawings depicted here—such as "Crystal House in the Mountains," "The Architecture of Framework of Space Open to the Universe," "Valley Transformed into A Flower," "The Crystal Mountain," or "The Rock Cathedral"—not only establish the distance between the aforementioned poles of "home as a building" and "home as a world," but the same annotations enliven our engagement with the drawings and then, finally, at least partially, resolve the tensions between signified and signifier—the ability to empathically comprehend the idea of the interconnections between the world and art.

MARKUS BREITSCHMID is a Swiss architectural theoretician and a professor of architecture at the Virginia Polytechnic Institute.

Philip Ursprung

Abstraction and Empathy: Hans Danuser's Volcano Series

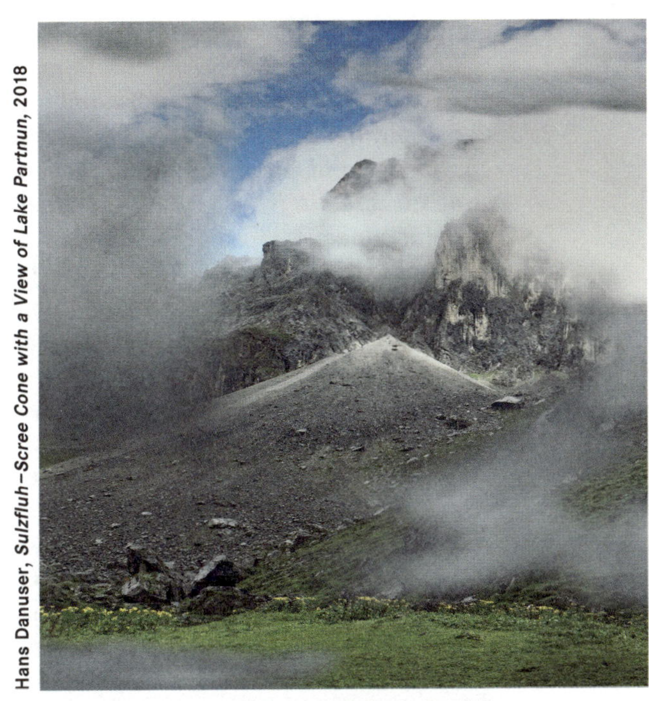

Hans Danuser, *Sulzfluh–Scree Cone with a View of Lake Partnun*, 2018

Hans Danuser's digital color photograph titled *Sulzfluh Geröll-kegel* (2018) shows a mountain landscape against a light blue sky streaked with patches of fog and clouds. A bright green meadow with yellow flowers extends into the foreground. In the middle ground is a cone of scree in various shades of gray, white and black. Towering in the background is the gray-bluish mountain massif. The fog partially covers the mountain's silhouette. The form and contour of the rock formation fragmentarily shines through the veil of clouds. At first glance the image of the stormy mountain landscape and the image composition, which follows the time-proven rules of the golden ratio, appear quite conventional. What is unexpected, however, is the shape of the cone of scree which draws the viewer's attention like a magnet. Sunlight shines through a break in the clouds, highlighting the figure of the cone like a spotlight. Its bright edge contrasts with the darker background. It looks like it was drawn with a ruler, as if man had intervened in this environment shaped by the forces of nature.

In their minds viewers complete the figure, making it a triangle. Placed with geometric precision in the exact center of the image, it seems as if the figure is taking the place of the almost invisible mountaintop. Instead of a picture of the Sulzfluh mountain, a general, abstract sign signifies "mountain." Viewers can simultaneously see the image and read the sign. The chiaroscuro of shades of white and gray creates an illusion of depth similar to a trompe-l'oeil. Given the two-dimensional composition of the image, it is not entirely clear whether the cone of scree is freestanding—in other words, whether it is a circular cone—or whether it extends from the foot of the mountain flank to the saddle. The tip of the triangle could be the apex of a cone, but also the vanishing point of a central-perspective view. It is highly unlikely for a circular cone—meaning something man-made, be it mining or tunnel construction waste or the waste of some other huge construction project—to exist in this location, yet it is impossible to obtain absolute certainty. Like an ambiguous image or *vexierbild*, the photograph stirs the imagination. The tension between image and sign, seeing and knowing mesmerizes the viewer.

Danuser took the picture with an iPhone. He probably didn't plan to photograph specific subjects during his mountain hike in the spring of 2018, in which case he would have probably brought a different camera with him. On the other hand, a professional camera on a tripod would have made it very hard to respond in a timely manner to the special formation of the clouds and capture the brief moment when the light makes the cone glow. In any case, as a tool the camera as such is less crucial to Danuser's practice than the presentation of the prints. Since he regards the photograph not as a neutral carrier of meaning but, rather, as a tangible, material object in space, he focuses his energy on the dispositif, that is, on the dimension, the framing, the printing technique, materiality and placement on the wall or floor.

Even when travelling light, Danuser inevitably carries with him the long history of artistic engagement with the subject of mountains. From Giovanni Segantini's light-suffused paintings of the High Alps in the 1890s, Ferdinand Hodler's paintings of the Savoy Alps from the early twentieth century and Ernst Ludwig Kirchner's colorful depictions of the Davos landscape in the 1920s to Ansel Adam's photographs of Yellowstone and Yosemite National Parks, Albert Steiner's black-and-white photographs of the Engadin in the 1930s and 1940s and Armin Linke's epic film *Alpi* (2011), a long thread of explorations of the subject of mountains runs through art history. Irrespective of this tradition, Danuser also pursues his very own project on the subject of mountains. Like his other projects, such as *In Vivo*, the *Frozen Embryo Series* and *Erosionen*—which could be described as "artistic research," if the term weren't so overused these days—it is a long-term project.

System and Fragment

The subdivision of his own oeuvre in series that often drag on for years is indicative of the romantic impulse pervading Danuser's work. He understands the oeuvre as a practice which comprises more than the mere sum of the individual parts. Each individual artwork in this regard has the character of a fragment whose role increases in complexity in connection with other fragments. Often rather opaque to viewers, the segmentation into series divided by numbers and subcategories is characteristic of his aim to combine the singularity of art with the generality of science. It is an ambitious endeavour, similar to what the architect and theorist Josep Lluís Mateo once described, in a different context, as a tension between "system and fragment."[1] And it may be compared to the seminal theoretical considerations the art historian Wilhelm Worringer presented in his dissertation, submitted to the University of Bern in 1907, in which he sought to grasp the tension between the terms "Abstraction and Empathy." To Worringer, whose studies drawing on Alois Riegl and Heinrich Wölfflin shaped the theory of abstraction, art and nature are two radically separate phenomena: "Our investigations proceed from the presupposition that the work of art, as an autonomous organism, stands beside nature on equal terms and, in its deepest and innermost essence, devoid of any connection with it, in so far as by nature is understood the visible surface of things. Natural beauty is on no account to be regarded as a condition of the work of art, despite the fact that in the course of evolution it seems to have become a valuable element in the work of art, and to some extent indeed positively identical with it."[2] Worringer's objective was to break away from a Eurocentric art history with its focus on classical art and develop a universal, time-transcending aesthetic allowing a coherent consideration of both non-European art forms and most recent European art. Although Worringer doesn't elaborate on it in his dissertation, this also includes the consideration of the then contemporary art of Expressionism and Cubism. As he put it: "Modern aesthetics, which has taken the decisive step from aesthetic objectivism to aesthetic subjectivism, i.e. which no longer takes the aesthetic as the starting-point of its investigations, but proceeds from the behaviour of the contemplating subject, culminates in a doctrine that may be characterized by the broad general name of the theory of empathy.... the basic purpose of my essay is to show that this modern aesthetics, which proceeds from the concept of empathy, is inapplicable to wide tracts of art history.... We regard as this counter-pole an aesthetics which proceeds not from man's urge to empathy, but from his urge to abstraction. Just as the urge to empathy as a pre-assumption of aesthetic experience finds its gratification in the beauty of the organic, so the urge to abstraction finds its beauty in the life-denying inorganic, in the crystalline or, in general terms, in all abstract law and necessity."[3]

> According to Danuser, the trigger for the volcanoes project was the abstract "delta" sign, a shape approximating an isosceles triangle, which the Zürich mathematician Andrew Barbour drew into the shaly sand during a 1991 excursion to Grisons.[4] Danuser photographed the drawing in the sand and subsequently used the image in various forms. The spontaneous act of scratching a figure into the sand with a stick—rather than with chalk on slate or with a pencil on paper—must have aroused the photographer's curiosity. It is reminiscent of the Greek origin of the word "photography," which means "writing with light," and of the imprint of rays of light on the light-sensitive emulsion of the negative. The triangle spontaneous drawn in the sand shows evidence of the stick's slightly irregular handling. Rather than a precise line, it consists of a small valley dug into the sand. The edges are raised like slopes. It is a kind of miniature landscape, much like the surface of an exposed photographic negative—or a developed positive—consists of crystal landscapes when seen under the microscope.

In itself, there's nothing unusual about someone drawing the fourth letter of the Greek alphabet, which also appears in various functions in mathematics. Yet for Hans Danuser the artist it becomes the starting point of a game informed by both chance and rules. Initially, he rotated the image in his series *Rotation vom Delta zum Berg.* The delta (one that is, to be sure, shown upside down) is twice turned by 90 degrees. At a later stage, the image of the mountain morphs into that of a volcano through the addition of colored hatching to the triangle image in the sand. The hatching results from the photographic paper being coated with color, a process patented by Danuser as "matography." The result is a relief of sorts which, in turn, evokes the surface of the photographic paper as a miniature landscape. Just like certain rock strata in the Alps come to the surface after softer layers have eroded, the colored hatches, dots and lines remain in place during the process of copying and developing the positive. In other words, the photographs are not subsequently colored; rather, the relief-like raised color layers have always been there. They remain in place like barriers at the edges of which the image copied onto the photographic paper's emulsion halts.

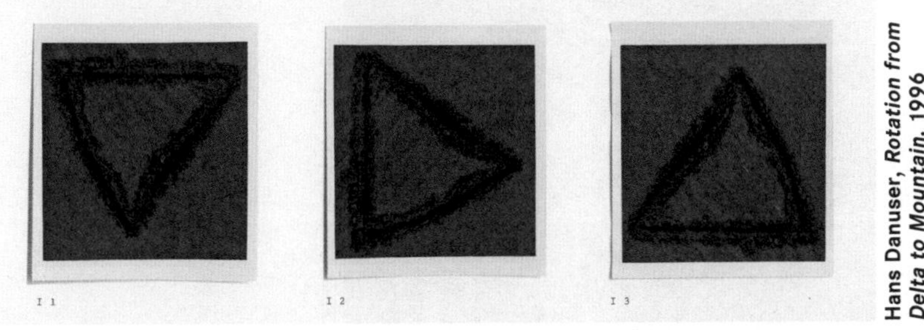

I 1   I 2   I 3

Hans Danuser, *Rotation from Delta to Mountain*, 1996

Tagged Mountains

If we accept that Danuser moves between the two poles of abstraction and empathy or the non-natural and the natural, then his interest in volcanoes is all too understandable. Volcanoes are mountains which, from a distance, look like abstractions of mountains. The unmistakable triangular shape of their cones sticks in every child's mind. Volcanoes create the land and transform it. They make the soil fertile. It would have been impossible, for instance, to feed the traditionally very densely populated island of Java without the incredibly fertile soils as a result of the island's forty-five volcanoes. Moreover, volcanoes have a tremendous potential for destruction.[5] The 1815 volcanic eruption of Mount Tambora released so much ash into the atmosphere that the following two years, which became known as "Years without a Summer," saw disastrous famines in Europe and inscribed themselves into collective memory.

The eruptions of Mount Vesuvius in antiquity and in the seventeenth and eighteenth centuries as well as the 1883 eruption of Krakatoa, the most devastating eruption ever, are among the epochal events of history. Even today, reports of volcanic eruptions are stirring, because they remind us that we are ultimately at the mercy of the forces of nature, regardless of whether they are human-influenced or not.

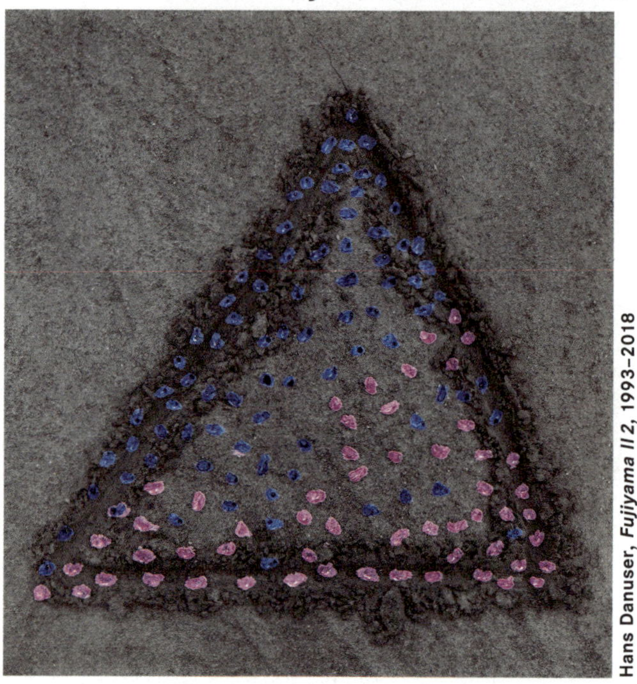

Volcanoes are huge figures against the ground of the landscape. They are neither landscape nor structure, neither dead nor alive. Some volcanoes serve as landmarks for the areas where they stand. Mounts Kilimanjaro, Fuji, Vesuvius and Etna are symbols. In other regions, for example in Chile, Iceland or the island of Java, volcanoes appear as systems. As a group, their impact is different than in the case of a single monument, for they suggest that the volcanoes are interconnected through an invisible network of magma.

Volcanoes are points of entry, openings. Their craters mark the transition from an outside to an inside, from the earth's surface to the interior of the earth, from the visible to the invisible. Entering a volcano creates a sense of partaking in the creation of the earth and being able to reconstruct the formation and transformation of the topography through volcanic rocks.

Standing at the edge of a crater is an experience that is fundamentally different from that of standing on the top of a mountain. A crater may have a highest point, but this can change abruptly with the next eruption.

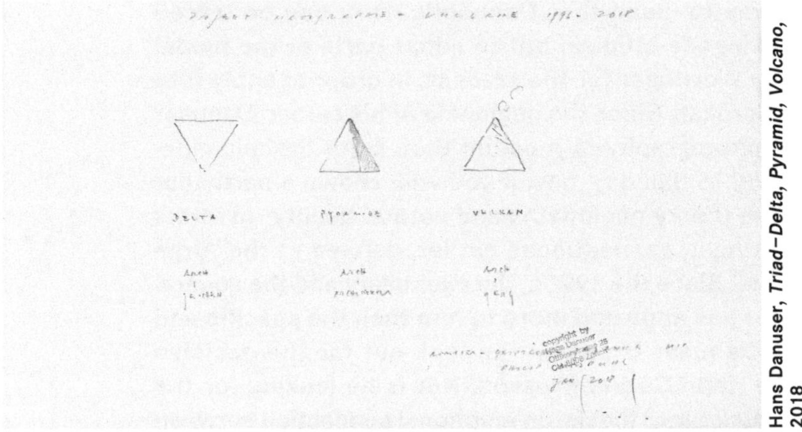

Hans Danuser, *Triad—Delta, Pyramid, Volcano,* 2018

It is not clear how the transition from mountain to volcano occurs in Danuser's work. In *Dreiklang* (Triad), a 2018 drawing, he notes how a delta first turns into a pyramid and then into a volcano. Danuser, who also has a penchant for counting rhymes in his work, i.e. for coincidences arising from fixed rules, doesn't provide reasons for his decision. When we recall Danuser's affinity for sculpture and architecture, we can understand that the pyramid serves as an intermediate stage. In a conversation he mentions that, in 1998, he went on a spontaneous trip to Egypt "solely to see the pyramids and leave immediately thereafter."[6] Once again, it is appropriate to cite Wilhelm Worringer for whom the pyramid was a central argument in his theory of the urge to abstraction. According to Worringer, the pyramid is a "perfect example of Egyptian artistic volition," as it "may equally well be regarded as a sculptural memorial or an architectonic shape."[7] He goes on to quote Alois Riegl: "The architectural ideal of the Ancient Egyptian undoubtedly attained its purest expression in the sepulchral memorial type of the pyramid. Before whichever of the four sides the spectator stands, his eye always perceives merely the uniform plane of the equilateral triangle, whose sharply terminal sides give no reminder of the extension in depth behind them. In comparison with this carefully considered and very acutely emphasized limitation of the outward material appearance within the surface dimensions, the actual utilitarian task-space-construction withdraws completely into the background. It is confined to the provision of a small sepulchral vault with insignificant entrances that are as good as non-existent when looked at from without."[8] The aim here is not in any way to claim that Danuser's work can be traced back to Worringer's studies, but to adopt parts of the model developed by Worringer for the present, in order to apply it to Danuser's approach. Since the beginning of his career, Danuser has viewed photography—a medium that, from the mid-nineteenth century to this day, has, if you will, shown a particular affinity for the theory of empathy and natural beauty—in terms of what Worringer, as mentioned earlier, defined as the "urge to abstraction." Since the 1990s, the exemplary and the general or the regular has appealed more to him then the specific and the unique. Danuser is not on the look-out for the decisive moment like Henri Cartier-Bresson. Nor is he looking for the Barthesian "punctum," that is, an emotional connection between the photographed object and the viewer.[9] Instead, Danuser wants to render visible forces and connections which elude the senses and conceptualization. Accordingly, his photography is not attracted to theater, film or video, but rather to sculpture, architecture and landscape.

> This may explain why, as a photographer, Danuser travels to the volcanoes and visits the pyramids not to actually photograph them but rather to assure himself of their actual existence. From the window of his studio in Davos he could at length look at the Schiahorn and photograph the mountain with its avalanche barriers. Another series is of the Eggberg, another mountaintop marked by avalanche barriers. The mountains in Grisons are not volcanoes. But from afar they may appear somewhat like volcanoes whose peaks also often remain without vegetation on account of the eruptions. Danuser chooses them as a subject for the very reason that they are obviously treated and altered by man. The avalanche barrier is not a blemish in the natural beauty, not evidence of some kind of defect. It rather shows what Danuser, ever since his exploration of the spaces of nuclear energy, gene technology, finance at the beginning of his artistic career and chance and the processes of erosion later on, never tires of pointing out: the places and the never fully well-defined zone where the human and the non-human meet.

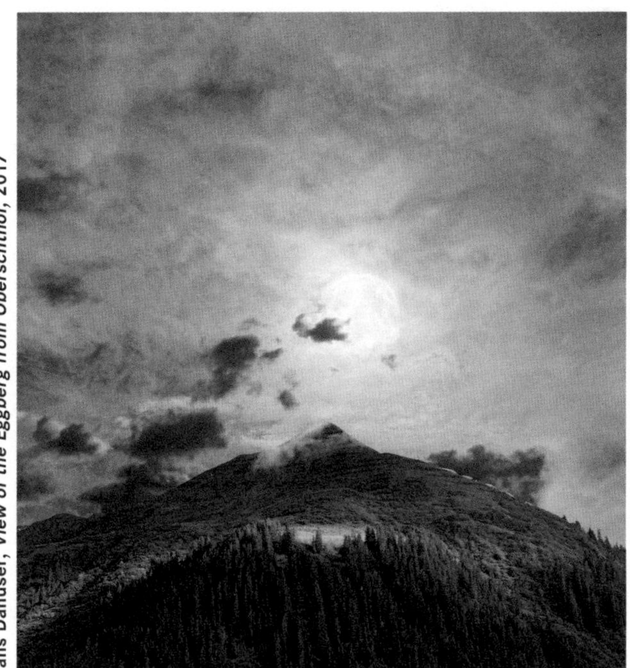

Hans Danuser, *View of the Eggberg from Oberschthof, 2017*

1 See Josep Lluis Mateo, *Sistema i fragment, Quaderns d'arquitectura i urbanisme* 158 (August/September 1983), p. 2 f.
2 Wilhelm Worringer, *Abstraction and Empathy* (Chicago, 1977), p. 3.
3 Ibid., p. 4.
4 The excursion with Professor Barbour and his team took place as part of Hans Danuser's architectural art project *Institutsbilder—Eine Schrift Bild Installation,* University of Zürich, 1991.
5 See Clive Oppenheimer, *Eruptions That Shook the World* (Cambridge, 2011).
6 Hans Danuser in conversation with Philip Ursprung, Zurich, June 2018.
7 Worringer, *Abstraction and Empathy,* p. 90.
8 Ibid., p. 91.
9 See Roland Barthes, *Camera Lucida. Notes on Photography* (New York, 1981).

**Finn Canonica,
Mareike Dittmer and
Sara Masüger**

"The city-mountain contrast is the consumption-production contrast"

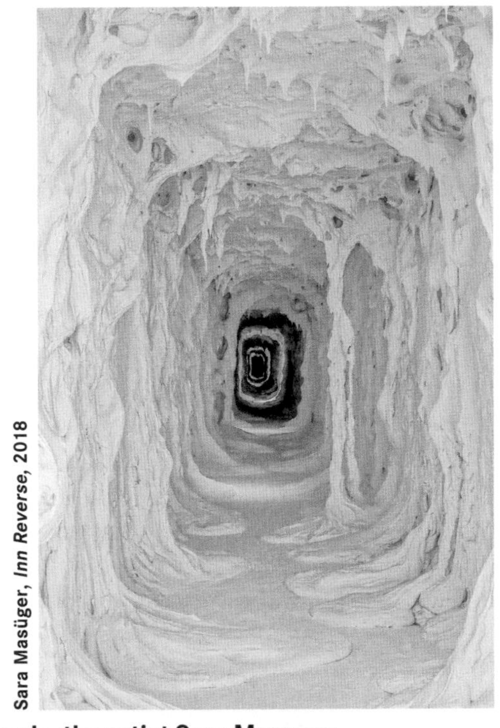

We meet in the Engadin village of Susch—the artist Sara Masuger, Mareike Dittmer, the director of art foundation CH / Muzeum Susch, and Finn Canonica, the editor-in-chief of *Das Magazin.* The idea is very simple: we want to sit around a table and talk about art and mountains and of course the Engadin as well.

Finn Canonica   Sara, you're a Graubünden native, or at least you have local roots, right?

Sara Masüger   Yes, that's correct. But I live and work in Zurich. Still, I have to say: whenever I come back here to the mountains, I initially feel quite overwhelmed by the scenery.

Finn   You've obviously got a thing for mountains. In 2018, you installed a massive rock formation in the Bündner Kunstmuseum in Chur: a piece of mountain brought into the museum. Visitors first had to grapple with issues of scale and dimension. And your permanent installation *Inn Reverse* is on display here at Muzeum Susch. The viewer steps into a kind of grotto, gazes through a long tunnel and looks directly at the Inn River whose waters eventually empty into the Black Sea. It's a complex

work about mountains, the sea, the water that connects everything. I tried to make a mental connection between your art
and Land Art, but yours is something totally different.

Mareike Dittmer   There really isn't a connection. What
Sara or other artists like Olafur Eliasson or Julian Charrière do
is exactly the opposite of Land Art: they are bringing nature
into the interior of a building. By contrast, Land Art brought
art into nature.

Finn   Yes, Land Art always competed with the landscape
in a certain sense, trying to transform the landscape into art,
but it was often easily overshadowed by the landscape. When
I look out of the window now at the mountains, that's hardly
surprising. Sara, for the *Earthroom* piece—that's the installation
in Chur we just talked about—I'm wondering why you used
imitation rock and didn't want to incorporate real stone, aside
from the obvious factors of weight and scale.

Sara   The question of whether it's fake or real, the resulting sense of uncertainty and confusion, is what interested me. If
it had been about how I managed to bring a giant boulder into the
museum, it would have become a story about transport and
overcoming the laws of physics. That doesn't interest me at all.

Mareike   I also find it boring to think about the purely technical feasibility of a work of art. Your grotto in our museum is
also artificial. It no longer tries to look as if it were real. That
was also the case with Eliasson's sun at the Tate. Whether art
is created outside in nature, or when natural phenomena enter
the exhibition space—in both cases the concept of monument-
ality plays a role. Sara's rock formations in Chur almost burst
the bounds of the exhibition space.

Sara   I'm interested in the way that size and scale
changes content. A mountain as one's counterpart—that's hard
to really fathom. But when does a sculpture become so large
that it becomes a space in itself?

Finn   Nature is often described as monumental, as overwhelming. Isn't it simply the case that we generally harbor a
romantic view of nature?

Mareike   Nature is vast, the individual is small. That's the topos of romanticism, conjuring up the image of Caspar David Friedrich's *Monk by the Sea.* And yet why do people climb tall mountains? Why do they dive into the depths of the ocean, embark on expeditions to the Poles? All these undertakings are monumental.

Finn   Monumental, or yes, "sublime." I think we want to experience nature in a sublime way. We are basically seeking this sublimity. Proust writes that just as he only wanted to see his favorite actress perform in classical roles, he only wanted to experience storms at the coast where they are particularly sublime.

Mareike   Sara, your tunnel here at the museum is much smaller than one expects, just based on photographs. But in images, it really does appear quite monumental.

Sara   I'm very interested in the constructed perspective, with the tunnel as a kind of illusory space. But my reference is always the body, how does something relate to the size of my body.

Mareike   Do you two also think of a flat landscape as being monumental?

Sara   The sky can be monumental, like in Holland. But for me, my work is not about absolute size. I like the idea of zooming in and out, both on landscapes and the body. The actor Klaus Kinsky once said that the only really interesting landscape was his face.

Mareike   Without a sense of scale, everything basically becomes a landscape, right?

Sara   Yes, a close-up of a face is also a landscape.

Finn   Sara, when our train came out of the Vereina Tunnel, you looked out of the window at the mountains and said: What a great archive of shapes!

Sara   It really is that for me. And the wonderful thing about the mountains is that, like a sculpture, you can walk around them and they always look different. Maybe that's why I like it so much in the mountains as a sculptor.

Finn   Can a mountain be considered a sculpture? The art historian Philip Ursprung believes that a volcano can be understood as a kind of architecture. That makes sense to me.

Sara   I like to look at the landscape with this kind of artistic perspective—but then I want to hurry back to the studio. That's where art happens for me. It doesn't necessarily have to be a landscape. I can put a stone on the table and see it as an archive of shapes.

Finn   I'd like to discuss another aspect. Whenever I travel to the mountains and go walking or hiking, I always feel like Jean-Jacques Rousseau: I become more relaxed about all the things that would otherwise stir me up and make me agitated. Maybe it's the mountain air. Or maybe it's because my gaze is more drawn outside towards nature, and not directed inside where the *Taedium Vitae* is waiting, as the Stoics called it, the weariness of life. Goethe wrote about this feeling quite beautifully in *Poetry and Truth*.

Mareike   We can't talk about the Engadin without mentioning Nietzsche. Nietzsche said that the thought process only really takes shape and reaches its highest form when we are in motion.

Finn   I can relate to this experience. Good ideas never come to me when I'm sitting on my chair in the office. Sure, I can manage details in the office, but the ideas always originate somewhere else, usually when I'm out and about and on the move.

Mareike   Movement is really the key word. Either a physical one, or the movement of thoughts and ideas in a conversation.

Finn   My best thoughts come to me while walking and talking to someone interesting. One of Kleist's essays is entitled *"On the Gradual Production of Thoughts Whilst Speaking."*

Mareike   The philosopher Marcus Steinweg cultivates this practice of "precipitous thinking," as he calls it. He never has a script, his thoughts are formed while talking. But of course this is also extremely dependent on language. I think it works much better in English than in German, because in German the verb always comes so late in the sentence. You are much less free to simply extemporize. The grammar of the language doesn't allow for that.

Finn   Perhaps that's why German philosophy became so important because you can't just babble away in German.

Mareike   That could well be. The word *Erscheinung,* for example, means more than just "epiphany" in German. But I'm not sure if that alone indicates more depth. Or the expression *in-die-Welt-geworfen-sein* used by Heidegger to describe our existence—being thrown into the world. Trying to capture that with a term like "thrownness" in English, well, that just doesn't really cut it.

Sara   I'd like to make one more remark about walking and thinking while walking. I think it has to do with the speed, the pace. When you're going somewhere on foot, it's an optimal tempo. You can register everything in detail, even though you're in motion. When I sat on a train for the first time after an epic three-month hike, I immediately felt sick.

Finn   It's a cliché, but I'm asking because I've never done it before: is it really life-changing to go on a hike lasting weeks or months?

Sara   I can only speak for myself. After months of hiking, I had a clearer sense of who I am and what I want.

Mareike   You speak of clarity about yourself. But it is also interesting that your works are often disconcerting, even just due to their materiality. It strikes me that one of the first reactions is always: Can I touch it? This handmade aspect triggers such a response.

Sara   I'm very interested in playing with uncertainty, this feeling of disconcertedness.

Mareike   Is that a strategy of yours?

41

Sara   I'm not sure if I would call it a strategy. I always
take ideas as just an initial impetus to get started. But the
work only becomes good, or at least good for me, when I lose
the idea in the process. But without the idea I would never
have gotten started in the first place.

        Finn   The idea is the initial path, which you later abandon.

Sara   Yes, it is indeed like that. Nice paths are good,
but it's even better to part ways with them. This is true for
artistic work and in the woods, but also in the mountains.

        Mareike   The alpine clubs will hate us. They don't like it
        when people stray from the paths.

Finn   That's the problem with Switzerland and all its
hiking trails. You always have to follow the yellow signs, usually
walking one after the other in well-trodden furrows. It's not
easy to talk to one other. That has often been my experience
in the Swiss mountains, at least on classic hikes.

        Mareike   Maybe mountaineering is about solitude and not
        socializing.

Finn   But you should never go on a mountain tour
alone! I'm interested in one thing: mountain climbing is often
about this aspect of getting to know yourself in extreme situations to gain a clearer sense of who you are. But isn't the
role of art to increase complexity? Isn't it wonderful when a
work leaves you feeling disconcerted and unsure? This can be
a personal uncertainty or a general uncertainty, a moral or
ethical uncertainty.

        Mareike   The idea of confusion is also important to my
        understanding of art. That's what I like so much about the
        Emma Kunz exhibition at the museum. Kunz never saw herself
        as an artist, and we know so little about her. Not even what's
        the top and what's the bottom in her pictures. They're neither
        dated nor signed. It's an exhibition that mainly asks ques-
        tions. Including a major one: When is something art, only if it
        is produced als art?

Finn   Yes, I quite liked that too. Actually, the more interesting question is: Where is art? The question "What is art?" is tautological.

            Sara   I imagine art as a kind of territory in which you either are or aren't active. Another metaphor would be that of a mountain: there are different ways to the top, but the path you choose, and whether you even reach the top, is not so important. The important thing is that there is this mountain.

Mareike   In Jean-Paul Sartre's autobiographical work *The Words,* there's this story about a mountain. The author is recalling his childhood. There was a friend of the family who was never in the center of things, but was immediately missed if he was absent. Sartre describes the man as "the mountain." He writes that he always wanted to be someone who stands out when he's absent. But Sartre also writes that with all his knowledge and everything he read and learned, he had created a kind of giant tunnel system and hollowed himself out. His knowledge destroyed his foundation.

            Finn   What a great image! Yes, the mountains are simply there, you almost forget about them, but if one were suddenly missing, we would notice it immediately because of the void.

Mareike   The author Robert Macfarlane wrote about *Mountains of the Mind.* You never just see the mountain, but also all the things we have ever thought about it.

            Sara   Nature is untouched while landscape is man-made. Can we make that statement?

Finn   I think so. Paradoxically, Swiss hiking areas are much more regulated than an abandoned industrial landscape where it's never clear who owns this gravel-covered plot with an oil tank and you're not sure if you can enter the industrial ruins or if you'd be risking your neck like in certain urban neighborhoods. Such places are real *terrain vagues,* a subject dealt with by the artist Lara Almarcegui.

            Sara   Do people think differently when they live and work in the mountains? I would venture to say if you grow up in the mountains, your inner landscape will be shaped by them.

Finn   There's the infamous text by Martin Heidegger, *Why Do I Stay in the Provinces?* → p. 158 Is there something to that?

Mareike   For me, it depends on what you want to do. Things are more concentrated in the mountains, the distractions disappear. The city is more inspiring because there's more excitement. For me personally, I was always drawn to Berlin because it's a very relaxed big city. In the mountains, and you know I live here in Susch, there's simply no distracting scenery around you.

Finn   What is distracting?

Mareike   The social space around you. For me, cities are places of consumption, not production. If there are three great readings being held tonight, why should I sit down and write a usable paragraph? The contrast between city and mountain is the contrast between consuming and producing.

Finn   It could also be an isolated house by the sea?

Sara   Yes, for sure. The older I get, the more I want to move to the mountains. But a friend told me that I wasn't old enough for the mountains yet, because stories have a way of lingering there.

Mareike   What did he mean by that?

Sara   The stories people tell about you tend to hang around in the valleys like fog.

Finn   Mareike, you were in London and Berlin, and now in Susch. Is that strange?

Mareike   Yes, but I didn't know it at the time. I was only familiar with the Harz Mountains. And I thought of myself as more of a sea person. When I visited for the first time, I was extremely impressed. There's no horizon line and the mountains are everywhere.

Finn   The city is a stage, and you always have to perform.

        Sara   In the city I often have the feeling that I have to
        be somebody. I have that much less in the mountains. Here
        you don't have to produce and set yourself apart, at most
        perhaps from a tree.

Mareike   I like London a lot, but it's all so exhausting.
That's why I like cities where you can do everything on foot.
Paris, for example, or Zurich. In London, I can't figure out my
position in the landscape, the cityscape, because the subway
network is utterly beyond comprehension. I have to be able to
locate myself in a landscape. It doesn't matter so much if it's
the city or the countryside. When I can walk and hike places,
that's what makes this localization possible.

        Finn   Swiss art production is very fixated on the mount-
        ains, especially the field of literature. Why is that?

Mareike   I think it has something to do with the size of the
cities. Zurich isn't really that big. You don't have these urban
experiences. It could also be that the city is simply too beautiful. The notion of the city as a Moloch doesn't even exist. There
isn't enough dirt, the hard edge is missing.

        Finn   The rural countryside and the provinces have
        come back into fashion, if we can put it like that. Global cities,
        the renaissance of the city—those were the buzzwords you
        used to hear at numerous talks and events. Now the pendulum
        is swinging back in the other direction. In their appearance at
        last year's Engadin Art Talks, Rem Koolhaas and Niklas Maak
        both affirmed their belief in the provinces. Their exhibition at
        the Guggenheim in New York is set to open in 2020 under the
        title *Countryside, The Future.* → p. 265

Mareike   It's good that the outlying periphery is being up-
graded. This movement is interesting, away from the center. Dis-
courses have now concentrated much more on minorities—do
you see a parallel to the sudden interest in the periphery?

        Finn   Interesting thought. This parallel you're drawing
        makes a lot of sense.

Mareike   It can no longer just be about the one majority opinion, which explains the movement out of the center and into the periphery. That changes everything. You have to communicate differently with your audience in the periphery. Looking at the museum, for example: we can't run the museum solely for the 5,000 professionals in the field who are constantly travelling all over the globe anyway. The museum is anchored here in this place and addresses a very diverse audience. One that is local, regional, national and international. The old monastery, the brewery, it's a very historical place. Then there's the architecture, and of course the art. Plus the people who visit just to see how this even came to exist, such a high-level museum in a small village.

Finn   It's one of the most beautiful museums in the world. A huge asset for the Engadin, Switzerland and lovers of art and architecture worldwide. There was the idea of signature architecture, Bilbao, Fondation Louis Vuitton. These are great buildings, but they also create a certain distance. They radiate something elitist. The museum in Susch doesn't have that at all.

Sara   Chasper Schmidlin, one of the museum's architects, has a gallery together with his cousin Gian Appenzeller in Madulein. Their gallery is in a converted stable because Chasper often finds the white cube to be a bit intimidating. I also recognize some of this attitude in the museum in Susch. The whole place is inviting and there's so much quality in the little details. Nothing comes across as pretentious, and you can also understand how the structure was built.

Mareike   A big difference is also the reversal of dimensions. From the outside you can only see a third of the museum. It's not trying to inspire awe. It doesn't say that if you go in there, you have to look at art for two hours. Of course, once you're inside, you can look at art for two hours if you wish. The hidden scale of the museum is a clever move from a psychological standpoint. The house is also like an organism. There was no master plan conceived by someone in New York. The oldest parts of the building date back to the twelfth century. The architects had to work with it, and the museum was developed from the inside out. The house is a challenge with twenty-seven rooms, and always these views to the outside. In eighty percent of

the rooms here, we are completely removed from the White
Cube concept.

Finn   What is the relationship between space and artwork for you, Sara, as an artist?

Sara   There's always a dialogue between the two. There
are places that strenghten the work and others where you
have to create the conditions for it. In any case, space has a
strong influence on work. Normally I finish the work in space
by installing it.

Finn   The white cube emerged from the idea that the
focus should be exclusively on the art. But in the meantime, I
find that such spaces often broadcast the message: Attention,
art! In my opinion, that's not always a good thing. That's why
I like places like the Galerie Tschudi in Zuoz. For me, it's one of
the most beautiful galleries anywhere.

Sara   Yes, it's great when art can take on new impact in
concert with the space. A white exhibition space is like a white
piece of paper. When works are extremely fine and delicate,
then of course they'll tend to be swallowed up in a barn.

Mareike   The place then also essentially becomes a work of
art. It will be viewed, even if no art is being shown.

Finn   This is also the case with Muzeum Susch. Even
without any art, I'd like to spend time in the building because
it's so beautiful. But now we've done enough talking and should
go climb a mountain while it's still light out.

Sara   Yes, definitely. Good idea.

Mareike   Okay, let's get going.

The artist SARA MASÜGER lives and works in Zurich.
Sara Masüger's permanent installation *Inn Reverse*
at the Muzeum Susch combines sculpture, architecture and landscape. Running underneath the
floor of the entrance hall in the Bieraria Veglia is
a narrwo tunnel filled with sculptural forms that
echo natural rock formations found in the Engadin.

MAREIKE DITTMER is the director of the Art
Stations Foundation CH / Muzeum Susch. With a
degree in Culture and Communication Sciences
from the UdK Berlin, she was involved in a number
of exhibition and publication projects.

Iso Camartin

Bumperfatscha

We don't just sit down at the table and dig in. Good manners
require that we speak to one another before we start to eat. We
wish each other—in the Western world, at least—"bon appetit."
That's a nice custom, and besides, appetite is a nice word. It
has to do with desire and craving, and if a meal doesn't inspire
any sense of desire, then something's clearly wrong.

> The Rhaeto-Romans used to exchange an even better wish
> before they started a meal. In the old days, before the interna-
> tional "bon appetit" took hold with them as well, they wished
> each other "bumperfatscha." Hiding in this word is the Latin
> *bonum per faciem:* May the meal be so good that it shows
> on your face! The faces of the people eating should become a
> mirror for the love, the care, indeed the art of those who pre-
> pared the food. With the first bite—if it was good, of course—the
> faces of everyone present lit up. The meal was a joyful event,
> and everyone could see that from the faces around the table.

The Rhaeto-Romans still like to eat well. In that they're no
different from other cultures' gastronomes. But, unfortunately,
the word "bumperfatscha" has fallen completely out of fashion
among them. Young Rhaeto-Romans don't even understand
it anymore.

> Wouldn't it be nice if anyone who goes to the trouble of serving
> up the best possible food for their guests could see not just
> hunger, desire and craving on their faces, but also the radiant
> message, "bumperfatscha": Your cooking is magnificent, just
> look at the delight on my face!

Nina von Albertini

Body Objects and Landscape
Sensibility and Responsibility

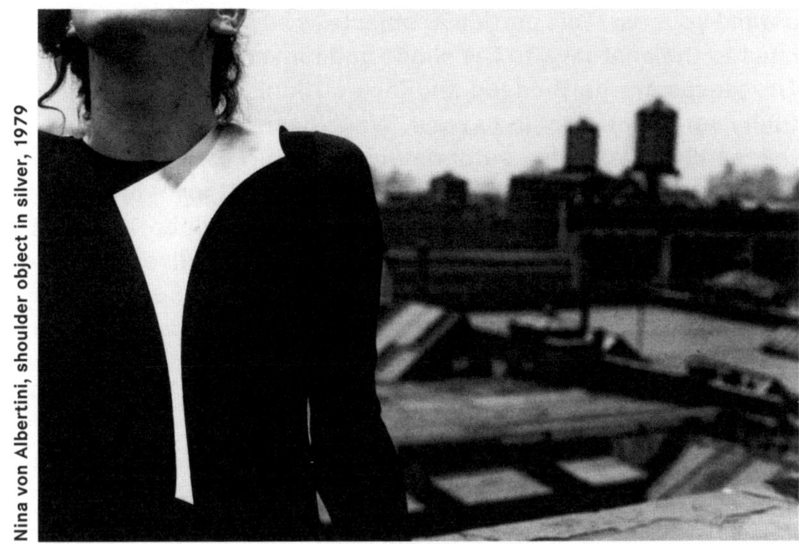

I am originally from the Engadin valley, my mother is from the Engadin valley, my culture, my roots are here, and in my life and my different activities it was always very important to me to be rooted here. So, I would like to speak about a few phases of my professional career. Early on, I was most interested in ancient jewelry and its craftsmanship. I worked with different masters in various places in Europe and the United States. I focused on archaic, ancient jewelry, its symbols and rituals. This definitely influenced my contemporary forms. I had no interest in the jewelry that was fashionable in my time, preferring instead something that had to do with our here and now and with us, self-assured women. I declared my pieces to be wearable sculptures, body objects. It was mainly silverwork, such as a shoulder object with clear lines and a smooth surface, or a later object for the back, with a very simple, rectangular structure. I concentrated on expressing myself through the body and these wearable objects. In other words, I wanted to give back to women a symbol or a ritual art piece inspired by jewelry of ancient times that had a function and meant something, such as belonging to a tribe, or having a certain status. By contrast, the jewelry we had in the 1970s or 1980s was often reduced to its pecuniary value. To wear my pieces, purchasing power is not the only prerequisite. Instead, you need a strong posture and a certain inner attitude–and so you can't wear them every day. For example, one object I created is an ear shell to put

around your ear. This particular object–as all my objects do–relates to the anatomy, to the shape and movement of the body.
The pieces are hard-edged and look striking, but they are actually very comfortable to wear. While designed for the body,
these objects are also autonomous sculptures.

> By this time I had begun to exhibit my work in galleries more
> frequently and was successfully collaborating with the world
> of fashion and publishing. But I realized that I did not feel
> like selling my pieces to people without a connection to the
> sense of my work. So I made a radical decision: I withheld
> my objects and decided to start studying agricultural engi-
> neering at the Swiss Federal Institute of Technology (ETH) in
> Zurich.

Back then, the ETH was still a quite conservative institution
in this field, and, after having lived in New York, Milan and
Paris, it was hard for me to integrate into such a setting. But
my roots here in the Engadin, as well as our family house, a
very old patrician house with a farm, located in the Domleschg,
helped me. At the university, I wanted to obtain theoretical
and practical knowledge and was interested in going further
into agricultural engineering. I realized that the basic re-
source for nature, for most ecosystems and especially for
products, is the soil and its fertility. Hence, in my studies, I
focused on soil ecology and processes and ventured into soil
physics. But there, I faced a challenge: while soil physics
usually use models and statistics as analytic tools, I wanted
to render physical and biological regeneration processes
visible (rather than quantifiable). For example, I wanted to
visualize the damage that soil compaction caused to the soil
structure and its fertility. By infiltrating blue water as artificial rain on grassland surfaces of different compaction stages,
I was able to show colored flow patterns of different regeneration stages on the soil profiles. These patterns indicate
the paths the water takes and where it is able to infiltrate.
The youngest patterns, just after ploughing, showed a sealed
plough layer and almost no interaction with deeper layers of
the soil. As a consequence, every time soil is ploughed or
compacted by heavy machinery, the soil organisms are
disrupted and disturbed, and soil fertility is impoverished.
Having been able to visualize these damages, I also wanted
to create awareness for the capacity for soil regeneration.
If we just treat soil a little better, if we change the way we

produce and harvest, working with less heavy machinery, the soil has immense potential. A flow pattern of the same piece of grassland four years after ploughing illustrated the soil's ability to regenerate: the upper layer was no longer sealed and disconnected, and the blue-tinted water was able to seep deep into the soil. Physical processes and soil organisms such as earthworms, insects, funghi and bacteria had reconquered and reopened the soil to water and air–to life.

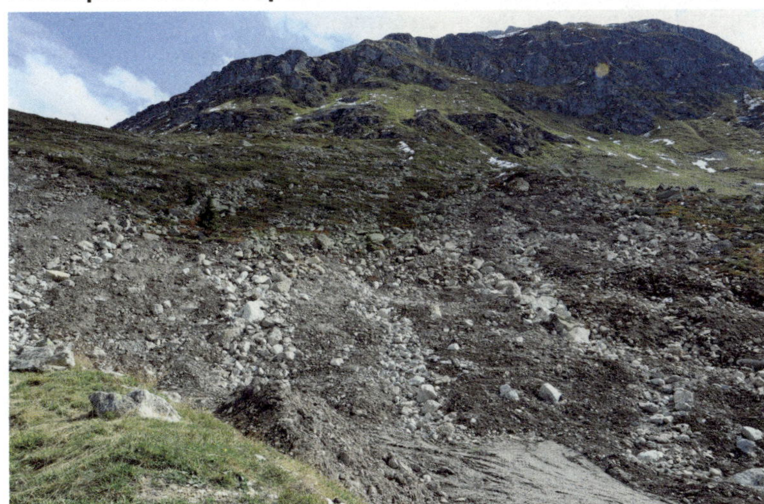

Nina von Albertini, A newly remodeled landscape at the Julierpass, 2011

The images I was able to analyse generated almost more meaningful results than would have been possible through quantitative analysis. And one of the very important assets of my research was its visuality since it enabled me to share my results not only with fellow researchers, but also with farmers. Through these images, famers would be in the position to see something they had never seen before–so in this respect my images opened up new dimensions.

After this phase of research into soil physics, and after I had lived with my family in Niger for several years, I came back to Switzerland to live in the Domleschg–a valley close to the Engadin–because I had to take over our family house and farm there. Upon returning to Switzerland, I realized that a lot of our soil and environment was being destroyed, especially in mountainous areas like the Engadin, where we don't have many resources and the few we do have are very vulnerable. A special challenge that our valleys face is tourism: the land is highly populated and we have a lot of construction going on because of second homes, and therefore the pressure

53

on land is very high. This is why it is extremely important to
create awareness in order to render people more sensitive
and knowledgeable about nature and the landscape.

> As an environmental engineer, my role within architecture
> and large-scale construction projects outside the building
> zone, such as roads, tunnels and hydro-energy plants, consists
> in implementing a respectful, aesthetic, logical and site-specific
> handling of the ecosystems and their soils in order to reduce
> negative impact on the environment.

In 2008, I was asked to contribute to the construction of new,
important road segments on the alpine Julier Pass. At first, I
hesitated to participate in this project because I feared my
role would be delimited by the rigid norms and rules that
dictate road construction in Switzerland. But then, the urge
to try and minimize the road's negative impact on the environment was stronger.

> It is in the context of this project that I subsequently developed
> a pioneering method, which enables the preservation of the
> natural and vital composition of vegetative ecosystems while
> also moving them for the sake of construction: soil transplant-
> ation. This method, which requires one to work with precision,
> yet on a large scale, allows the relocation of entire clusters
> of soil into new locations together with the vegetation that
> forms part of them: grass sods with, for example, alpine roses
> and which, together with the stones embedded in it, can
> continue to grow in close-by places.

With this strategy, which is indeed highly cost- and time-effi-
cient, I was able to integrate soil- and landscape-protection,
with the demands of road construction and traffic regulation.
It is thanks to such inventive and sensible methods, that construction does not need to signify destruction anymore. And
this is important, since there is evidently an urgent need to show
more sensitivity and knowledge when intervening in nature.
If we adhere to sense and sensibility, instead of ignorance
and brutality, nature can be preserved.

> As Jacqueline Burckhardt has noted, my work as a jewelry
> designer and my work as an environmental engineer are actu-
> ally not so far apart from each other: just as I follow the
> anatomy and character of my subjects when making body
> objects, I also respond to the formations and intricacies of
> nature when working with soil.[1] Both of these activities are
> principally based on sensibility and understanding for forms

and shapes. This attunement, in turn, enables me to work with the anatomies of bodies and soils, rather than against them.

1 See Jacqueline Burckhardt, "In der Bergwelt,"
  DU Magazin, no. 846 (May 2014), p. 67.

Philippe Rahm

Climatorium:
A Museum on Global Warming

The Climatorium, a 3500 m² building, is the visitor center of Taichung Central Park in Taiwan. It is located in the middle of the park, on its eastern boundary. The complex consists of a café, an information office, toilets and educational spaces and exhibitions on climate change. These include a public reception room opening onto three climatic chambers of about 200 m² each, to which three themes, heat, humidity, and pollution, are attached: themes that have also prevailed in the general composition of the park. The architecture of the Climatorium itself, its constructive mode, assumes and reveals the role and primary climatic mission of architecture. It is composed of four physical layers placed one inside the other: four filtering climatic planes placed according to a concentric climatic gradation, from the most exterior and natural to the most interior and artificial, from the most varying and uncomfortable to the most permanent and comfortable.

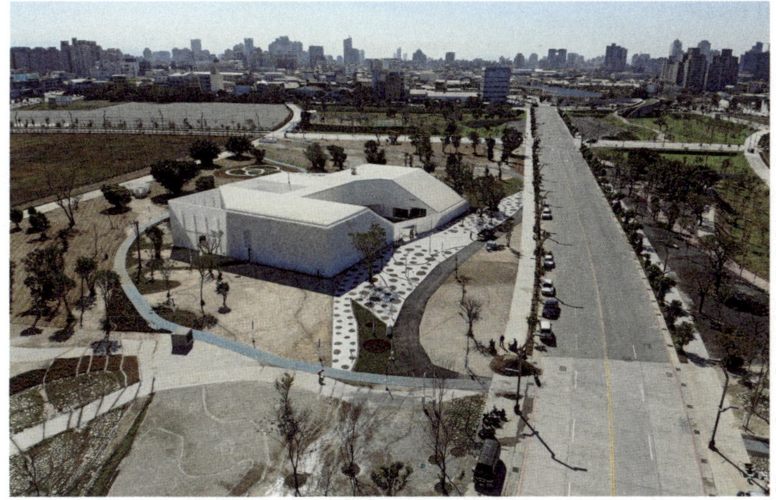

Climatorium, Central Park, Taichung, Taiwan, 2019

Taichung's climate is extremely hot and humid. In December, the coldest month in Taiwan, the daytime temperature averages around 24°C, with peaks as high as 31°C in recent years. The relative humidity remains at a fairly high average year round. November is the driest month, with a relative humidity of 60%. Summer temperatures are highest in August, with an average daytime temperature of 33°C and recent peaks of up to 38°C. The relative humidity during summer is on average 80%.

Because man is a homeothermic animal, he must maintain a body temperature of around 37°C, because the enzymes necessary for the biochemical reactions of human metabolism, present in the billions in our body, can only function optimally at a temperature between 35.5°C and 37.6°C. According to speculations by chronobiologists, the existence of the sub-Saharan man two million years ago, who existed on the highlands of East Africa where the average air temperature remains constant all year round at around 22°C, explains the way in which the human body can tolerate an external temperature of 22°C, considerably colder than the body. This temperature of 22°C establishes the upper limit of the thermal neutrality zone, which is between 20°C and 22°C. Any variation in external temperature to below or above 20°C to 22°C will increase the basic energy expenditure to combat the risk of the body's core temperature falling below 35.5°C or rising above 37.6°C, known as thermoregulation. And of course, the greater the difference, the greater the effort needed from the body to warm or cool itself.

It is because of this homeothermic condition of the human body and its suitability for a sub-Saharan environment with an outside air temperature of around 22°C that man needs to remain in an outside temperature of between 20°C and 26°C, which allows him to maintain a body temperature of between 35.5°C and 37.6°C. When the outside temperature drops below 20°C or rises above 26°C, man combines his own bodily means, the various thermoregulation mechanisms, and external ones: among others, clothing, constructed shelter, or even migration. Architecture is therefore not autonomous and cultural. It actually falls within the range of physiological means that allow us to maintain our body temperature at 37°C. It is one of our responses, along with food, clothing, and migration, to a significant drop or increase in temperature, alongside the internal mechanisms of vasodilation, sweating, muscle contractions, or catecholamine secretion. To keep our body temperature constant, we implement different reactions, be they natural or cultural, microscopic or macroscopic, biochemical or meteorological, related to food or urban planning. In this original thermoregulatory mission, architecture then appears as a larger form of vasoconstriction, or conversely, digestion appears as a slightly smaller variant of architecture. Ultimately, architecture is nothing more than an augmented form of body thermoregulatory mechanisms, or an augmented, exogenous, and artificial form of thermogenesis and thermolysis.

More often than not, the climate of Taichung is uncomfortable because on the whole it is too hot for the average human metabolism. The human body is better suited for a cooler environment, such as that of the African highlands of the Olduvai Gorge, situated at an altitude of 1400 meters. In hot and humid Taichung, which is at an altitude of 100 meters above sea level, the human body is constantly under stress to release the excess heat it produces that the outside air, already too hot, does not accept.

In Taiwan, the role of a building is first to passively reduce excess heat from the outside climate, by lowering the amount of radiant heat, through a roof and walls that block or limit sunlight, by preventing rain and runoff water from entering the interior through waterproofing, and by separating the heat from the outside air through airproofing. Then, the building permits the creation of a thermally insulated space pocket in which air can be cooled, i.e. lowering the indoor temperature until it reaches the thermal neutrality zone at 22°C and also offering the benefit of lower humidity levels. All these efforts to reduce excess conductive and radiant heat and moisture are achieved by using materials of different layers and thicknesses, precisely chosen to meet a mission: blocking light, blocking water, blocking heat. Thus, each filter layer composing the facade of the Climatorium remains isolated, detached from the others: water supply, heat supply, sun supply, public access supply, are all treated as independent components, forming a specific geometry. The facade is not a simple line; it thickens, expands, curls, stretches, contracts, divides, and splits into multiple independent lines.

The first layer of the facade, the outermost, is a white aluminum grid whose role is to provide a physical and solar barrier while remaining visually transparent, with its large frame made of open cubes at two ends of 20 cm by 20 cm. It defines the large perimeter of the Climatorium and establishes a first privatization base; two sliding gates allow the complex to be opened to visitors during the day and closed off at night. Between this first layer and the second are both covered and open spaces that can be used for gatherings and for the outdoor terrace of the café, plus another covered space and a back yard for service. This first physical limit draws a first degree of interiority in a gradual progression from the outside to the inside, from the largest to the smallest. It is a first layer through which rain, sun, heat, and wind still pass, but which sets physical boundaries of ownership, according to the opening and closing hours of the Climatorium. Inside this first layer, a second layer—the water-proofing layer—unfolds, sometimes glued to the first layer, the grid, sometimes detaching from it, thus generating intermediate external voids: those of the courtyard, the café terrace, and the back yard. This second layer blocks soil moisture and rain, and filters sun and air with a waterproof polymer; painted white to obtain a high albedo, it reflects incidental sunlight to prevent it from turning into heat when in contact with the material. Inside this second layer is the third layer, the thermal insulation layer, made of recycled PET wool covered with a textile finish. This layer is sometimes detached from the second to open up spaces between the two: spaces protected from light and rain, but still not thermally insulated, and without air conditioning, only natural ventilation. Sometimes this results in the spaces being a little too hot but we accept this because of the functions they serve.

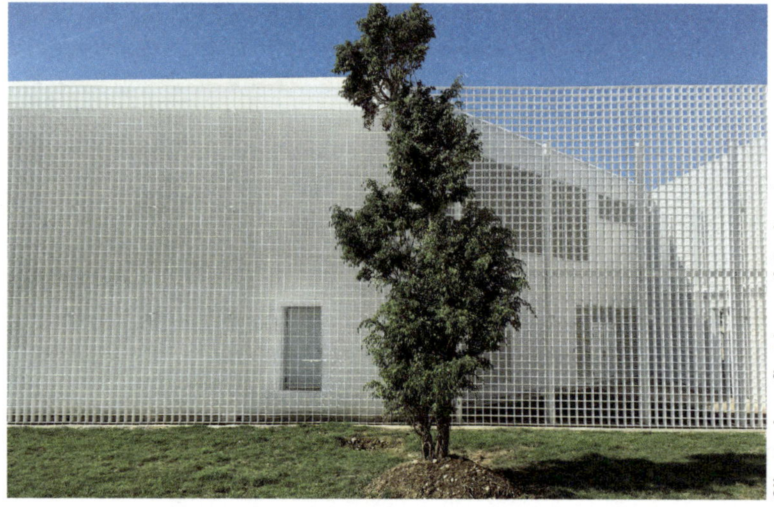

Climatorium, first layer of the facade

These spaces, which are a little removed from the outside but still not completely "inside," correspond to corridors, toilets, storage spaces, technical rooms: those places that you only pass through, where you never stay long enough to feel uncomfortable from excessive heat. Here, in the shade, the floor, ceiling and walls are entirely covered with aluminum and steel—materials that are cold to the touch and have low emissivity, i.e. visitors are not subjected to the heat that would be radiated by materials whose temperature is the same as that of the air. Inside the third layer, the thermal insulation layer, are the most comfortable spaces, fully insulated, and the only ones in which the air is conditioned in order to lower the temperature to around 22°C. Here you can find the park's information center along with information on climate change, plus places to have coffee, and offices. Finally, at the heart of the building, is the fourth and final layer, made of concrete that secures the structure of the building and braces the entire construction. Inside this fourth layer are three Climatoriums, each reproducing a particular climate: colder for the first (Coolium), drier for the second (Dryium), and less polluted for the third (Clearium), thus providing three ideal climates where the usual problems of Taichung—excessive heat, humidity, and air pollution—are overcome.

Coolium

The Coolium is the spatialization of a cool climate. Inside a 16 by 10 meter room is built, in real time, the cooler altitude climate of Jade Mountain (Yushan), which is located in the center of the island of Taiwan. The village of Alishan, at 2190 meters above sea level, enjoys a high-altitude subtropical climate with average temperatures ranging from 10.3°C in winter to 18.4°C in summer. Alishan's geographical position mean it has cooler annual temperatures and lower humidity than Taichung, at the lower altitude of 110 meters above sea level. Even at latitudes near the equator, the higher you climb, the lower the air temperature. Achieving altitude is thus one way of cooling down in summer in the tropics. During the hot and humid monsoon seasons, in both summer and autumn, Alishan enjoys a milder and drier climate than that on the plains. During the winter months, its climate is cold and dry.

The Coolium not only reproduces the cool climate of Alishan but it also replicates three parameters: temperature, humidity, and light. Temperature and humidity data are captured in real time at the Alishan weather station and transmitted immediately to the temperature and humidity sensor inside the Coolium. The temperature inside the Coolium is continuously adjusted by the air conditioning system in order to correspond, in real time, to that of the village of Alishan. The temperature and humidity of the air inside the Coolium also mirror those found at the same time in Alishan.

In addition, light intensity sensors installed on the mountain range record in real time the constant variation in the sun's luminosity, which depends on the time of day and the passage of cloud and fog, for example. The Taiwanese mountain where Alishan is located is called Jade because of the color of its summit, which is snow-covered in both summer and winter and thus resembles jade, a milky gemstone ranging from white to green that is very popular in China. We reproduce this intense white light from the top of the mountain: both the incidental light and that reflected by the snow. For this purpose, a set of fluorescent tubes have been situated on the floor of the Coolium that emit light with a spectrum similar to that of the sun. Alishan's variations in light intensity are transmitted to Taichung via an electronic control that monitors the light emission of these fluorescent tubes, lowering or increasing it according to the actual light variations on the mountain.

Thus the cool climate of Jade Mountain and its light, at an altitude of 2190 meters, is perpetually reproduced in the Coolium, at an altitude of 110 meters, allowing visitors to Taichung to make an instantaneous journey, like a motionless climb to a higher altitude.

Dryium

Taichung has a hot and humid subtropical climate. Most of the year, the humidity level in the air is very high, around 80% relative humidity, which hinders the physiological process of cooling by the body's natural perspiration, preventing heat inside the body from being evacuated due to the rapid evaporation of beading sweat on the skin.

Nevertheless, the relative humidity rate tends to decrease during the months of October, November and December, reaching more comfortable levels of around 60% relative humidity. The body is able to return to sweating as a mode of thermolysis, allowing a better evacuation of heat. Thus November 21 stands as an "ideal" day in Taichung, because it is central in the least humid period of the year and, moreover, is cooler. Tour guides encourage visitors to visit hot and humid countries during the dry seasons so as not to suffer from the uncomfortable excesses of air humidity. As we know, dry heat is more bearable than moist heat.

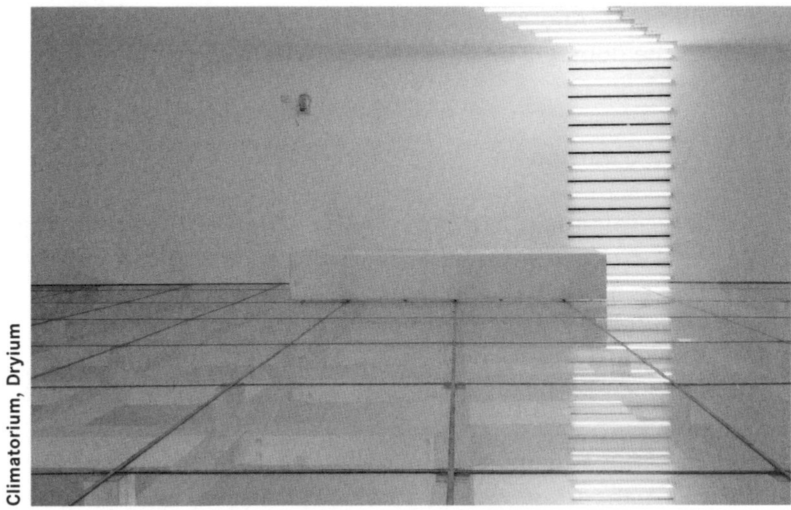

The Dryium is the eternal spatial construction of a single less humid day in Taichung, namely November 21, that is recreated and repeated perpetually: like an endless day, occurring throughout the entire year. The sensors inside the Dryium communicate with the air conditioning machines so that they can accurately reconstruct the variations in humidity and air temperature from November 21 in the Dryium's interior. The air conditioning turns on or off and modulates its power in order to adjust the humidity and temperature inside the Dryium space and replicate external conditions recorded on November 21, 2018.

> The 18 by 10 meter room, 6 meters high, is entirely white. It is crossed horizontally in its center by a transparent glass floor that divides the room into two equal volumes, 3 meters high, like a skyline. Above, on the ceiling, is depicted the Taichung sky on November 21 and below, under the glass floor, as if the ground in Taichung were transparent, is the sky of the Pitcairn Islands, in the South Pacific Ocean, on the other side of the globe.

On the walls, floor and ceiling run fluorescent tubes of "daylight" color temperature at 5500° Kelvin, whose trajectory follows that of the sun, simulating its course according to the azimuth and angle specific to November 21 in Taichung. Depending on the time of day, only a few fluorescent tubes will be lit at exact locations, following the changes in the position of the sun on November 21 in Taichung. At noon, for example, only the seven tubes in the center of the ceiling will be lit. At sunset, only the seven tubes on the west wall, at glass floor level, will be lit. And at midnight, only the seven tubes in the middle of the floor will be lit, able to be seen through the glass.

Clearium

Taichung, like most major cities in the world today, suffers from pollution due to industrial emissions of toxic gases and fine particles in the air.

These harmful particles accumulate in our lungs faster than the rate at which our bodies can filter and evacuate them effectively. The effects of this exposure to toxic gases and particles have both short- and long-term impacts on our health, including asthma, nausea, cognitive decline, decreased physical performance, the risk of stroke and some cancers. The phenomenon is more intense at times when the wind is not blowing and when it is not raining: conditions that intensify the stagnation of particles. The reported mortality figures caused by such pollution and the decrease in life expectancy are now alarming.

The Clearium is the atmospheric reconstruction of an unpolluted environment, of pre-industrial air. Inside, the Taichung climate of 1832 is recreated: a time before the industrial revolution began to produce and intensify air pollution, causing global warming through the emission of CO_2 from the combustion of coal and oil. In the Clearium's engine room, two air filters collect and filter air from outside. One filter cleans the air of nitrogen oxides (NO_x), ozone (O_3), and sulphur dioxide (SO_2), and the other traps the harmful fine particles suspended in the air (PM_{10} and $PM_{2.5}$). This cleansed air is then constantly cooled by 2°C to emulate the temperature in Taichung in 1832, before the increase that we know today due to global warming. The global increase in atmospheric temperature due to human greenhouse gas emissions since 1832 is now estimated at 1.5°C or even 2°C.

Cleansed and cooled, this air is blown into the Clearium from the edges of the ceiling. Because it is always 2°C cooler than the outside air, this air drops into the room and remains there, without mixing with the outside air (the Clearium ceiling is open in the middle).

As the room is partially open to the Taichung rain and the sun's rays, the humidity level is modified by creating a kind of "cloud" layer using an artificial water mist sprayed over the roof. From time to time, due to the fine vaporization of the droplets, a cloud is produced. This cloud connects the current climate to that of 1832, which was more humid and cloudier. Global warming leads to a reduction in clouds due to a decrease in the evapotranspiration of plants on the planet, which close their stomata to conserve more water in the fight against excess heat. In the Clearium, visitors can experience how the Taichung climate was before global warming and air pollution from the industrial era began. Thus the Cleairum creates a uchronia:, that of a contemporary Taichung that has not been affected by global warming.

Cecilia Bengolea

Lighting Dance

The history of movement is the history of evolution. Astonishingly far back in that history, multi-celled gelatinous creatures evolved nerves that coordinated cells and transformed
tiny contractions, contortions and twitches into propulsive
pulsing. These were the first movements. Later, neurons con-
vened into an electro-chemical storm of repurposed signaling—
bearing the first marks of what we would now identify as a
nervous system.

> Then, about half a billion years ago, Cambrian animals first
> watched, seized and fled from other animals. Senses, nervous
> systems and behaviors escalated an arms race against the
> senses and behaviors of others. And amid such explosive evolu-
> tion, it might be reasonable to assume that speedy, grasping
> creatures evolved often and developed the greatest neurolog-
> ical complexity. But surprisingly, of all the basic animal body
> plans (phyla), only arthropods (insects, crabs), vertebrates and
> one subgroup among mollusks—cephalopods—evolved com-
> plex active bodies. Which is to say that only vertebrates and
> cephalopods developed large, complex nervous systems.

These two nervous systems developed independently, so
much so that each is truly alien to the other. Many hundreds
of millions of years later we still encounter, in both brain and
body, beings that are familiarly strange, yet strangely familiar.
Bone-free and shape-shifting, the octopus's body is one of
pure possibility. Dynamic, fluid and unconstrained by the skele-
tal armor of a nervous system housed within a skull, octopuses
can configure their bodies in ways we can barely imagine—just

one example being their ability to flow through cracks the width of their eyes. Their skin senses light and can respond allowing the body itself to become a chromatic billboard of instantaneous communication.

Vertebrates share the architecture of an inherited nervous system. Cephalopods are different—so different, in fact, that in terms of structural intelligence our most common ancestor was a worm-like creature of the pre-Cambrian era. With neuron numbers comparable to those of mammals, octopuses' brains are distributed within their bodies; their limbs harbor nearly twice as many neurons as their central brain. Neural loops may give the arms their own form of memory. An octopus is so suffused with its nervous system that it has no clear brain-body boundary. Not only is it carrying the dream of protean form but it is of an alien intelligence to match.

Dance may be our most advanced forms of bodily expression. Unlike sport or other related forms of physical communication, dance demands that we consider the figure as pure medium devoid of functionality. In dance the segregation of movement and knowledge is the least strictly enforced. So-called physical memory plays a vital role as the brain functions that typically trigger discrete actions become, in long, fast sequences, so overloaded that the body has to take over. Detaching itself from the command sequences is what allows a dancer to move in ways that appear directed by something other than the head— the same mechanism that allows a boxer to throw survival mode combinations of the kind of intricacy forfeited by the situation he or she may encounter. Accessing physical memory is in some very distant sense delving into what Peter Godfrey-Smith calls the "other minds" of cephalopods, creatures that over 600 million years ago made an independent voyage into complexity.

Adaptive physical intelligence may well be the indirect quest of most dance, but it is the basis of my practice that has been centered around the creation of new bodies of thought. The other mind that is the focus of my attention is less about what Deleuze and Guattari would term the body without organs than a body without boundaries, a fully eroticized being born of a state of constant rehearsal. The spirit and rhythms that infuse this body move in several directions at once. Often they are found played out in transient or boundary places such as the side of the road where passing cars choreograph another kind of risk. Sweat and tropical rain further dissolve the boundaries between inside and outside, reminding us perhaps that inner body fluid is an electrical conductor that functions for the body in ways similar to the synapses of the brain—creating new pathways and communication highways redefining sentience. Electrical rhythms pulse through this body and the landscape it inhabits. Working on steps is just one part of the endeavor to synchronize and compose the self within a state of greater liquidity. The beginning and ends of traditional dance and sex are here forgone in favor of an actualization of a polymorphous erotic identity marked by a body not in a state of realization but of rehearsal, of constant becoming, of deferred gratification and spiritualized pornography.

And so where most dance fetishizes the extremities—hands and feet—to emphasize the boundaries and the physical distance between command and action, thought and expression in Dancehall and the other forms that fascinate me, I discover something else. The movements I'm drawn to are those in which the body is driven by a physical intelligence of its own. Through ritual and repetition, arms, legs and torso seem to develop independent memory. Relieved of the cumbersome call and response mechanism that separates action from thought, the body begins to describe a life of its own—perhaps something like the kinetic sentience from which we vertebrates were separated so many million years ago. And so the dance form that fascinates me the most, may also carry within it the message that just because evolution built minds twice, over doesn't mean that we should give up on trying to close the gap.

Isabel Nolan

"...for ever and ever
and infinite and super-infinite
for evers."

Having been asked recently if I draw every day, I admitted that my only daily work practice is lying on the floor. Sometimes it is out of tiredness, but chiefly it is because when thinking I love to be horizontal. Being flat on my back affords less latitude for fidgeting than standing or sitting; and cooperating fully with the force of gravity, I imagine I ruminate more freely.

Occasionally I'll drift into that altered hypnogogic state that precedes sleep, when uninvited images, alien ideas arrive to mind. It can be a weirdly fruitful time for entertaining unstable thoughts, for generally mentally rearranging the world whilst reality is up for grabs. Perhaps this might be the reason that the English word "lying" means not only being supine but untruthful too.

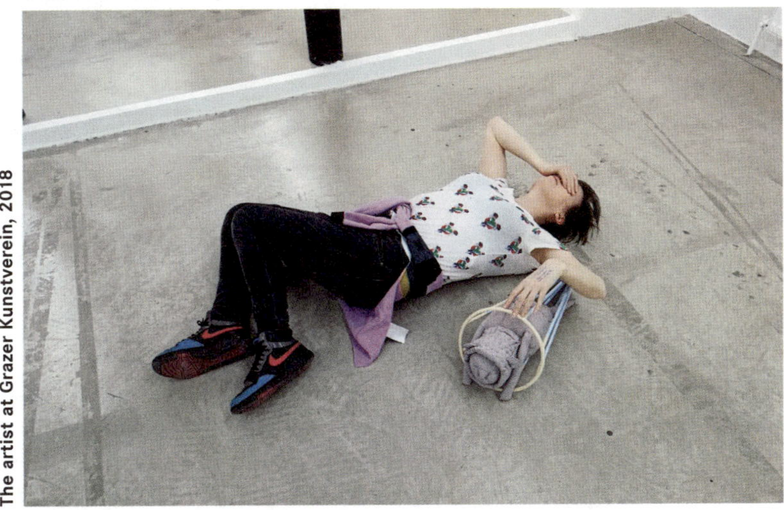

Physical lowness or horizontality is often used as a metaphor for lacking control, for surrendering. Taking something lying down; not standing on one's own two feet; sleeping on the job: they all imply a failure to be in command. I sometimes feel that increased proximity to the surface of the earth makes us beautifully inventive, our duplicitous minds gratefully receptive to subterranean and protean lies. It is no wonder we often get lost in thought.

Images of horizontality and lowness are often conflated with an idea of the Earth as a changeable, corrupt, realm; and similarly associations with carnality, sleep, and death run deep. This might be irrational. It is also ubiquitous in thousands of years of Western human thought. In marked contrast, the sky is a symbol of eternity, uprightness, freedom, divinity and grace.

This prejudice, all that is up is good and a horror of that which brings us down, pertains, I suspect, directly to the way grace is often discussed as if it is a corrective to the offences of gravity. Verticality or height, it is assumed, give us the reason, the control or spiritual grace that our low animal nature wants, that it both lacks and desires.

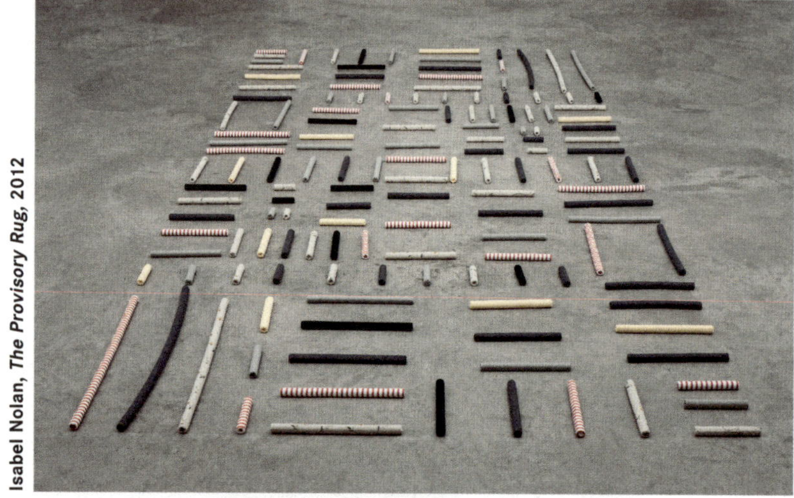

In any case I suspect it is neither true nor false to say that grace is in conflict with gravity, as asserted by Simone Weil and the organizersof this gathering, but many assumptions follow from the inference that it is.[1] I am interested in the ways that works of art test that hypothesis, but first I want to think about Lucy.

In 1974, some 3.2 million years after her birth, approximately 40 percent of the fossilized skeleton of a member of the species Australopithecus Afarensis was found in Ethiopia. It is thought that Lucy, as the discoverers named her remains, died at about twelve years of age, a mature young adult standing at 1.1 meters tall. Her lone ankle suggests that Lucy was flat-footed but it is her valgus knee, her knock-knee, which is the key indicator that this homonin walked on two feet. Her name in the Ethiopian language, Amharic, is Dinkinesh, which means "You are marvellous."

After our ancestors had, as a species, stood up, humans, extinct hominins like Lucy perhaps, began to inhabit this distinction between the earth and the sky, between up-down, and body-mind. The world, in upright Western thought at least, became discontinuous with itself. Hierarchies of space appeared, leading us to see the sky as something out there, as above,

rather than something enveloping the earth and surrounding us.
Our bodies, our feet in particular, came to represent that part
of us which is constrained by nature, in contact with the earth,
the world of change, death and decay: whilst our minds, our
souls looked to eternity for answers.

> Australopithecus were probably equally comfortable moving
> through trees as on foot. Several unanswerable questions come
> to mind. Did Lucy have a sense of up and down? Might a being
> who lived 3.2 million years ago have had a concept of gravity
> and grace? An understanding of what is meant by reality and
> correspondingly of unreality, or imagination? Did she unthink-
> ingly sense that she was of the world, or feel, as most people
> do, somehow separate from it?

Lucy's state of mind is immensely intriguing, in part because
of how important being upright is to human thought. She is
also a means for me to flag my foolish fascination with the idea
that once we occupied a world not formulated in terms of
these binaries, of earth and sky, gravity and grace, body and
mind, and our cursed/blessed in-between-ness, but as a continuum and ourselves indivisible from it. It is a secular take on
an image of prelapsarian bliss.

> By checking the reality of such constructs with works of art,
> I believe we can find connection where there seems to be
> difference or opposition.

Usually the relationship between gravity and grace is couched
as a negotiation of control, as freedom and agency overcoming
involuntary constraint. However beauty is not necessarily
predicated on grace, or on transcending gravity; rather it may
be the fusion or confusion of both gravity and grace which
affirmatively affirms our human in-between-ness, or blurs the
distinctions of the reality we inhabit.

> With this in mind, as a human who thinks quite a bit about verti-
> cality whilst happily lying on the floor, I'm going to discuss some
> things, made by people other than me, (but which I've responded
> to in my own work): works that I sense undermine simple divi-
> sions, and revel in in-between-ness, and even in confusion.

38,000 BCE

I first saw Löwenmensch's image online many years ago. They
were a he, then a she, but consensus has shifted again to he,

and though known as Lionman in the Anglophone world, I prefer Lionhuman.

> Lionhuman above all else looks to me like a being who works hard to join the heavens and the earth. He was made, I sense, by someone who suspected that the world is not necessarily simply what it appears to be.

He has a cave lion's head and forelimbs and the body of a short-legged human. Lionhuman was carved from a mammoth tusk around 38,000 BCE. He is acknowledged to be the oldest fabricated, figurative sculpture. Reconstructed from 268 fragments, he is exquisite, all 31.1 cm, with his cracks, gaps and mystery. He lives in a museum in Ulm but finally we met in real life when Lionhuman was displayed in the British Museum as part of a show titled *Living with the Gods.* Having obsessed about him for so long I was tactically prepared to be disappointed.

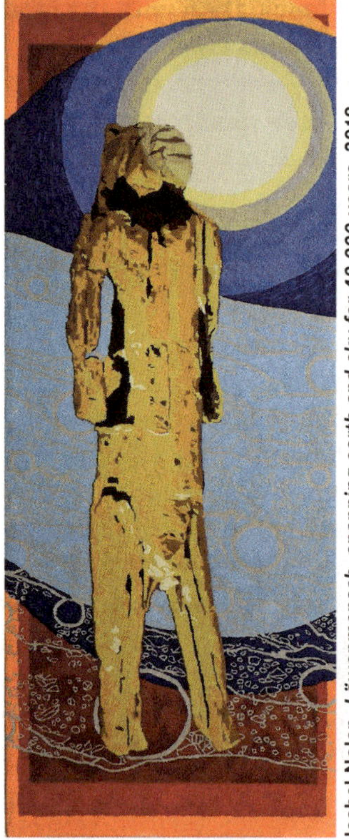

Isabel Nolan, *Löwenmensch, spanning earth and sky for 40,000 years, 2018*

> *Living with the Gods* was a show, which posited that "beliefs in spiritual beings and worlds beyond nature are characteristic of all human societies." Lionhuman was cast in the role of poster boy for the exhibition and given pride of place, the first

piece in the display. Frequently, the artefacts of the upper ice age are correlated with enormous metaphysical claims; the birth of religiosity; belief in the supernatural; even the emergence of our humanity or a soul that separates us from the animals. The birth of spirituality, the dawn of our truly human nature, of symbolism or otherworldly belief seemed an immense weight for Lionhuman, the oldest piece in the show, to carry. I cannot help but wonder if perhaps this figure has more prosaic or profane origins. It could be a nascent artistic provocation gleefully testing the nature of reality. Or a proto-scientific exercise, a peculiar document produced by someone wondering what the offspring of a lion and a human might be like. Lionhuman might simply be the protagonist of an ancient bedtime story. A story told to encourage small, unruly humans to go to sleep lest the Lionhuman come.

It looks like the work of a homonin who had discovered that narrative and meaning are as malleable as the clay, the wood, the animal matter, the grasses and even the stone of their surroundings. This is an enormous claim but not a metaphysical one. Ivory was slowly shaped and something wholly unreal was brought into being, into reality. Early humans at some point discovered their capacity to rearrange the substances of the world and make it meaningful to them in wholly new ways.

Lionhuman's mouth turns up a little on one side. He looks thoughtful. His unnatural stance looks purposive, as if a human posture gifted him with reasoning intellect. Perhaps even 40,000 years ago, verticality was already a signifier of rationality, of animal instincts left behind. A lion's head is elevated, the animal's power, its captivating terror somehow tamed by the human form. Standing on tiptoe, straight legged, straining to escape the earth, or its nature, perhaps it is a story of grace overcoming gravity, of reason overcoming instinct. Equally it might tell of power drawn from an animal nature, of self-consciousness superseded by killer instinct. We'll never know. A vacuum of information surrounds its production.

Lionhuman can't stand on his own two feet. He must be propped up. I imagine his creator carrying him about like a baby showing Lionhuman all the ruptures that his appearance made apparent in the world: between human and animal, earth and sky, body and mind, between the horizontal and the upright, gravity and grace.

Whether such gaps were exaggerated or closed by Lionhuman's uprightness and in-between-ness, undoubtedly objects such as this changed reality and what the world could mean.

440 BCE

For a time I had a fixation with, a crush on, a badly damaged sculpture which is housed at the Kunsthistorisches Museum (KHM) in Vienna. Carved around 440 BCE, a Roman copy of a Greek original, Doryphoros' curtailed potency, his almost pornographic ruin and contrapposto elegance seem a perfect conflation of fantasy, reality, power and intimacy. When you orbit the work, the inhuman but radiant stone flesh suggestively invites you to touch, but his forbidding, derelict perfection insists you keep some distance. Here gravity and grace are in customary tension. The lightness of the sculpture belies the substance of stone.

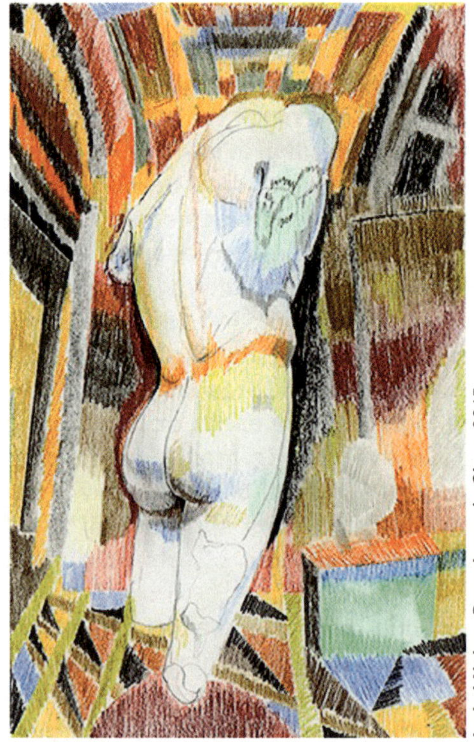

Isabel Nolan, *Doryphoros in Glory*, 2015

My infatuation with it was in part, I suspect, because of its location in a physically and culturally high, upright, and in ways, domineering, building. Temples, cathedrals, and museums, edifices that use height to impress, to worship, to intimidate, overwhelm me. It's a great, oftentimes libidinal pleasure to surrender to the force of a building that defiantly, brilliantly and beautifully harnesses gravity to inspire feelings of grace.

On the thresholds of these places, without needing to consciously think it, I'm aware that shortly all the atoms that temporarily shape me will be deployed elsewhere in this increasingly disorderly universe. This cosmic irrelevance is not quite the awe, or revelation that Gustav Semper, chief architect of the KHM, intended with his high-minded schemes but such aesthetic intimations of oblivion make me terribly receptive.

Whilst navigating these places my appreciation, my nervy pleasure, eventually dissipate. The knowledge that this active surrender to the commitments of church fathers, monarchs, industrialists and autocrats is deeply problematic builds. I'm no longer drifting, but stalking through these highly cultivated spaces. Compelled and alienated by the ferocity of civilization. In those moments, feeling as if I have ceded all control to external splendor, I become prey to infatuations. And my love for these places, combined with the immense, distant, authority of the location makes me crave intimacy.

When the ostentation of Vienna, the grandeur and upward sweep of its architecture, the sickening concentration of riches and objets d'art, succeeded in dazzling, captivating, overwhelming, and making me feel both ignorant and poor, I became physically obsessed with this maimed warrior from the KHM's collection. Instead of trying to understand the draw and history of this statue so that I might find new work to work on, new thoughts to think, I was just wondering what it might feel like to be naked in front of it; and if I could dare to make it happen, just to be held by the gaze of a sightless thing.

Like Lionman, Doryphoros is free from the burden of a specific identity. He is a sculptural archetype. Once he would have carried a spear; he still emanates the aura of a proud warrior, but he is sadly disfigured and very old. There is so much about him that remains unknown, space in this instance that was filled only by my libidinal imagination. Entranced by his graceful gravity, I was having low thoughts in high places.

One September day in 2011, after descending from the vertiginous heights of London's St Paul's Cathedral, I skirted the interior walls, avoiding the oppressively high and empty but God-shaped dome, and happening on this statue of poet John Donne was part pleasure, part relief.

Donne, I found out later, had been the Dean of St Paul's. In April 1631, one month before his death, he modeled for this memorial sculpture. A painter was hired to make a life-size drawing and though gravely ill with stomach cancer, Donne knotted himself, head to toe in his burial shroud, and stood on a specially made wooden model of a funeral urn.

The resulting full-length portrait was set by his deathbed. And one year on, an altogether unique, upright funerary statue, carved by master craftsman Nicholas Stone, was installed in the cathedral.

Instantly I was struck by the silken surface of the stone, the gravity-defying ruffled fabric and of course Donne's face. He meets death not with a requisitely dutiful expression of piety but with a look of private rapture; the gaunt face of the drawing is made dreamily youthful. A hint of a smile lifts the corners of his mouth. I find him beautiful.

But what sustained my attention were his knees, which are slightly but unmistakably bent, his smooth kneecaps separated by vertical, labial ripples of fabric. This bend introduces an animating moment of uncertainty, of downward movement to the upright statue, completely disrupting its modest graceful piety. His knees suggest an ordinary fallibility. Maybe due to the onset of fatigue, of doubt, his joints yield a little to gravity's sickly pull.

Donne was not posing for an ordinary ecclesiastical portrait in stone but acting out his future resurrection. He's a lover on the verge of a long desired consummation: caught between earth and heaven, on the verge of witnessing the everlasting dawn, his lips curving ready to kiss Christ and hands stirring in anticipation of disrobing. Donne is enacting a quiet ecstasy, his fierce hope of dwelling bodily *"for ever and ever, and infinite and super-infinite for evers."*[2]

Maybe his legs are not weak but tense: the knees not bent with illness and age but flexing, ready to take a momentous step from the urn, which perhaps he defiantly, even ironically mounted. With that thought, the urn transforms from a morbid

pedestal into a classical springboard to the next dimension.
The gravitational dip of his knees gives Donne the energy, the
momentum, the grace required for his heavenly transportation.

> This desire to face change, to stage manage his transition
> from life to eternity with a performance in stone, is testament
> to receptivity. A delicate monument to fear and vulnerability,
> to human in-between-ness, carried out with imagination, style,
> even wit. His willingness to perform in extremis, to will what
> is unimaginable into reality, is beautiful.

It is a work of grace transfigured by gravity.

1969 CE

> The main component of this final work is a wooden table held
> approximately 45 cm off the ground. Two bent ply and steel
> chairs, side by side, support its back legs. The tabletop is
> penetrated, between the front legs, by the pointed hat of a
> large model of a Disneyesque dwarf, who is mostly terracotta
> brown, but has some blue paint on his collar and hat. The
> dwarf faces forward and so gives a direction to work. Four
> other chairs at floor level pursue the table. Up top, two more
> rest on its surface. Other elements include empty wine and
> champagne bottles, fake fungi, and a disarrayed tablecloth.
> On the mouth of at least one upright bottle rests a plate.
> There is some other crockery dispersed about.

Attached to the table's underside is an upside down paint-
daubed, stuffed dog. It has eggshells on its inverted tummy.
Suspended around it are handkerchiefs; each pinched at the
center, they hang from wires under the table surface, bobbing
about in a figurative sense like a gang of textile ghosts. Stuck
to various surfaces of the table are scribbled notes, small
drawings and a substantial number of photographs.

> *Dwarf Parade* by Paul Thek was first displayed in 1969 but
> was remade and reshown in various guises with quite startling
> variations, at times involving potted plants, a stuffed swan,
> pillows, logs and candles. Each instance is a perplexing con-
> catenation of things; the parade of the title is echoed by the
> way the diverse objects array themselves in a bawdy line, a
> line drawn in the world by the work.

There is some sense of it originating in the interruption of a
raucous party; booze was consumed, the order of things was

upended, spillages and odd inversions have occurred. Things went badly for the dog. I conventionally imagine that the dwarf was the host; his rictus grin and blank eyes draw mine to the suspect toadstools. In each variant the tabletop somehow got smashed over his head. He and it are stuck with each other.

It's tempting to keep listing the constituent parts, to try to draw all these elements together, construct a complete picture, come up with a cogent interpretation, but it goes nowhere. Yet the whole shambolic, ambulatory object coheres in a profoundly peculiar and confusing way. I think that it is trying hard to make some progress, to transcend its condition but cannot, or will not, conceal its shame and suffering, its reliance on alcohol to escape earthly woes. The work is playful, it is tragic; it is bizarrely uplifting. Trapped by its own efforts and comical condition, parading dysfunction, and death, it is celebratory and degraded. It is beautiful. Joyous, unruly, and disobedient, each element escapes the senseless tableau just as much as it comprises it. This seems a very human and in-between condition.

Seeing it in Kunstmuseum Luzern in 2012 I had the sense of being fully present, alert, but also finding its reality so fascinating, so consuming, that there was no room for my own thoughts. I circled it, got down on my knees to study it from below, trying to not miss any element, any detail. I vividly recall how utterly moving, arresting it was, and all the while I knew how ludicrous it was to be so touched, so physically engaged, so captivated and bewildered by a cluttered table penetrated by a cartoon dwarf in a big white room in Switzerland. I was in a state of intense and thrilling ignorance.

It makes the world absurdly present, testing and disrupting reality with glee and rigour. When a work is this good, occupying space in such a singular way, utterly possessed of its own particularity, understanding falters. The work demands and defies our scrutiny. This image looks like a document of some crazed corner of reality but it feels like the daily failure to ever really understand the world.

When gravity and grace are in such perfect disarray, an artwork makes the borders of our own conceptual frameworks somehow visible, exposing them for the constructs they are. The sense of actively surrendering to the generous strangeness of the work is intense: a thrill attendant on negotiating our relationship with oblivion, with reality. Moreover there is the mental and physical difficult demand of looking and looking when you know that sight alone is nowhere near enough to take in certain works. Your skin, your body is feeling the work too. That is beauty.

Now.

I have had for many years a sense that the gravitational forces exerted by artworks operate not on the Newtonian principles that pertain in our lived experience on the surface of the earth, but rather work more in line with the language of general relativity. Of course this is without scientific basis; nevertheless, I've had a few unforgettable encounters with artworks, with objects that convince me that they can alter the shape and passage of space and time. Time passes unevenly in a rapture of being with the work; slowly attending with one's whole being, the world closes in. Space bends, light shifts, and an hour goes in the slow blink of eye.

With these protracted moments of perplexing revelation and self-surrender, an intense encounter with reality is made, an undifferentiated meeting with the world, such as Lucy/Dinkinesh might have taken for granted. And I think such beauty enables us to love the reality of the in-between human world even whilst we hate it.

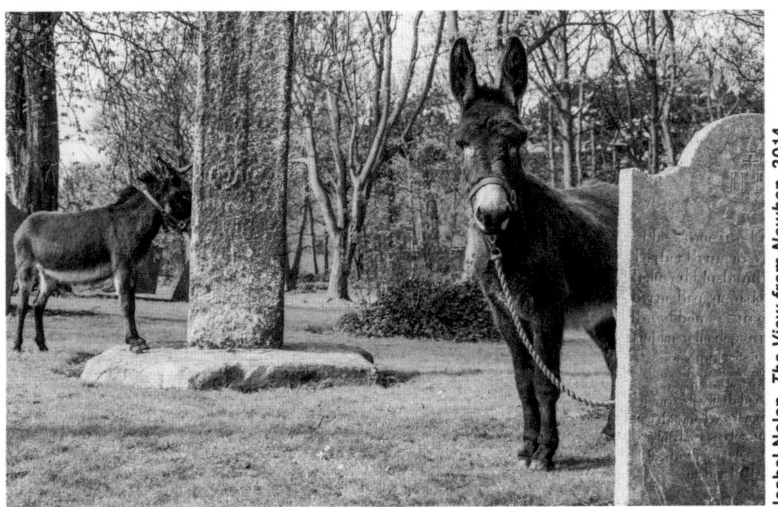

Isabel Nolan, *The View from Nowhen*, 2014

1 Engadin Art Talks, Grace & Gravity, 2019.
2 Donne, quoted in Philip Cottrell, "John Donne, Undone, Redone," in *Death, Burial and the* *Afterlife: Dublin Death Studies*, ed. Philip Cottrell and Wolfgang Marx (Bray, Co. Wicklow, 2014), p. 53.

Michael Schindhelm

The Artist, Leadership and Contemporaneity

Nowhere is talk of contemporaneity as pronounced as in the arts (literature, music and theater, etc.). The term, in the sense that art deals with it, doesn't exist in politics or business, say. In this context it is interesting that in German we regard what is *Gegenwartskunst* (art of the present) and *zeitgenössische Kunst* (contemporary art) as synonymous. Contemporaries share this conception of the term in accordance with a certain present. Contemporaries do not necessarily share a past or a future. Their commonality consists of a here and now (and in English we say "contemporary art" and "contemporaneity"). This identification with our contemporaries should have implications for the role of art and artists in society.

> Art clearly operates with a peculiar temporal terminology. If we interrogate its role in the current world (this society) as well as the (dis)functionality of decisions and leadership in this world (this society), then this specific temporal terminology is relevant.

> The problem with time:

The phenomenal durability of the fleeting in modern life allows it to pass by in a flash. Constant scarcity provokes the question: What time are we actually living in? The diktat of current capitalism is of continual movement. It is unswervingly loyal to the future. We should have it and nothing else in view. The present disappears. We have no time, i.e., the present has slipped from our grasp.

> This present nonetheless offered the generations of only the last century the security of living in an unmistakeably defined, socially structured time. One belonged in a time and this was inscribed clearly in each individual biography.

Not to put too fine a point on it—today we live *before* time. Time has become anonymous. It is no longer experienced as *our* time. Instead it's just *current* and drives everything forwards. It has lost its social character. We thus observe how the immediacy of human community is abandoned in favour of rampant nostalgia (and the subsequent populism, for example) or an equally rampant progressive escapism (sci-fi, cyber-mysticism, new age, etc.). The difference between social and current time is to be found in the fact that current time connects people primarily through the scarcity of time. The society of material excess is one of temporal shortage.

Yet being connected through time has been and is important for people and society. According to Jeremy Rifkin, man is the only living being "tethered to time." This connection to time is dramatically endangered by the state of continual movement, if it has not indeed already disappeared. The lack of present is particularly striking. The present has, over the course of recent decades (and the most recent in particular), become, bit by bit, a prelude to the future. What prides itself in relating to the present, a speculative part of the art industry, for example, tries instead to always be ahead of this present. Fleeing before the present.

So what time are we living in, or living in advance of? The future may tell it differently. An audit of the current day tells us the following: this is the time of fake news, climate change, over-population, Instagram, escapism, veganism, disruptive tech-nologies, the end of Western dominance, massive improvements in the quality of life in so-called developing countries, Brexit, Alibaba, the Marvel cinematic universe, Spacex, etc.

There are three topics in cross-section across this (and similar) audits of the current day. These are *productivity, institution and communication.* These cross-sectional topics are just as relevant for today's happenings in general as they are for art and its potential to play a part in these events and potentially re-define them. *I see the key potential of contemporary art in its capacity to connect time, or indeed to overcome the alien-ation of social time. The current, pressing role for art consists in contributing to the transformation of a society in which time is scarce, into one in which there is an excess of time.*

Productivity:

Research and practice assume to the same extent that tradi-tional production and value chains will be radically challenged, by new technologies in particular. What have already been sometimes swingeing consequences of digitalization for the arts such as literature or film are well-known and have been detailed. Audience habits have equally been thrown under the wheels of this radical change. We still read, for example, but "differently." The idea of social media raises the likelihood that the process of reception itself has become more attrac-tive than the (usually ephemeral) product produced, or the object of reception. Current developments in the field of social design based on "collaboration," "participation," "networking," "adaptation," "collapsing," etc, as well as the sheer flood of technological possibilities for design (of art products) have triggered a production flow in which the products and their production can scarcely be differentiated. Benjamin's term of reproduction depended upon the duplication of what was an initially genuinely produced original. Current (re)production, however, needs no original (and the consequences in the field of authorship are currently being discussed at length). The product is just a milestone in the process of reproduction. If we may make a comparison with biology: the classic product is, to a certain extent, the individual of productive life; repro-duction, on the other hand, ensures the species is maintained. Reproduction is never pure repetition because (as we have known at least since Kierkegaard) the routine of repetition always leads to new results or products.

> The process design inevitably proves to be more important than the product design. Today's prosumers allow the flow of reproduction of news, entertainment, education and art, etc. in one continuum.

Institution:
Traditionally, the process of reproduction was maintained by organizations. To employ our biological metaphor again, prod-ucts (presentations, books, paintings, etc.) could be regarded as individuals, with organizations as the species.

> Art organizations, as well as the whole art and culture industry, find themselves in a transformation process, the end of which we cannot fathom; the current form of this process is defined by us in general as a *cultural plasma*. Not only are production and reception changing, but inevitably also decision-making, directing and following processes, how resources are distrib-uted, evaluation and mediation, as well as how responsibilities are administered.

High culture is an erratic cultural landscape in need of reform that is the result of centuries of praxis and interaction of society and art; within it exist inherited hierarchies as exist inher-ited criteria for evaluation and mediation. The marked lack of education of (elite) cultural managers in relation to the role and potential of all that culture which is not high culture is striking. The cultural institution's crisis leads us to the question of leadership, in a literal sense. How can we develop a relationship between base and apex anew, between producer and consumer, or the relationship of the I to the we? How can established culture liberate itself from the splendid isolation of elitism, how can less well-established cultures free themselves from a defensive position of being underestimated and injured, etc? How fruitful, how accepting and how collaborative is, or could, commercial culture be?

Leadership and following must be rethought. For this, an alternative concept of communication is required.

Communication:
I propose a thesis for contemporary art in this regard: *I communicate, therefore We are. We communicate, therefore I am.*

Fundamentally we understand art as being, amongst other things, a technique that helps us to differentiate ourselves from one another and either to communicate these differences to one another in exchange, or to overcome them entirely. Art is, in this sense, communication. Communication predicates that the person communicating has both an image of themselves, as they do of the other. Through communicative influence, these kinds of images become exemplary. Art is, amongst other things, this kind of communicative influence.

From our perspective social media are well placed for an observation of the current transformation process in communication. Images or messages operate like products (see above, under Productivity) as the elements of the flow of the reproduction of communication.

The ultimate goal is, as a rule, no longer an individual message but the mediation of messages, a continuum of exchange of images which leads to the formation of social relationships and, possibly, social behaviour. Because, as a rule, communication takes place in multiple directions, a network of prosumers of messages and images emerges. The continuum first becomes relevant for the question of leadership and following when stable relationships between prosumers result from this exchange. These relationships become stable by virtue of the fact that they are not based on ephemeral temporality but that a robust present has transpired between those communicating.

The interplay of art between producer and recipient, or between prosumers, can be observed in relation to this very aspect of stabilizing, and conclusions can be drawn regarding the possible societal effect of art. How can contemporary art achieve this stabilization of the relationship with its following? The process could be illustrated thus:

> A continuum of reproducible messages emerges in an exchange employing art images of oneself (the artist-I), of others (he/she/it) and of a community (we/institution/environment), messages which are not limited to the moment of exchange, but leave traces. Both the exchange and the form of exchange that the artist employs make him or her a *role model*. Using the qualities (skills) described below, the artists thus develops an interactive and participatory process design, with or independent of a cultural institution. In this, certain actors are qualified as peers and influences (traditionally these were/are mediators, critics and academics, for example) who, interactively with artists and/or cultural institutions, stabilize the exchange of messages. Through the artist's position as a role model and because this process of exchange can be reproduced, an overarching trust emerges between artists, influencers and prosumers (audience) as is intrinsic in functioning relationships of leadership and following in general. The network structure of the continuum leads to an interactive and dynamic leadership–following relationship that can also weather conflict or shocks.

The emergence and maintenance (stabilization) of such leadership–following relations requires, as already mentioned, certain competencies that are mediated through engagement with art. I define artists with this capacity as contemporary artists, or indeed *role models*, who are capable of realizing the successful process design of this stabilization. They develop this capacity on the basis of particular *qualities* that empower them and which therefore must be cultivated and promoted in the context of teaching and research. Initial outlines of these qualities are the following:

> Identity:
> Artists engage more explicitly than other people with the particularities of individuals. The general attitude is one of "I to we." The artist's capacity to practice art allows him or her to both articulate these particularities and to communicate them (see communication).

Motivation:

Artists are driven by their imagination, more so than others. In strict accordance with Pina Bausch's motto (that what is interesting is not how the dancer moves, but what moves them,) it holds that fantasy is the starting point of the artist's effect. Sloterdijk spoke of the four stages of the imagination, (see his speech for the Salzburg Festspiele, 'Der Tau von den Bermudas'). This must no longer be timely, but it is certainly interesting to attempt some research on fantasy in the age of globalization and AI and the role of fantasy in a new concept of leadership.

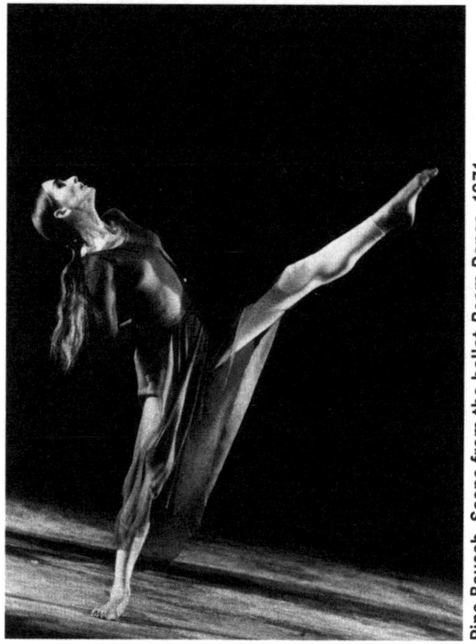

Pina Bausch, Scene from the ballet *Poem Dance*, 1971

Communication:

Artists speak a language of images, each their individual form. This connects the individual in a non-rational manner with a society and makes life as an artist possible. An artist's semantics is ambiguous. In this is a nascent power in light of the multi-optional, no longer differentiable, nature of reality today.

Integrity:

Thanks to the forms of identity and motivation described above, the artist has a particular relationship to his or her environment.

The artist develops a sense of the codes of his or her "class" and solidarity with their peers. Michelangelo, David Bowie or a colleague in Indonesia may seem to have more in common with him or her than the people around. With this the artist describes a particular relationship in space and time that has far-reaching implications for political engagement or social responsibility, etc.

Professionalism:
Artists continually question their own professionalism. The profession is a calling to challenge oneself and to take risks. The artist lives with the paradox that success may not rest in the product, but the process, of creation. Where imagination is in play, uncertainty reigns. The artist does not regard uncertainty as something to be avoided, but as natural agency.

Tomás Saraceno

Aerocene Manifesto:
Aeronauts Unite!

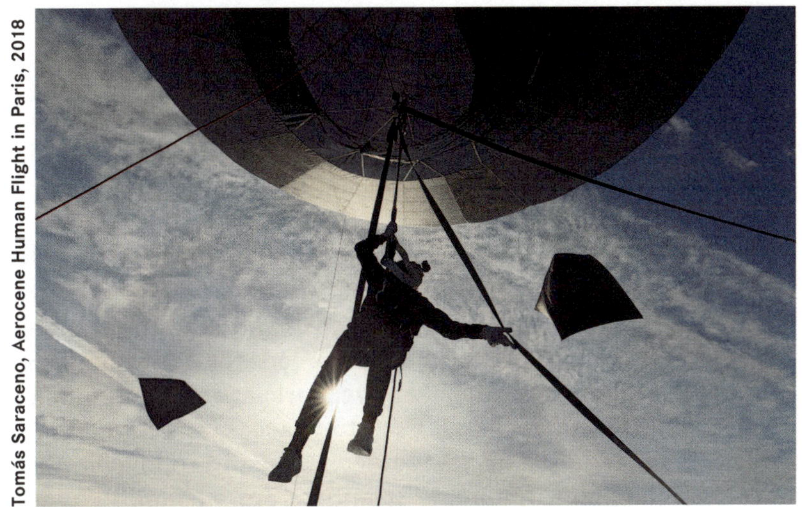

While fossil fuel based industries endeavor to colonize other planets, the air, this interface between us and the Sun, is controlled by the few and continues to be compromised: carbon emissions fill the air, particulate matter floats inside our lungs while electromagnetic radiation envelops the earth, dictating the tempo of digital capitalism, in the era of global warming. Yet, a different epoch is possible, one of interplanetary sensitivity through a new ecology of practice. Towards this, collective ideas must form, by asking: How would breathing feel in a post fossil fuel economy? And what are our response-abilities to be on air? How can geopolitical borders be challenged in an age of climate inequality? How to participate in a new epoch beyond the Anthropocene, towards the decarbonization of the air, and independence from fossil fuels? Together, we call for this new epoch, which we have named *Aerocene.*

> Aerocene imagines space as a commons, a physical and imaginative place cleared from corporate control and government surveillance. Aerocene promotes de-securitized, free access to the atmosphere, the last earthly layer created as a result of the interplaying forces of the Sun, gravity and the earth mass. Aerocene is a proposal—a scene *in, on, for,* and *with* the air.

The launch pad towards this new epoch is an aerosolar balloon, a Do It Together (DIT) entrance to the aerial, whose only engine is the air and heat of the Sun, floating as a result of temperature differentials between the two air masses, anywhere from 2 degrees up. In such a way, it calls for a new embodied cosmology attuned with the Sun, the life-giving star that has been turned into a threat by clouds of black carbon that absorb solar energy and make our planet warmer every day. These self-stabilizing aerosolar bodies float differently from any airborne plant or animal. Once inflated with air, they are able to elevate into the sky, thanks only to the Sun heating the air in the interior, afterwards relying only on the wind to drift along aerosolar journeys.

> In this way, Aerocene performs in stark relief to the industrial activity that has injected large amounts of carbon dioxide, aerosol particulates and hot air into the atmosphere, as a result of fossil fuel combustion processes. While naturally occurring clouds are crucial atmospheric agents that reflect a portion of the sun's energy back to space, cloud formations now stand corrupted by new categories of anthropogenic clouds, to such a point that some scientists are pushing to add them to the International Cloud Atlas.

Through their relentless metamorphosis and movements, terrestrial clouds play a generative role in regulating the planet's average temperature. Deciphering the language veiled in their shapes, it becomes possible to read the various morphologies dictating weathers both present and future. In the age of the Anthropocene, it has become possible to ignore the tumultuous variation of the natural world, to usurp its control by jet plane and railroad, cutting through wind and storm with petrol, riding floods with motorized engines, ironically contributing, in the propulsion of greenhouse gases, to the increasing unpredictability of the weather phenomenon. Aerocene, as weather-dependent, re-builds a less anthropocentric relationship with the environment, becoming a way to exit from our epistemic isolation and re-entangle ourselves with the milieu, in this case, the weather. Floating airborne without carbon emissions, these aerosolar journeys speculate about what kinds of nomadic socio-political structures might emerge if we could navigate the rivers of the atmosphere, reconsidering the ways in which borders are set up by humans, and the power of national institutions to decide who can transit: policies that dramatically affect vulnerable subjects, humans and non-human life forms. This is to become *airnomads*, moving from *Homo economicus* to *Homo Flotantis*, who is attuned to planetary rhythms, conscious of living with other humans and non-humans and who learned to float in the air, adrift with the wind.

Human and non-human life forms suffer from climate change, experiencing a wide range of impacts, not least their enforced mobility in search of survival, as nation states around the planet re-assert their geopolitical borders. What are the rights of pass, the corridors we need to open, in order to restore the right to roam? How can we overcome the paradox of decisions made by the few, simultaneously forcing and inhibiting migration? Aerocene calls for an interspecies right to mobility that could reconnect with elemental sources of energy and with other planetary atmospheres, breaking the boundaries of the sublunary and expanding the critical zone of all air-dependent life. We suggest a model for a landscape that balances and harnesses our relationship with the unlimited potential of the Sun. This realization requires a thermodynamic leap of imagination, just like during an eclipse, when only in the absence of light we become aware of our scale in the shadow of the cosmos.

Researchers in industrial and social ecology refer to "sociometabolic regimes" to define the epochal shifts in energetic relationships between humans and their environment, establishing a strict correlation between these relationships and specific sets of social values. They have also argued that two of the main kinds of metabolic regimes have been solar based, the ones of hunter-gatherer societies and agrarian societies. Despite the existence of societies that still rely on such relationships with the Sun—together with all the other species that populate the Earth—these are threatened by the domination of the current metabolic regime, the one based on fossil fuels, the mark of the Anthropocene. Increasing globalization is pushing this regime towards its end, engendering the disappearance of clouds by the very same energy supplies on which an aggrandized fossil capital productivity depended, raising the urgency to rethink how we can coexist with the planet and its resources.

Julian Charrière and Nadim Samman

"As We Used to Float" (Excerpts)

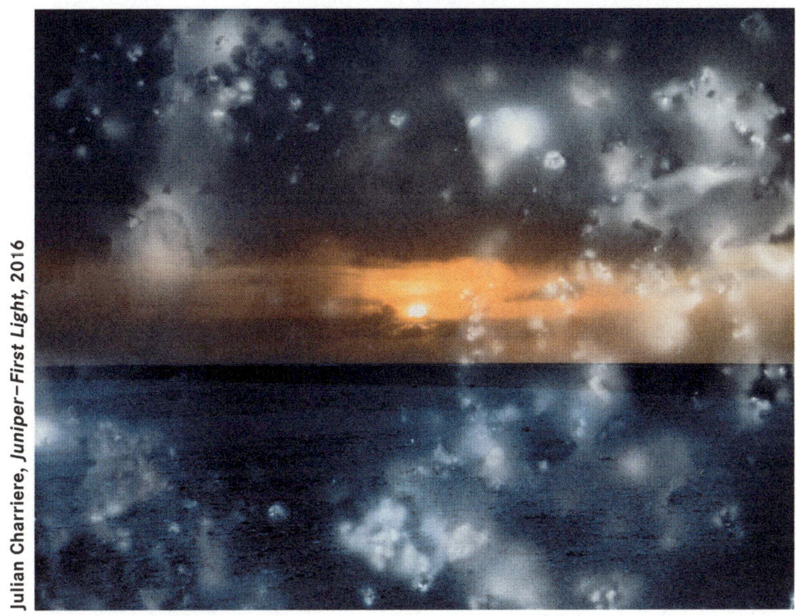

The Narc

Diving the wrecks of Bikini Atoll requires intense preparation. As they lie some sixty meters below the water's surface, only the successful performance of a host of specialized scuba processes can deliver you to them and bring you back without the bends. The aim of this kind of diving is to operate at the limits of the feasible, in terms of depth, time, and human physiology. It is a system for managing the greatest degree of risk while remaining in control and achieving objectives underwater. Technical Diving is a practice wholly concerned with the outer regions of safety, defined *technically* as opposed to recreationally. The theoretical aspect of this sort of diving involves studying the interplay between physics and biology relevant to a person's consumption of multiple gas mixtures over the course of a single dive. Breathing regular air at pressure causes progressively increased degrees of physiological impairment the deeper you go, due to nitrogen narcosis. It also ushers in the risks of oxygen toxicity, based on the partial pressure of the breathing mixture. Switching gases to avoid both of these factors is the name of the game. But this practice requires an understanding of when to switch and at which depth. Such

95

factors are unique to each dive profile and must be planned every time, individually. Switching too soon or at the wrong depth, or miscalculating the length of time needed for any stage of the decompression procedure, is no benign mathematical error, but can bring on fits, paralysis, incontinence, bubbles in the brain, and even death.

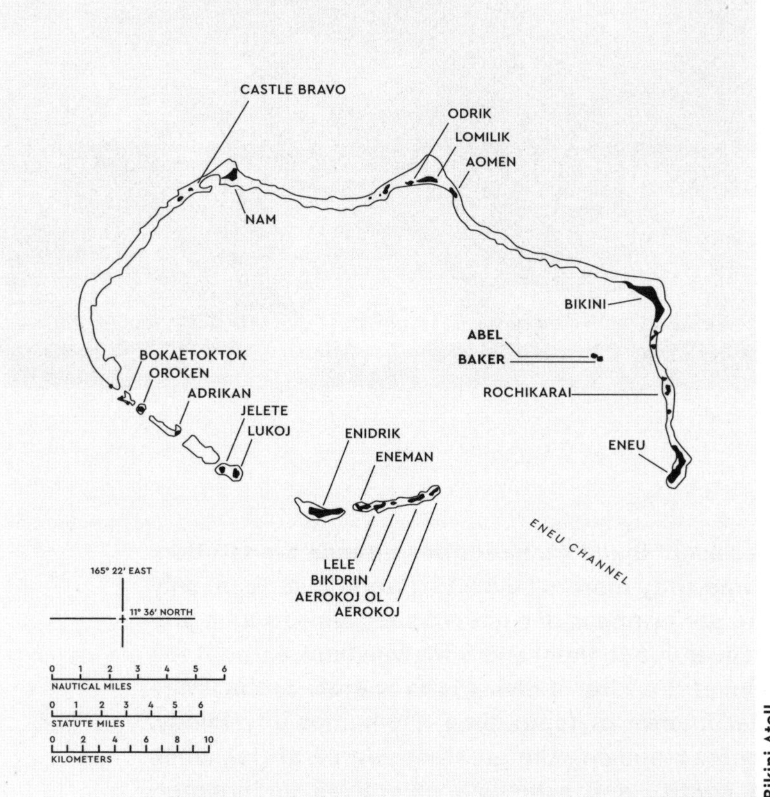

In addition to the theory, there is an exponential increase in gear. You don't use a Buoyancy Control Device (BCD), which is a kind of a plug-and-play system. Instead, you put on "wings"– a kind of streamlined harness incorporating a thin steel plate and numerous metal rings for attaching things. It looks closer to rock climbing equipment than something for scuba, and requires a lot of attention to set up before each dive. You strap two tanks onto the back of it instead of a normal single. To the front, you clip another, containing a higher percent oxygen mix. Instead of two regulators you have three. You also need three delayed surface marker buoys (DSMBs): one to deploy during decompression, another if you have a problem and need to alert the surface, and a third in case you lose one. In addition to your first dive computer, you wear a backup. And if both fail, your dive plan is also written out on a slate, which you strap to your other forearm. You carry a spare mask and two torches. You wear a knife on your leg, should you need to cut yourself out of a tangle, and whatever other tools your mission requires—in our case, cameras and lights.

Laden with all these things, underwater, you need to be comfortable and in control. You also need to be much more aware of your buoyancy than on a recreational dive, as the border between safety and danger can hinge on a meter during decompression. To maintain your depth, precisely, you need to be alert to your body, noticing subtle changes in pressure before you have to look at an altimeter. With so many objects to take care of, you cannot be constantly checking throughout the forty-something minutes you spend hanging on the line.

At the end of the theoretical and practical training, our instructor, Nico, says that he is passing us. According to the terms of his insurance, thus far he has only brought us to forty-five meters and no deeper. Now that you are newly minted technical divers—he states with a wry smile—I'll take you down to sixty, *just so you can feel it.* This seems like a figure of speech. So far, everything appears the same, whether at twenty, thirty, or forty. Once you pass that second atmosphere, at ten meters, and have equalized, your inner ear is set up. He tells us that the plan is to jump in and go straight down until we hit depth, then we will ascend. *Just a bounce,* he says.

We tip backwards over the side of the zodiac and purge the air from our wings, descending headfirst for a few seconds amid a rumble of bubbles. We feel a squeeze around our necks as the pressure increases, as well as the swift chill of the thermocline, sitting high-up in the water column.

As we slide down a little deeper into the water, righting ourselves, it takes on the green-brown color of crocodile skin, and before long visibility is just a meter, our fins barely visible through the fog. We are sinking, but apart from the initial visceral register of the pressure, there is no way to tell that we are moving, except for the altimeter function on our computers, ticking away. In less than a minute we are at forty. Forty-one. Forty-two—and there is no bottom, just blurry darkness.

At this rate of descent, you start to think that you will soon hit your limit and that, as a matter of necessity, it is time to slow down. So, you inject some air into your wing—a conservative amount, so you don't shoot up like a rocket towards the surface. It has no effect, and the computer keeps ticking the meters away. Deeper. Still negative buoyancy. You reason that the pressure at this depth is greater than anything encountered in training, so you give it double. No result. Still falling, now scared. The thought of sinking further into the yawning chasm, beyond recovery, is horrifying. At fifty-five meters, you are charged with adrenalin, alert and trying to work it out, when—all of a sudden—you are dunked in a pool of insanity. A wave of intoxication breaks throughout your bloodstream; your brain is enveloped by a tsunami of nitrogen, rendering you dizzy and confused.

What makes the intoxication so terrifying is that you possess just enough awareness to know that you have lost the thread—that you are unable to make a plan, barely able to make sense of the numbers on your computer. You are out of control and the abyss is taking you. In panic at this realization, you start to breathe more heavily. And with heavier breathing comes more narcosis—a downward cognitive spiral. Now you are hyperventilating. You can't get enough air out of the regulator. It feels like the device is the problem—stopping you from getting the breath you need. You feel like spitting it out, opening your mouth wide and drinking the air, even though the still-useful part of your mind knows that this is the worst thing you could do. You know, too, that freaking out is a grave mistake, and so you panic even more. You kick your legs because you no longer trust your wing. No escape. Fifty-nine. Sixty. Sixty-one—and you turn to look for Nico, gesticulating wildly to indicate that you have lost control; that you are fucked up. Later, Nico says he saw the fear of death in your eyes. Once Nico sees it, he takes over. He firmly grabs your shoulder, extending his arm and locking his elbow—placing maximum distance between his body and yours while keeping hold. The reason for this, we learned in our rescue training, is that panicking divers have a tendency to claw at the person trying to save them, sometimes ripping away their mask or regulator, perhaps even trying to steal the latter, abandoning themselves to shameful instinct. He holds you there and stabilizes your depth. Then he looks you in the eye and holds you with his gaze, making you understand that he is in control; that *somebody* is—delivering you from the anxiety of having to take care of yourself. This done, the panic is gone–despite the remaining narcosis. A few seconds, then a simple gesture: a thumb pointing up, indicating that we should now ascend. And we do, slowly, meter by meter. Sixty. Fifty-nine. Fifty-eight. His hand still gripping your shoulder. When you reach forty, though still intoxicated, you can feel it start to drop off, like you have passed the apex of its bell-curve. You can see, now, that you will not fall any deeper into the trip. You are ready to take back control of your life. You point to yourself, then offer Nico the classic hand sign for OK. He lets you go and the rescue part of the dive is over. All that is left is to make a controlled ascent.

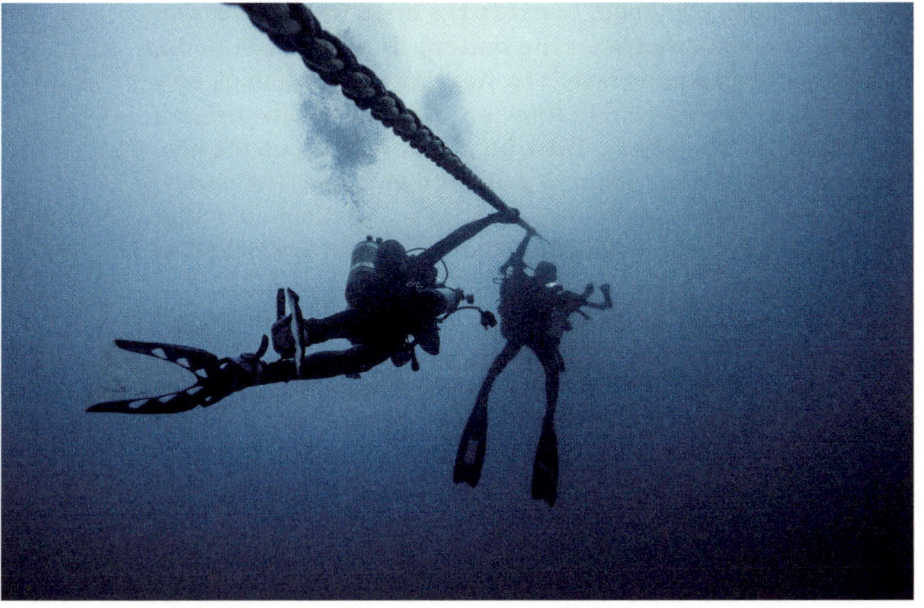

Saratoga

The Windward's engine is idling somewhere above the wreck of what was once the largest battleship in the world. Our training ended thousands of kilometers ago and yet, here, before we begin our jump, we are receiving a lesson in what it means. Technical divers can handle their own affairs, which is to say, realize their objectives, safely, on their own. John is about to deliver a case study. Throwing himself over the stern he disappears into the blue with a heavy rope over his shoulder, one end of which is attached to the bow. He will carry it a full fifty meters through the soup, towards the shadow of a massive wreck, lying somewhere on the bottom. There, he will find a part of the dead ship to lash it to, heaving the cord, thick as a sailor's leg, into a reliable knot so that the Windward can function as a sort of buoy. Then, he will climb back up the line. Only when he is back onboard will our dive begin. The performance gives us chills. We begin to rig up, making sure that each hose is properly clipped in, that our vents are locked or open as necessary. You want to make sure that your BCD can inflate, so you test it. You want to make sure that it doesn't leak, that you can achieve buoyancy, before you jump in carrying so much weight. The tanks are heavy, and if your wings fail you can be pinned to the bottom and drown. You also want to make physically certain that both tanks—and not just one—are fully open, as your pressure gauge is only partial and cannot report on both. You want to establish that the valve in your regulator isn't stuck—that it will deliver air to your lungs. And that your buddy's works too. You also want to make sure that the deco bottle really does contain the enhanced oxygen percentage used to calculate your dive plan, so you employ a sensor device to verify. You want to check that each of the tanks has been marked with an appropriate color, so that you can easily recognize which bottle is appropriate to sustain your life at a particular depth. Never mix tanks. Once you review the full package of your exoskeleton, every screw and hose, you want to be ready to go. Hobbling under the weight of our tanks, hunchbacked, towards the edge of the deck. Ready? Yelling—*Ready?* Giant strides off the side of the boat. The water makes us alert, and when we're all together a hand signals that it is time to sink. We swim under the Windward's hull, acned with shellfish, feeling the pulse of its engine through the water. We approach John's bowline and begin to climb it, downwards, headfirst. The water is thick. A plankton bloom—one of the most intense in decades. We continue our descent into darkening water, pressure building inside our heads, following the rope, deeper, and deeper, until, eventually, a blurry geometric volume begins to appear. A school of jacks pass on the left. Deeper. Gray reef sharks overhead. Our dive computers count away the depth. Time runs quickly underwater. Meter after meter the picture gains focus. Time to let go of the line. We're floating—no, flying—above a horizontal plane. It's clearly man-made, though the outward texture appears organic. A deck. Not just the deck of a ship, but a landing strip, and we are falling out of the sky towards it. We begin to modulate our speed, adjusting the buoyancy of our wings in order to put down lightly, feet first, like birds, on the runway of the USS Saratoga. At a length of 264 meters, the Saratoga is so long we cannot see its end. Designed to carry seventy-eight aircraft, including thirty-six bombers, it was twice torpedoed in its two decades of Pacific service, twice repaired, then put back to work, only to be crippled by a kamikaze assault at the battle of Iwo Jima. Repaired once again, it became a training carrier, before serving as a transport for prisoners, until it was finally subjected to two atomic blasts, in 1946. The first barely damaged it, while the latter put it here, on the bottom. Once we have collected ourselves together, we push off from it with our feet, abandoning verticality, and begin to swim along the runway, scanning it with our cameras. Slowly, at first, a little uneasy. Then, as more of the wreck's character is disclosed, slightly increasing our pace. Further. Continuing, on and on towards a murky vanishing point, we begin to discover that it is collapsed in places, opening into chasms exposing the ship's inner compartments. As we catch glimpses of equipment and hatches, cabins for sleeping in, and others for weapons, it is clear that, despite being dwarfed by the lagoon, the Saratoga is a world of its own. We move to the starboard edge and peer over. Though it is only twenty meters until the bottom, it looks like an infinite void, giving the impression that the wreck is floating in the water. Further along, the ruined control tower resembles a decaying Gothic cathedral. Tangled and draped in ropes and cables, it makes for an eerie sight—every piece of rigging coated in a thick green slime of biomass that billows in the current. There are no sharp edges anymore, only an indefinite zone of disintegration. The ship is not a form. It is an atmosphere, a cloud of particles, a blurry, narcotic cosmos. The nightmarish topography holds us in its grip, drawing us along. More massive depressions. Holes, cavities; impacts of the bomb or the weight of water–something powerful. We push onward along the man-made plane. Seconds. Minutes, watching the clock and the pressure in our tanks. Still swimming, the runway breaks into a massive rift. A kick of the legs puts us upside-down, and sinking three meters into the depression, allowing a view into the wreck's guts, the wrong way up, through a cross section of a corridor. The last thing we can make out is a lamp covered in grime, before the tunnel dissolves into a haze of blackish green. Another breath and a pull of knees towards our chests, so that our lungs' volume, and our body positions, effect somersaults. Heads the right way up, we float back up to the level of the runway and resume our path, advancing until we reach the end of the runway, which scoops upwards like a ramp. This is where the airplanes would lift off. We breathe out, kick out over its tip, into the blue, and fall. Ten meters. Another ten. Plunging until we can see the sand. A quick jet of air into the BCD, fins out in front, just a little twist of one to effect a final 180-degree turn, then touchdown. Facing back from whence we came, standing on the bottom, looking directly up at the bow–thirty meters of steel and coral bearing over us from beneath an abyss. A shadowy horror. A building. A sea-scraper, or the mandible of a prehistoric whale about to close in and swallow us, completely. How long have we been staring at this thing? A minute? Five? We're obviously dreaming, here, on the bottom. Time is fluid at these depths, but a spark of reason alerts us to our computers, whose beeps now assert that we are behind schedule–a serious error for our first deco dive. We lift off and start to ascend, slowly, until we are just above the landing strip, whose desolate plane we follow in search of the bow line. A female tiger shark hovers into view from behind the half-sphere of a gun turret. Don't be afraid of sharks, we've been told, over and over again; be afraid of the bends. She turns around and disappears behind a curtain of plankton. Continuing, George–guiding–seems unable to find the rope, our link to the world above. We catch each other's eyes and question, without any need for sign language, whether a mutiny might be in order. Normally, once you have reached the bottom, you rely on visual recognition of the topography–

coral heads and rocks—in order to navigate. Amid the flow, you try to situate yourself in relation to fixed points. In a second, everything can turn. The current can change direction and, without keeping an eye on things, you can drift away without knowing it. Eventually, you will notice that nothing looks familiar. In a second, even beautiful scenography can take on a mean aspect, reminding you that you do not belong. That is when you need to remain relaxed. The safety principle dictates that there must be no quick exit. No matter how much you want to leave immediately—to escape something, or return to the surface, where you imagine the situation is more welcoming—you shouldn't. An impulse to quick flight is more dangerous than many things down here. Now we are at a place that looks familiar, but not from the dive's beginning. Are we turning back on ourselves or actually heading for the rope? Perhaps George knows what he is doing, but it does not seem clear to us. Then, a tower appears—more recognizable than other details. Perhaps it is what we are looking for. We direct ourselves towards it. Then we ascend its vertical wall, past a shaft before reaching the place where the bow line is attached. The dive computer doesn't look good. It is certainly time to go, but we cannot rush. Hands on the rope. Checking the dive slate. One minute to rise five meters. One minute to rise some more. Two to rise further, and so on, the rope yanking intermittently. We climb, and climb, and we watch the clock; and we check the slate to make sure we are on plan, until the point where we must let go and swim for the stern of the Windward, loose in the current, looking for the deco bar that is our dock. The bar is a steel structure that resembles an oversized crowd-control barricade, upside down and suspended below the waterline, off ropes attached to each corner of the stern. Its last horizontal beam begins at three meters below, its second at six, its first at nine. Now hanging onto the first, we're like fish caught on a longline, or ragged sails on a mast. A breath. Exhaling. A slow rumble of bubbles offered up to the juddering thunder of the boat's engine, which charges the surrounding water with vibration. You feel it in your skin, despite the insulation supplied by your wetsuit; in your guts; in your skull: a low frequency ripple through viscera. A pulsing snarl. This is a safe place, though, your subaquatic pier. An intermediary between your scuba rig and that other technical edifice meant to keep you living at sea: the boat. Hands on the steel scaffolding, we feel relief. But the next thought is that we need to hang on, here, for forty-five minutes in the bouncing water. The current pushes us around, the added drag that we supply serving to twist the bar on a diagonal axis, so that its left side is no longer behind the boat, but pulling underneath, towards the propeller. While this mean-looking corkscrew is not running, being in such close proximity to it quickens our breath. As the bar pulls further in, the swell pushes the stern about a meter upwards and the rail is ripped from our hands. Lucky. Altitude isn't the only hazard: being yanked up against the underside of the boat's iron husk, or having the prop crash down on one's head is also a concern. It's hard to keep at nine meters, give or take a half meter, with the bar dancing so much. Even this close to air you are still, practically speaking, further away than it might seem. Distance from the surface isn't measured in fathoms, but time. Patience is the order of business. After twenty minutes of reflecting on the fact that this will be our lot for the next fifteen days, we're able to move to the six-meter bar. Now it is time to change bottles. You take a big breath, then your regulator out of your mouth. You bite down on the stage bottle's colored one and inhale a new mix. This time it is nearly pure oxygen—Nitrox 84. It feels medicinal, filling your lungs, trickling out from them into your bloodstream, exciting every molecule in your body. You feel the narcosis lift; the dream abates. Awake, again, you can almost smell the sausages being prepared in the galley above. Three meters. Now you are almost relaxed. Only a few more minutes before it is time to go. The computer is ringing. You slowly emerge, up into a newfound psychological calm, though the water's surface is churning. You don't care how rough it is. The Windward is see-sawing, port to stern; the ladder that you need to reach is stabbing at the water. You double kick, like a dolphin, launching yourself at it and grab on. As soon as you do, it yanks you out of the water like a slingshot, up towards Brendan's strong hands, which lift you onto the deck.

NADIM SAMMAN is a curator, art historian and
editor based in London.

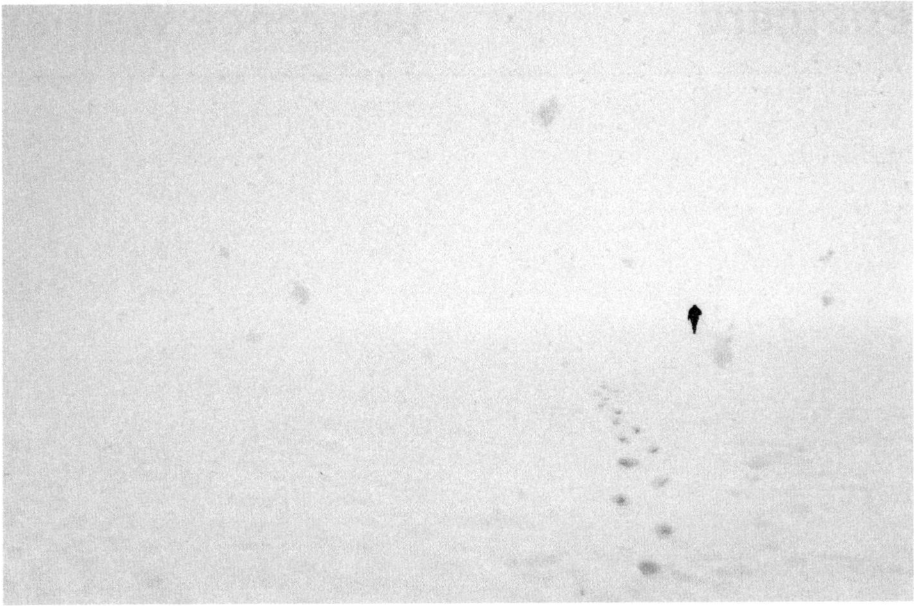

Julian Charrière, *Oberengadin*, 2017

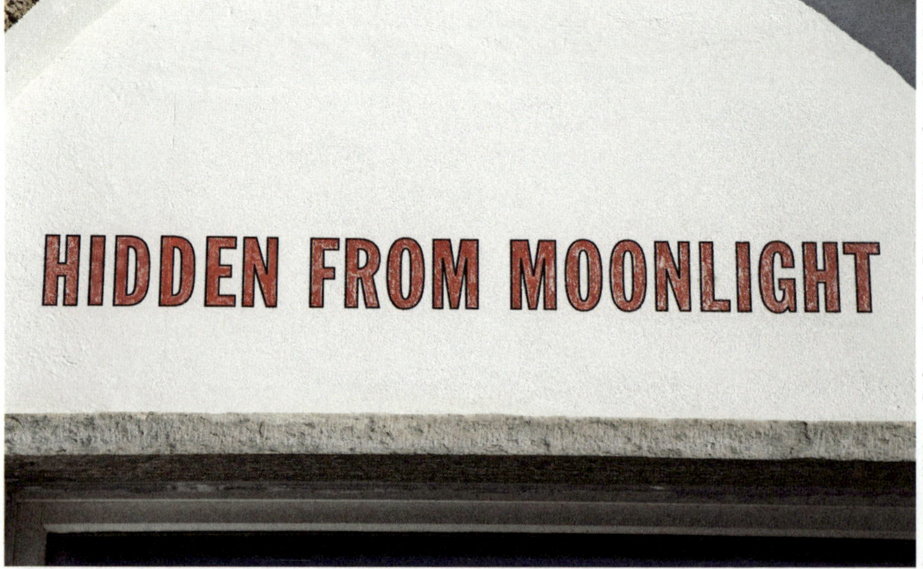

Lawrence Weiner, *Before the Sun Rises / Hidden from Moonlight /*

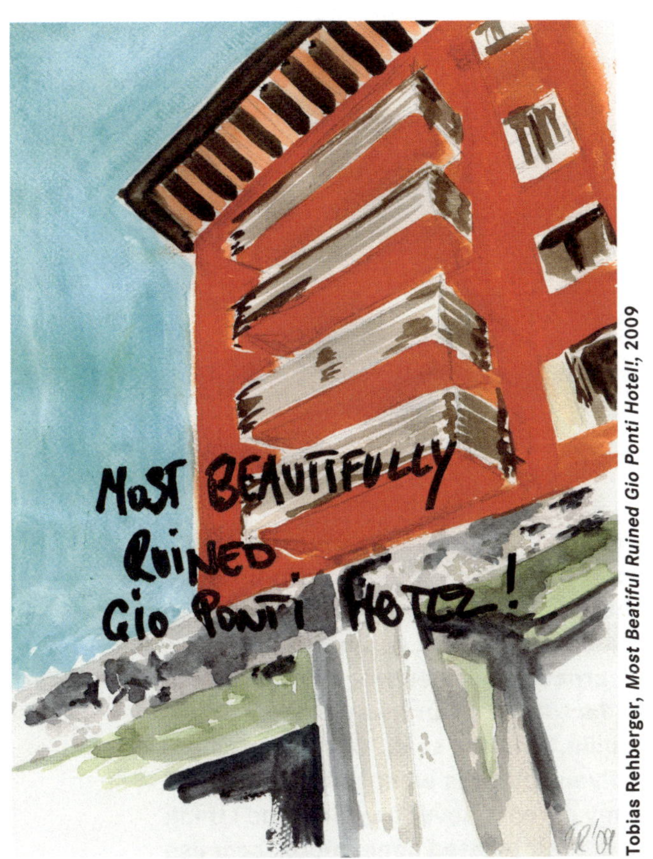

Tobias Rehberger, *Most Beatiful Ruined Gio Ponti Hotel!*, 2009

In the 1930s, the Italian architect Gio Ponti was commissioned by the Italian government to build eighteen hotels in the Dolomites, along a 160-kilometer line connected by cable cars. He completed only one, the Hotel Paradiso near Merano. In the Val Martello, on a site 2160 meters above sea level and difficult to access, he built a 250-bed palace with all possible comforts that was occupied by the Wehrmacht during the Second World War, reopened in 1946, and finally closed due to bankruptcy in 1947. Gio Ponti's plan to transform the ruggedness of the mountains with a network of wellness temples failed. In general, many proposed projects remained visions. Perhaps because the Alps were too big for some.

Postcard   Cerith Wyn Evans

What I know about the Engadin actually was revealed to me anecdotally during a phone call I made to my cousin because I was concerned about her husband's health. I don't speak to her very often, so she said, "Where are you now?" because quite often I'm only concerned about her when I'm overseas and just worry about the fact that I'm far away. And so I said, "In a valley called the Engadin," and she said, "Oh, I know where that is. Do you know that your parents went to the Engadin?" I thought, okay, because my parents never traveled, and I think this was on the occasion of their belated honeymoon, because my grandfather died shortly after they married and so they cancelled their original honeymoon. And I said, "When would they have been there?" She said, "Well, I don't know, in the late fifties," and I said "Could it have been in 1957?" and she said "Yes, it could easily have been 1957." Then I remembered seeing photographs, slides, transparencies, that my father had taken, which I got after he died—the whole collection, since he was a photographer. And I said, "Joy"—that's her name—"I don't think this is really possible." She said, "You know, you might well have been conceived in Switzerland." So, possibly, my relationship to the Engadin has been a profound one for the last fifty-two years.

Claudia Comte

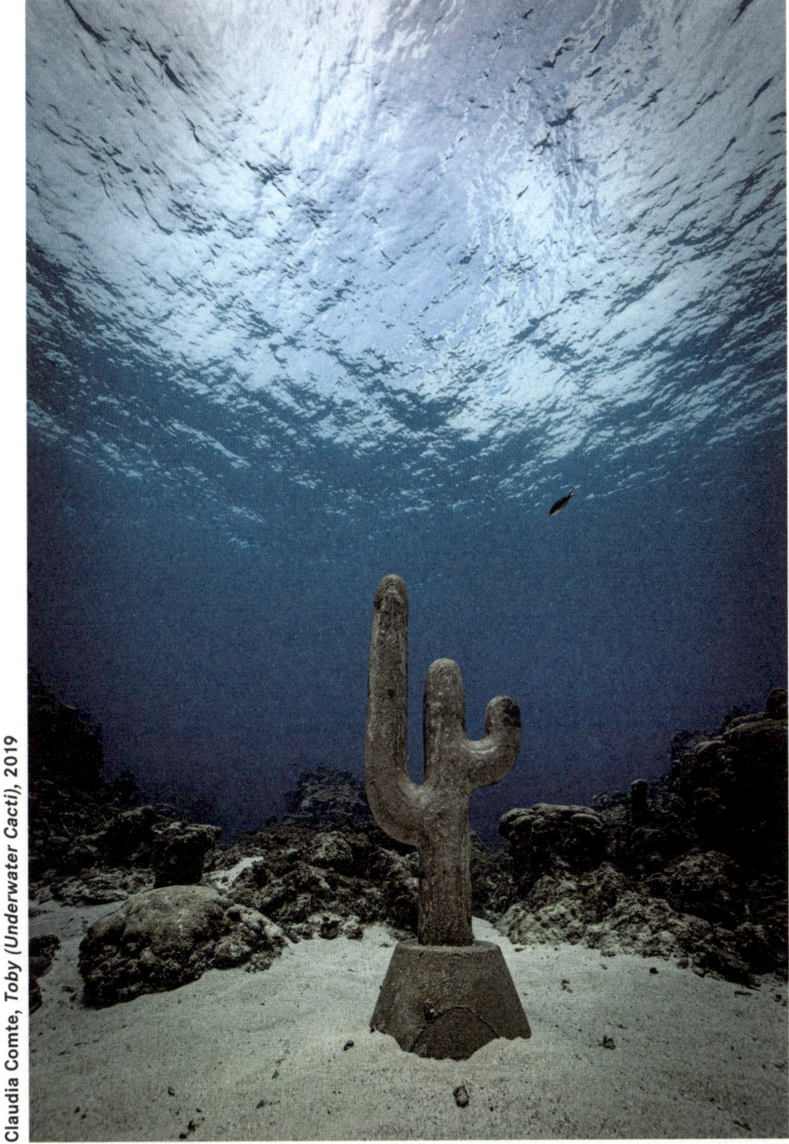

Claudia Comte, *Toby (Underwater Cacti)*, 2019

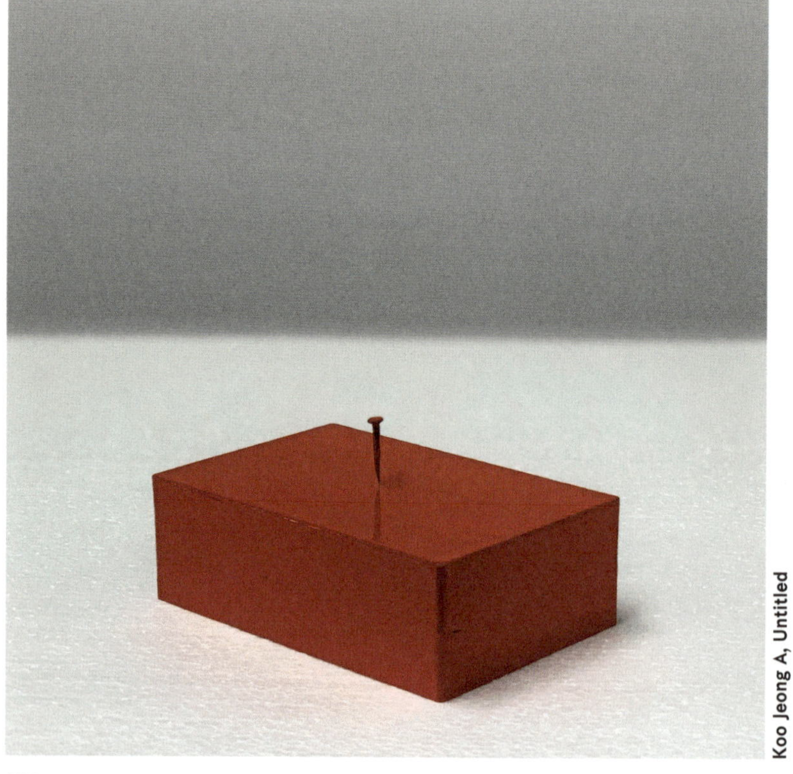

Koo Jeong A, Untitled

Scraffito window frame, Zuoz

Scraffito façade with doorway, S-chanf

Bethan Huws, Series of small notes from
architecture in the Engadin, 2005
Scraffito of bird, S-chanf

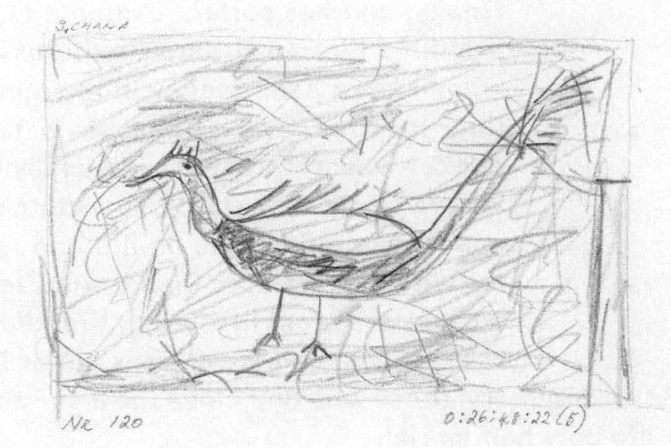

In the autumn of my life, I am constantly reminded of situations which are enriched by themes that were discussed at E.A.T. As a movie person, I notice in the most mundane events in life a reflection of the great movies I have seen. It starts in the morning, with my cup of coffee, which always reminds me of Jean-Luc Godard's quintessential and philosophical coffee scene in *2 ou 3 choses que je sais d'elle.* And it ends when I am falling asleep, hoping that I will have no close encounter with Bunuel's razor blade which cuts through an eye as smoothly as the clouds through the moon in my dreams.

Art enhances our life. When I stroll with my dog through the snow in the Engadin, I cannot do so without thinking of Christopher Wool and his painting *Run Dog Run,* or William Wegman's ubiquitous dog photos. Or when my new dog Louffy is daydreaming in a shadow inspired by Edward Hopper, I remember Fischli and Weiss's great sentence in their sculpture *Grosser Topf:* "What does my dog think?"

Sometimes, when I observe a lost little sparrow sitting on a perfect branch of a tree, I automatically see my own private slide show of the "best of" images from the bird pictures of the French artists Jean-Luc Mylayne. Sometimes when I see a white horse in the fields of Samedan, it reminds me of the scene in John Huston's 1967 film *Reflections in a Golden Eye,* in which Marlon Brando rides a white horse through the woods at midnight, hunting a young naked soldier while his angry wife, played by Liz Taylor, is sleeping with his best officer friend. Movies–as art and life–can be so tacky and cruel, yet still be great!

Finally, another perfect example of cruelty: Robert Bresson's profound film *Au Hasard Balthazar* always comes to my mind when I see a poor donkey in the meadows of the Engadin. The film–inspired by Dostoyevsky's novel *The Idiot*–follows a donkey which is treated sadistically by its various owners. This is pure transcendental cinema at its finest. I could go on and on with these reflections on life and art. But not without finishing with a quote from Claude Mauriac's book on Marcel Proust which I wrote out in my very first diary: "Ceux qui n'aiment pas la Provence, ne peuvent pas aimer l'art."

So, in summary: those who don't love the arts–and E.A.T.–have a life only half as rich.

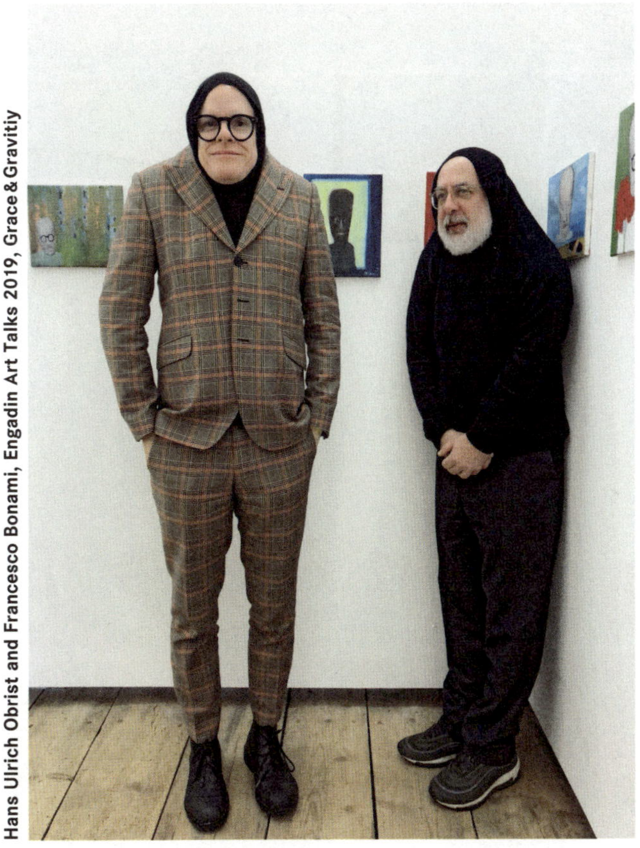

Hans Ulrich Obrist and Francesco Bonami, Engadin Art Talks 2019, Grace & Gravitiy

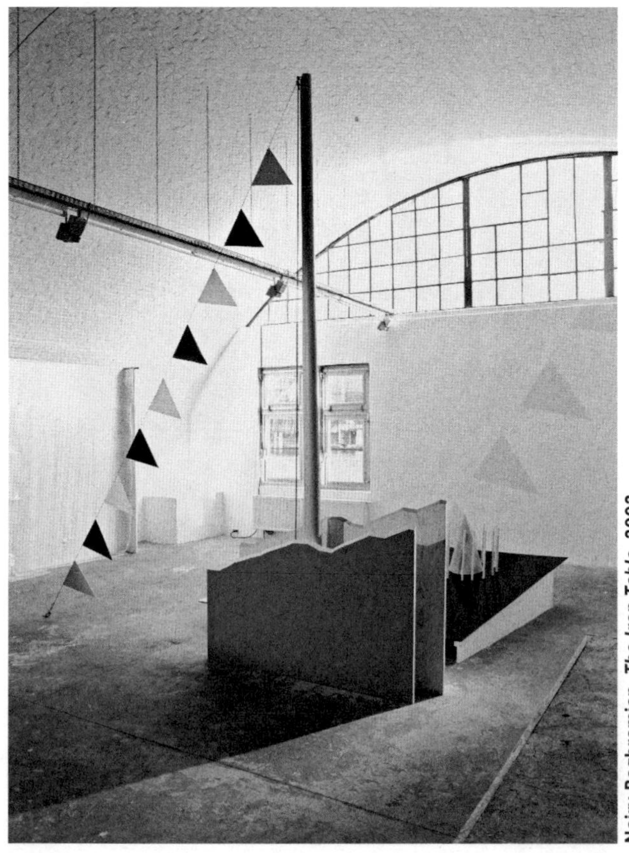

Nairy Baghramian, *The Iron Table*, 2002

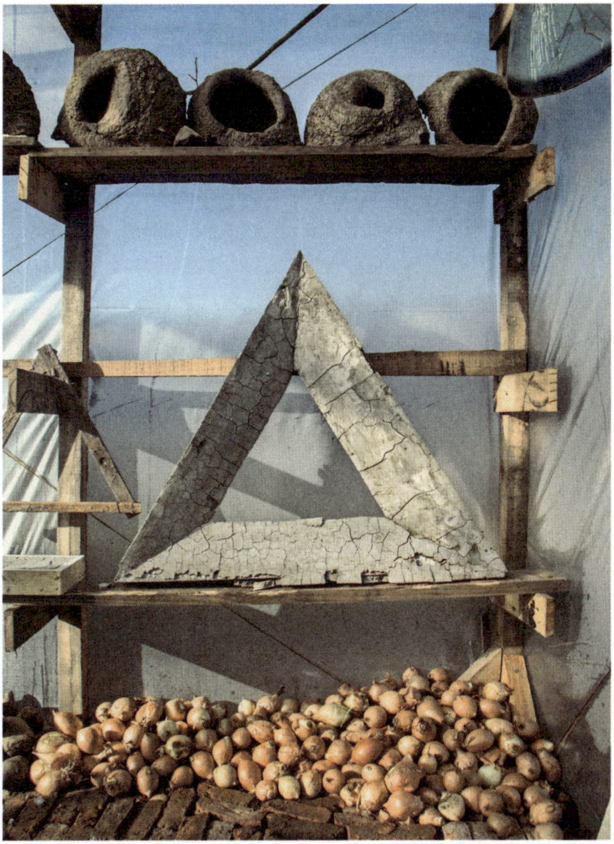

Adrián Villas Rojas, *Brick Farm*, An experimental collaborative studio located at a traditional brickyard on the outskirts of Rosario, Argentina, December 2012–ongoing

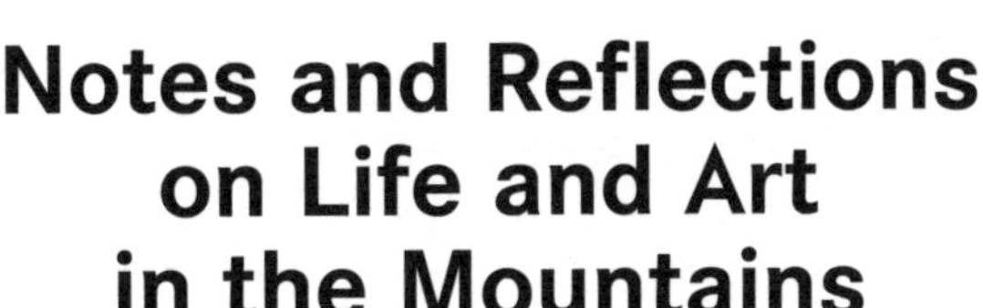

Notes and Reflections
on Life and Art
in the Mountains

Sublime Smell

The question of how it smells in a particular place in the world is one that never arises of its own accord. Scents naturally impose themselves, if present at all. They tempt and beguile, and it is no coincidence that they supersede colors as an attractant. It would seem that they are independent natural phenomena, comparable to mushrooms. Quite mysterious. With a world of their own.

Joachim Bessing

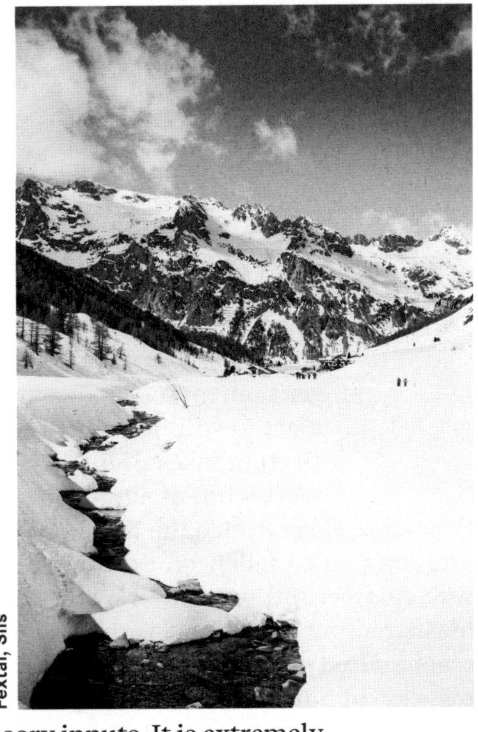

In nature, scents are one of many sensory inputs. It is extremely difficult to recall them in comparison to all the other sensations. Scents remain fleeting and elusive. In our memory of a place, they blend into an overall impression, one that might be defined by other predominant tones (for example, memories of New York will contain the distinct melody of its police sirens). In the hierarchy of sensory perceptions, scents seem to be at the very bottom. Visuals and sounds, and of course tactile stimuli, including water and wind, are formative for memory as well as its epileptic sisters, our dreams, whose slumbered sphere cannot be penetrated by scent. Which explains the long-established existence of electronic smoke detectors. Scents rank lowest in the hierarchy of digital communications. Meanwhile almost everything non-verbal can be transmitted wirelessly: moving images and voices, even heart rates. But the possibility of transmitting, or even just storing and subsequently retrieving a digitalized scent, similar to a photograph, is nowhere in sight. There is no Wikipedia for scents. So in order to tell you what it smells like in the Engadin, I must travel there in person. Physically, not virtually or theoretically. But that begs the question from an olfactory perspective: to which Engadin? To the wintry white version, when the valley is covered with snow from the highest peaks down to the villages below? At least that was always the case when the winters were still cold and snowy. I remember the smell of snow from those days—the special, dry cold I now feel in my nose when I recall the wide, glittering fields of yore. And the warmth of the winter sun on my face.

Or perhaps summer when the soil is warm and an aromatic blend of gentian, arnica and other floral scents floats above the meadows, like a sweet jelly you could ideally smear right onto a slice of bread. Instead, the bees hum and the grasshoppers chirp non-stop. Warm wood and warm stone—we know this phenomenon from scented candles and from cake: molecules start to whir as temperatures rise. The hard becomes soft, the fleeting takes flight. Scents are ephemeral. Like speech. Both a mere whiff of air.

Of course, there is also the Engadin of autumn, but my choice had long since fallen on September. Indian summer. By the way, Adalbert Stifter's novel by that name is quite interesting: his incredibly beautiful descriptions of nature extend over several hundred pages, but the writer deprives his narrative of any mention of how it smells there, around the Rosenhaus.

After a train ride that took me from Frankfurt am Main via Zurich and through the seemingly endless Vereina Tunnel, I arrived in Zuoz in the Engadin, late in the afternoon on the first of September. The first sample I inhale on the platform, just as the train has pulled out, is not exactly odorless, but I do not manage to distill a characteristic fragrance from the overall impression. It smells of track bed ballast and tar. There is a faint ringing of cowbells in the distance, though I cannot make out the cows themselves on any of the slopes around me, plus a herd of sheep that I do catch sight of as a swarm of light-colored dots, but cannot hear. These two sensory impressions are registered by my consciousness, which tells me I should be able to smell the grass in the pastures that belongs to the construction of these scenarios. But alas, I cannot actually perceive the scent of meadow grass all the way from the station.

It is said that the soul, an organ of consciousness, travels at a different speed from the rest of the body, although it is a part of the latter. The ability to perceive scents seems especially soulful to me. After the long train journey, I am not surprised that my sensory system has to slowly unfurl like a butterfly's proboscis before its feelers can tune into the Engadin.

On the footpath leading uphill from the railway station to the hotel, I am happy to see that the buildings begin to thin out after only a few houses. Expanses of green become visible. When we are asked how the Engadin smells, it is curious that we automatically think of the scents emitted by unspoiled nature. As if the scents produced by civilization have no place in our idealized image. But there's kitsch looming, I think to myself, sniffing casually at the imposing minimalist door front of a new Engadin-style building. The door is a rather atypical fourteen square meters in size and consists of a broad expanse of rough and rustic looking wood, though when my nostrils hover over the surface, it proves to have been sanded silky smooth and probably even polished, and only afterwards carefully turned matte again. The fragrance of the wood resonates, profound and rosy, touching a deep string within me. I listen to the leitmotif of the Engadin. Without a doubt, the door is made of Swiss stone pine. The greeting in the local vernacular is allegra. In the nineties they named a women's magazine after it in Germany. In Zuoz and the other villages of the valley, the houses have names. The same as the surrounding mountains, but of course there is no need to ask which of the two was there first. My hotel is called Castell and looks from afar like a mixture of both: a towering structure of rugged stone, but exceedingly cozy inside.

Passing earlier through a small section of forest, the trail took me through a stand of larches and over a clear brook. The water tasted cold and clear, like a pebble I had removed from the freezer and put straight into my mouth. Not only are the sense of taste and smell inseparably linked, but the field of cell biology increasingly operates under the assumption that tasting means smelling—and vice versa. My grandmother Margarethe, unfortunately now deceased, once suffered a total loss of her sense of smell in the course of a respiratory illness. As a result, she could no longer taste anything. The condition lasted almost half a year. As with the meatloaf Kirsten Dunst tried in *Melancholia*, all foods tasted "like ashes." Memories were of no help. My grandmother, otherwise a woman of consistently strong nerves, was pushed to the brink of suicide by a world that had been stripped of color.

From my room on the top floor of the hewn-rock castle, I have a direct view of the local mountain. Its name is Piz Mezzaun and it appears to be pulling a sheet of vapor from around its neck up over its face. I can already imagine the longed-for exhaustion from the mountain air, but I want to intensify it with hard effort so I can sink into the mattress like a stone pine tree trunk and rest in deep dark slumber until sunrise. The basement level that was blasted into the mountainous rock contains a hammam steam bath.

A stylistic incongruity? No. It is simply another side of the Engadin. The air in the labyrinth of wellness is saturated with hot steam. Breathing becomes a physically conscious act of creation, drawing the bucket full of eucalyptus deep into the lungs. Then a respite on a chaise longue, with flung-open windows looking out onto a meadow under the evening sky. Again from far away, the crystalline ringing of cowbells. With each breath the creature takes. That is silence. It does not get any quieter in real life.

I woke shortly after sunrise. The outside temperature was 13° in the shade, air pressure: 1,009 hectopascals, humidity displayed at 78%. The hotel has installed barometers and other measuring devices at numerous spots. I never have to search long to find one of the (mechanical) weather stations. Perhaps Adorno once tapped on a barometer glass with his finger in this very location. The Piz Mezzaun is now completely enshrouded. The windows of the breakfast room, too, are covered with thick swaths and veils. Every now and then, a gap emerges between them and a fragment of the mountain is visible: either in gray or green. I cannot help but think of clouds and wonder why they sink so deep down into the valley until I realize that the valley itself is high up (at around 1,700 meters). A piece of the cheese that I have chosen on account of its name tastes wonderfully like flowers. I even think I can make out the specific flavor of chamomile, and an image of a cow comes to mind, with its broad, shimmering, mushroom-shaped muzzle munching its way into the sea of flowers in an alpine Engadin mountain meadow—which curiously seems to present itself as the perfect idyllic image. The cheese produced in this way is called "Engadin Forte." It comes from the highest dairy in Europe, the Lataria Engiadinaisa in Bever (1,711 m), which I am mentioning because I was to pass by it a little later. Catching sight of it, I wished I could have opened the railcar window, as was formerly possible before the widespread adoption of air conditioning. As if climate control and air conditioning were all that mattered in life and on our travels! The supply of scents is likewise vital to human existence.

And so, deprived of experiencing how it might smell around the Lataria, I arrived at the valley station for my cable car journey up to Muottas Muragl—a mountain that incidentally breaks with the regional nomenclature of Piz as a first name. The Engadin locals must know the reason why, but I forgot to ask. Surrounded by the wispy clouds that were now being driven down the valley towards Sils Maria faster than in the morning, nature seemed to have become a sponge overnight. Dew has a specific fragrance which, if bottled, would become a hit among city dwellers, making them smell fresh, healthy and well-rested. In Zurich, I know a collective of soap makers whose liquid soap—which is biodynamically produced, of course—has the uniquely delightful scent of an herbaceous meadow mixed with a few arnica blossoms and chamomile. The perfumer has thus taken a partially shaded meadow by a lake in the woods as the inspiration for the soap's olfactory profile. After lathering up, consumers should stay away from any cows in the Lataria's service.

Up on the Muraglstein, I was released into the big wide world after a steep and swift ride with only a few others. Apparently, a person must only spend a few hours in a valley before they open their heart to the surrounding peaks and wish to spread their arms and simply sail away. Suddenly the world is far, far away. Up here the sun is shining while the clouds hover further below. Through a hole in the cloud cover, I gazed down at the airfield, then the car traffic, and it was as though none of that mattered anymore. Hardly a day spent here in the Engadin, and I could emotionally comprehend why Adorno had retired here all those years ago. The female students in Frankfurt had bared their breasts to him. No dialectic was of any help: that was the argument. And he dragged himself to the Engadin, to the elephant graveyard of great intellects. Far away from the world, yet simultaneously the essence of the world. Depending on the point of view.

A gentle ringing lures me deeper into the sparsely planted rocky landscape. Juniper, in particular, thrives here, which I was able to taste at the breakfast table in the form of a bitter syrup called latwerge. The berries taste flowery. The only thing missing is tonic water (which my consciousness is quick to mentally supply; even including ice cubes and the effervescent sound of the bubbles). As cows are strictly vegan, the animals themselves, like the meadows where they leave their dung, remain almost neutral in smell; in contrast to goats and sheep,

which feed on a similar diet of grasses and herbs but develop an
extreme, intense characteristic odor, which in turn, unlike with
the praiseworthy cows, also permeates their milk. This is a subject for debate, but it remains a matter of taste and is therefore
not worth the effort. From time to time, a single flower grows in
the grass, as if in a jewel case. I come across an especially beautiful arnica of a sunny yellow color that the sun itself could never
match, sprouting from the chocolate brown of a cow patty.

> This morning, I read in the Posta Ladina, the local Engadin
> newspaper, that a bumper crop of wild mushrooms has sprout-
> ed up in the surrounding woods and meadows. And indeed, on
> the way to the Castell, I discovered some large ones in the small
> patch of woods near the stream, even a red and white-spotted
> fly agaric toadstool, but it had already been nibbled on (deer
> are into this high, according to Carsten Höller). Up in the peaks,
> however, there is no sign (except for two tiny pale ones with
> caps sitting on a substrate of cow dung). The cow as an ena-
> bling force—Hinduistic notions, like the hammam, also have
> their place in the concentrate of world and civilization found in
> the Engadin. I have the constant urge to imagine how everyday
> life must have been in this wonderful landscape 150 years ago;
> in other words, how people coped as earthly citizens made in
> the Upper Engadin. As in *La vita—La natura—La morte*, that is
> how I imagine it. In this light, amidst the same scenery, unfor-
> tunately just not as beautiful.

Viewed from above, frogs look like people in a curious way. Even
just in terms of how they move. This occurred to me when I was
observing a young frog that had hopped onto the cupped palms
of my hands. There were hundreds up there, at an altitude of
two and a half thousand meters, in a narrow brook whose water
trickles downhill. Why there and why frogs—no one knows.

> The next morning revealed completely different conditions: a
> cloudless sky, the sun has broken through. Traveling to Samedan
> on the Rhaetian Railway, which has a reputation in Zurich for
> being unpunctual at times. And from there by bus to Sils. When
> passing through St. Moritz, I avoid looking out of the window
> as much as possible, even though it also counts as part of the
> Engadin. Yesterday, after coming back down into the valley, I
> went for a walk in the Staz forest, where an intense aroma of
> stone pine greeted me from the other side of the bridge over the
> En or Inn, raising my spirits and prompting me to quicken my
> pace. Yet the sillage of woody fragrance was not of natural origin,

but caused by the felling of timber on the other side of the bridge. In the forest itself, I paused several times to listen to the growling of the undergrowth, where spotted nutcrackers and squirrels break the pine nuts off the cones and nibble their harvest. These cones are Bordeaux red and dark lavender in color covered with glossy cherry bark resin, so not yet gnawed on: works of art, which I leave untouched, beautifully polished as they are. Also partly, because they lack virtually any scent.

Blueberries can still be found in the woods. That was the case yesterday at Lake Staz as well as today in Sils Maria in the woods on the lovely peninsula, which starts right behind the cow pasture. Firs and larches and stone pines. The larches are covered with lichen, which I think of as mushrooms of the air. The fact that it is still so nice and warm, an Indian summer with this feeling of melancholy, announcing that all this, the mushrooms and berries, the cones and nuts, the warmth of the stone and the soil, the ringing of the cowbells, the scintillating flash of the golden turret on the one house in Sils—all this will soon be frozen and enveloped in a blanket of snow. It is coupled at the same time with the wild hope, which we in fact know to be more: that all this is sure to return again after some time. That the spring version of Engadin will reconstitute itself, just like the summertime Engadin that follows.

I took a swim in the lake, which was green in color (due to the limestone in the rocks) and must have been near freezing point. It is a matter of feeling. Drying myself in the sun on the warm grass, I sniffed my forearm. It was the smell of me and something different, something I could only be when here. And which I had never been anywhere else before.

JOACHIM BESSING is a German writer and journalist.

In the Engadin with Nietzsche's Pain

I came into a quiet house. Here again in my place of sanctuary: the Engadin. Friedrich Nietzsche called it "my incubator," the place where he fit completely, corporally. The philosopher came here for seven summers seeking relief from his pains: from migranes, nausea and aching eyes. He rented a room in the home of a family in Sils-Maria, spent weeks and months in this bedroom and left it only to walk. He was alone here and enjoyed, above all, peace: from society, from his duties and to a degree also from his pain.

Simona Pfister

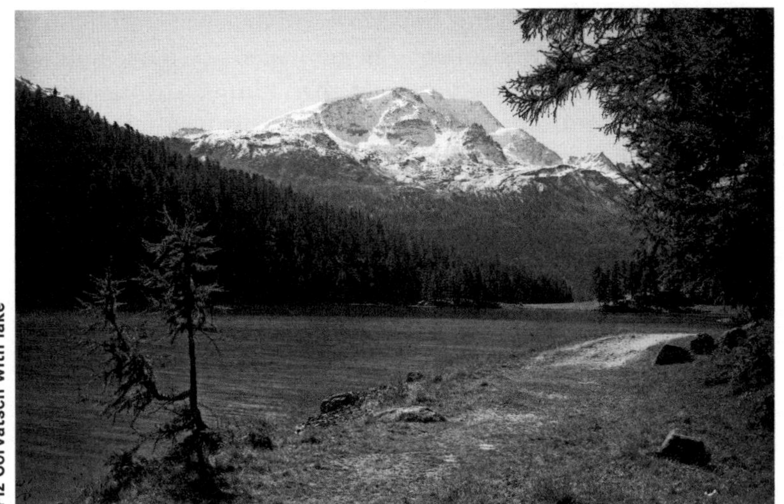

I want to try this too in the coming days, here in Punt Muragl, in my family's house, empty, where since I was small I have always felt an odd sense of peacefulness. I have not been here for years nonetheless; neuritis prevented me coming, or at least I thought it did. I thought I was too weak to travel, that the pain in my eyes, the headaches and stomach problems would be too severe. It sounds like a bad joke: the very pains that I believed were insurmountable obstacles on my path to the Engadin were those that brought Nietzsche here. So, from tomorrow, I want to do as he did: be alone in the Engadin with my aches and hope that the mountains help me live.

At six o'clock I get up and nothing is to be heard. No people, no machines, not even a bird. Everything is absolutely still; the living room is empty and the kitchen sleeps. I cannot remember when I last woke to such calm. While the water starts to heat, outside it dawns; today the sky is clear and a magnificent mountain landscape stands before me. Like a billboard stretched across the window. Right and left, cliffs lead to peaks. They seem so close and yet unreal, as if all those boulders were only an illusion. Between the mountains lies the countless larches of Staz forest. The tips of the trees sway in the wind; it is a dense, dark green carpet. Yet the trees too seem unreal. It is as if I can see everything out there, but never fix it, never quite make it through to it, as if this view should always remain an image and never my reality, as if this landscape were a presence that may always be there, but never for me.

After my tea I sally forth for a short walk, then I take a light breakfast and sit myself down to work. I keep to Nietzsche's daily routine: rising, tea, walking, breakfast and then work; after lunch another walk, this time longer—he managed up to five hours, I do two—working again afterwards, then dinner, sitting quietly for two hours and finally sleep. He lived this way for months, with slight variations, finding in the rigid structure relief for his nerves and from his pain. And in truth the morning walk helps my headache, work is easier; I feel more productive and during my long walk in the afternoon I'm overcome with ideas, even when I repeatedly believe that I am physically exhausted, too tired and want to return home. Sitting quietly in the evening seems at first onerous, too much like hard work; I would rather go straight to bed and be released from my pains by sleep. But I sit there obediently and all at once the time passes quickly, without my being able to notice what occupied my thoughts.

When I go to bed, I do so calmly and my thoughts are free, which has not been the case for a long time. It is as if I have to bring something additional into my sick body in order to regain the clarity of the healthy, the feeling that is self-evident for the well that their own existence is there for the taking. Nietzsche too wrote from the Engadin that he had to be strict with himself every day and every hour, for only thus could he, being sick, achieve anything at all. In fact the strict daily regime helps, paradoxically: complete rest does not reduce the pain, instead there is an ascetic cycle of rest, work and exertion. It makes demands on the body, but not where it hurts but rather where it can still achieve something. These are not the quotidian external duties and expectations, not all the things that I—and Nietzsche— have and had to do to prevent the pain, in which prevention appears like one's own weakness, not being of sufficient stature to take on the world. No, instead of living in accordance with exterior structures that demand something, which only works if there are continual concessions to the pain, thus making our bodies appear ever sicker, ever less accessible, he lived and now I live alone, according to my own, challenging, structure, one that suits our afflictions. So I feel stronger than I have for a long time. I do what I want to do and do not struggle in vain with what I have to do. I feel healthier without being any less ill.

But for this do I need, did Nietzsche need, the Engadin? Why did he not live in this manner elsewhere? Naturally, though, he was alone here, and here I too can be alone. The Engadin is, however, the very landscape that reflects this state, this freedom in the rigidity of one's own daily routine: here one is actually released from all the duties and expectations of the lowlands and both enclosed by the severity of the stony peaks and liberated by the breadth of the valley. One has a perspective of fresh air and of new possibilities. And this life feels exactly like that: instead of the narrow outward duties in the lowlands there is new freedom in one's own rigor in the mountains. This landscape and Nietzsche's rhythm—they are blood relatives, for who lives thus, really does fit here.

> But there is yet another reason why the Engadin helps the sick—indeed anyone who is subject to any kind of pain—and it has to do with the peculiar presence of the mountain landscape, the feeling that I have as soon as I open my eyes: the feeling that I cannot truly grasp what I see. Again and again I look out, again and again I fail, I believe that I have not really seen the mountains, that I have to look once again, so I look again and fail again. For the short time that one needs to direct one's gaze to an object, to see it and to grasp it, does not exist here, the landscape does not allow it. For in every glance the mountains appear to already be there, to have already been there, faster than me, faster than I can look, faster than my powers of comprehension. So I look out longer, I try to secure the mountains with my means, to grasp them, but they are already different, they have changed, as if newly created, and so I start from the beginning again. They have always been there, eternally and lasting, and yet they are new in each glance, caught in perpetual transformation—this is how the mountains evade human powers of comprehension and ask too much of our customary sense of time. Instead they are a presence of their own, an absolute presence, that in every sight offers eternal present and a contemporary manifestation of the eternal. And this leads to the billboard feeling, to the sense of not having grasped everything, of not being able to get through to reality, needing to look out once again. And this is not simply the case for a particular viewpoint, which one could leave, like any location. No, this landscape and this feeling mark the view wherever you are in the Engadin. If you are here, you cannot evade the particular presence of the mountains, but must look again, trying again to fix them.

This is why the Engadin helps pain. For pain too has this temporal peculiarity; pain is an absolute presence. In every instant the ill person feels, first and foremost, their pain; all else comes, in comparison, later, even one's own thoughts and words. With its penetration the pain is always first, always faster, already

there and seems to have always been there. And should the in-
valid want to fix it, to describe it, grasp it and thus hold it apart
from him or herself, then the moment is already gone, the pain
has already raced ahead and is in front of thoughts and again
in a different form and so once again anew, that which evades
customary thinking, representing its own, absolute present.
This makes pain particular: whoever lives with it must submit
to its temporality and is, through this, always at a remove from
the world, not really a part of their surroundings, because they
are enclosed in the presence of pain, in comparison with which
all else is deferred. And every attempt to record it will fail: the
pain is faster and one's thoughts continually chase after the
concept of what occupies one entirely corporally, but can never
be grasped in thought.

> Only these mountains and this landscape, that which has an
> equally significant presence, can help. Because here there's no
> time in any given instant to capture one's suroundings, because
> in any given instant the landscape is absolutely contemporary,
> there is for once something that is as fast as, that keeps astride
> with, my pain. Surroundings that cannot be grasped in that
> moment measure up to that within me which is ahead at every
> moment, and, for once, a coincidence of pain and mountains is
> produced that reduces the pain, because it alone no longer de-
> fines the present. What is without and what is within are, for a
> moment, equal, and I am less alone, because I am no longer alone
> captive to the absolute presence of the pain, but it is in a dead
> heat with the totally present surroundings. And thoughts are
> freer, not because the pain has gone, but because the Engadin
> shares its presence and thus frees my thoughts from the con-
> tinual race to catch up. My body is in synchrony with the world
> outside, the landscape and the pain are concurrent and I am a
> part of my surroundings. "I am related to this nature. I now feel
> the relief" is how Nietzsche described it. He and nature: "we do
> not marvel at each other, but are instead in confidence." In step,
> on a par, the mountains, like the pain, are always already there
> and as a result I am freed, my thoughts clear.

The next day I travel to Sils-Maria and am moved to the point of
ridiculousness by the beauty of the lake, the sky and the mountains. In fact I only wanted to come here in order to see the
Engadin from the place where Nietzsche stayed, to follow his
path around Lake Sils, but now I really feel like him, when in
countless letters he continually writes of the "most beautiful

day" and "most powerful blue" and these words sound like clichés, and for the serious German philosopher at least somewhat shallow and cheerful. Now similar words occur to me when I want to describe the landscape, postcard phrases. The same is only the case for me when I want to describe my pain and hear myself speaking in hackneyed phrases: "It hurts, really badly." My words and my thoughts are simply not adequate for these presences, not that of pain, nor that of this landscape.

All at once I no longer want to try it; for the first time I no longer want to capture the pain in order to defend myself against it. Instead I let it be, level with the mountains, ahead of me, intangible, but all right. So I walk in the direction of the Chastè peninsula and the Nietzsche stone and at last think other phrases and feel other things—even if these are only laughable emotions.

"The Despisers of the Body" is the title of one chapter of *Thus Spoke Zarathustra,* a book the concept of which Nietzsche developed during his first summer in the Engadin. Nietzsche wrote that those who would despise the body commit a grave error. They literally despise that which they actually are, the thing that enables any thought, even their scorn: the body. For Nietzsche, reason, the spirit, thoughts, the I—whatever one wants to call it—is a product of the flesh, just an abstraction created by the body. Therefore the body dictates what the spirit thinks, and can think at all, let's say, when in pain, the comprehension of "pain" and thought about it, having to think about it.

This is why the Engadin was and is so important for all writers, thinkers and artists who suffer pain, even if that is only weltschmerz. They too are essentially their bodies; their thoughts and works are products of their corporal being. And if this body is in pain then they are occupied, caught and imprisoned in this pain, in its total presence, their thoughts and feelings continually racing to catch up with it. They need the equally present Engadin, which is eye to eye with their body, which shares the temporality of their pain. In step with the pain-filled body, it merges with it and thus relieves and liberates thoughts, feelings and oneself—the product of the body.

A body in pain does truly fit here, in the Engadin, its "incubator."

SIMONA PFISTER studied history and religious studies and works as an author and journalist in Zurich.

The Blue of the Ether

In the eighteenth century the question of the sky's color came to the mountains. Travelers to the alps scaled peaks in search of blue: to observe, measure, and paint it.

Annina Boogen

Wednesday, April 4, 1979, Zollikon, in Ernst and Ursula Hiestand's
studio.

> Ernst: "I can't believe it, that I'm actually holding the de Saussure in my hands!"

Ernst looks closely at the new banknote, turns it over and holds
it up to the light. Ursula sits opposite him at the desk.

> Ursula: "Orell Füssli really did apply the new printing techniques well."

> Ernst: "You're right about that. And the blue. The blue of the de Saussure is a dream. I'm really proud of our work!"

Graphic design duo E + U Hiestand won second prize in the Swiss
National Bank's 1970 competition for a new series of bank-
notes. Ernst and Ursula Hiestand's series was even shown alongside the winning series at documenta 5 in Kassel.[1] Because the
Hiestands' designs contained innovative developments in technical security they were ultimately chosen for implementation.[2]
On April 4, 1979, the new twenty franc note, with de Saussure,
was brought into circulation.

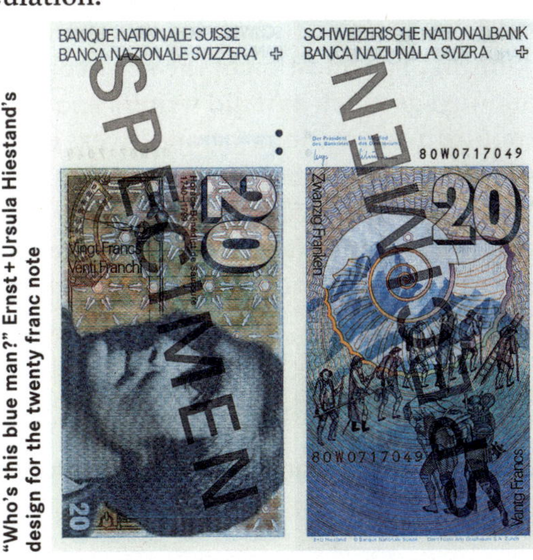

"Who's this blue man?" Ernst + Ursula Hiestand's design for the twenty franc note

Horace-Bénédict de Saussure (1740–1799), depicted on the bank
note designed by Ursula and Ernst Hiestand, was a natural scientist and mountaineer. He became renowned for his research
trips in the Alps and the four-volume work *Voyages dans les*

Alpes, published between 1779 and 1796, which resulted from these.[3] In these four volumes he presented (scientific) observations collated on his travels through the Alps. He also dealt extensively with the question of the color of the sky—and not by chance. In the 1780s he developed a gauge with the sonorous name of "cyanometer" expressly for this purpose, with which the intensity of the blue in the sky could be measured.[4] The instrument consisted of a circle on which could be found fifty-two shades of blue between white and black. These shades served as reference colors in order to define the blue of the sky in a particular place at a particular time. The question of the sky's blue as a natural phenomenon was apparently a conundrum that the Alpine environment in particular inspired. In the *Allgemeine Encyclopädie der Wissenschaften und Künste* (General Encyclopedia of Science and Arts) from 1831, for example, is written, under the heading "Himmelblau" (sky blue):

"And how dissimilar this blue can be, even at its zenith, in the same place at different times! How dissimilar at the same time in places that lie higher or lower! Even chamois hunters and alpine shepherds have often marvelled at how the sky grew ever darker, the higher up the mountains they climb [...]."[5]

In the eighteenth century the Alpine environment was used intensively as a laboratory for the natural sciences—be it for the study of geological theories, botanical research, or landscape painting. The question of the sky's color plagued natural scientists just as much as it did writers and artists. It was a subject of enquiry from various perspectives: in theory (understanding sky blue), "scientifically" (measuring the blue of the sky) or in "aesthetic" practice (painting the sky). Moreover, other general questions, about the function and the significance of scientific observation, coalesce around the cyanometer.

Understanding Sky Blue

Wednesday, April 4, 1979, Zollikon, in Ernst and Ursula Hiestand's studio.

Walking past, Barbara, Ursula and Ernst's fourteen-year-old daughter, sees the twenty franc note on Ursula's desk and picks it up.

Barbara: "Who's this blue man?"

Ursula: "It's Horace-Bénédict de Saussure from Geneva, one of the first mountaineers and an important Alpine researcher in the eighteenth century."

Ernst: "Barbara, do you know why the twenty franc note is blue?"

Barbara looks at her father.

Barbara: "Do you know why the sky is blue?"

Yes, why is the sky blue? And why does it appear to be darker when one is scaling a peak? Leonardo da Vinci (1452–1519) even posed this question. His manuscripts contain insights about the origin of sky blue, as well as manifestations of smoke and fog, some of which he garnered from experiments. Da Vinci had experienced how the sky becomes darker the higher one climbs up a mountain. He attributed the phenomenon to thinning air and concluded that the sky above the atmosphere must appear black. Da Vinci's interest in this question was due to his particular, artistic perspective: in landscape painting he had encountered the problem of atmospheric perspective.[6] Thus he established certain rules in his treatise on painting:

> "So that a painter who has mountains to represent in a landscape, ought to observe that, from one hill to another, the tops will appear always clearer than the bases. In proportion as the distance from one to another is greater, the top will be clearer and the higher they are, the more they will show their variety of form and color."[7]

The treatise further contains the coloristic rule that the blue of air has the effect of making distant mountains look blue. This phenomenon, which creates the impression of distance, is called "blueing."[8]

> Horace-Bénédict de Saussure asked himself similar questions to those of da Vinci's more than two hundred years later. The naturalist suspected that the sky's blue came about from the "opaque mist and vapours floating in the air *(vapeur opaques)*" which acted like a reflective filter.[9] Only blue light was not filtered out by these opaque vapours. He further speculated on a connection between the amount of opaque vapours and the blue tone. His explanation for the darker color at the summit was a lower level of vapour in the air (today we would call this humidity) in comparison with the valley floor.[10]

How air is perceived in color was debated in scientific academies at the close of the eighteenth and beginning of the nineteenth century. In this there were two fundamental, opposing theories: one theory suggested actual existing blue elements in the air; and a competing theory proclaimed the origin of the sky's coloring as the blue luminosity of an opaque medium (in front of a dark background).[11] De Saussure was an important player in this discussion, as he was the first to introduce a measuring instrument into the debate.

> In "Schreiben des Herrn Professor von Saussure an den Herausgeber, seine Reise auf den Col du Géant betreffend" (A letter from Herr Professor de Saussure to the editors regarding his trip to the Col du Géant),[12] which was published in the *Magazin für die Naturkunde Helvetiens*, he remarks:

"I believe therefore that when the sky appears […] darker, this comes about because then it's [the atmosphere's] unusual thinness and transparency does not allow it to reflect enough rays: one then sees moreover, so to say, the black of the celestial sphere; and this very black gives the sky the darker shading it has on the Montblanc."[13]

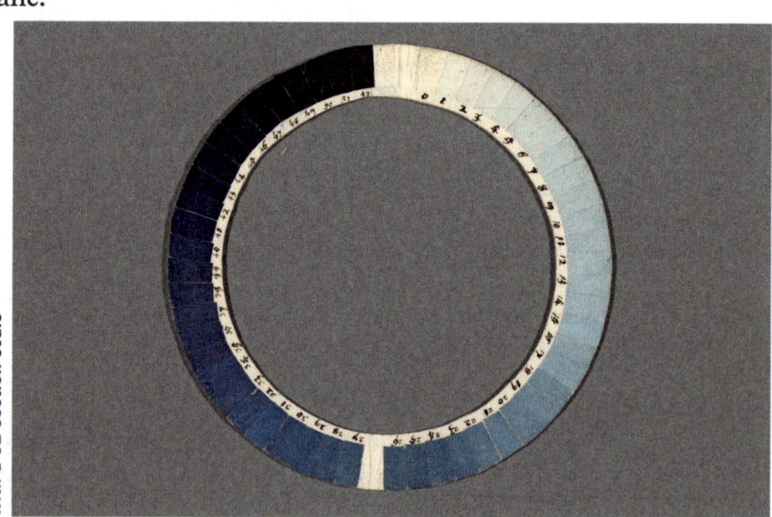

Horace-Bénédict de Saussure's cyanometer with a 52-section scale

De Saussure thus placed the blue of the sky—and also on the cyanometer—between daylight (white) and night (black). This ordering offered, at that time, a new perspective on connections between colors which de Saussure derived from his meteorological studies. The idea of comprehending black (darkness) and white (light) as the two extremes of a range was also adopted by Johann Wolfgang von Goethe (1749–1832) in his work *Zur Farbenlehre*

(Theory of Colors) published in 1810. Goethe refers explicitly to the cyanometer both in the essay *Von den farbigen Schatten* (On Colored Shadows, which can be regarded as a part of Goethe's *Theory of Colors* and which was likely to have already been written in 1793) and in *Theory of Colors* itself.[14] According to his *Theory of Colors*, the color blue is closest to darkness. For Goethe, blue does not conclude in black, but instead in darkness (and moves first into violet). Nevertheless, it is apparent that de Saussure's theories were of significant importance, not just for the practice of color standardization, but equally in the discourse of color theory.[15] Rather than merely positing a hypothesis, de Saussure wanted to investigate it empirically and undertake measurements.

Measuring Sky Blue

Wednesday, April 4, 1979, Zollikon, in Ernst and Ursula Hiestands' kitchen.

> Ernst: "Barbara, did you know that Bénédict de Saussure actually scaled the summit of Mont Blanc in the summer of 1787?"
>
> Barbara: "Yes, I read that before, but he wasn't the first. Two mountaineers were already there a year before!"
>
> Ernst: "You're right, of course, but because he could prove that Mont Blanc is the highest mountain in Europe with his barometer measurements he became much better known than the other two—I don't even know their names."

De Saussure took an early model of the cyanometer with him to climb Mont Blanc in 1787. This consisted of sixteen colored pieces of paper in stages between the poles of white and black. Stage one indicated the darkest tone, stage sixteen the lightest. At the summit, de Saussure measured a stage two blue, i.e. a very dark blue. At the same time his son, in the valley in Chamonix, measured a lighter blue, stage five.[16]

> Three years later a more elaborate version of the cyanometer was in operation and, with its fifty-two color variations, it allowed a more specific identification of shades of blue. It additionally

took on its circular form at this time. De Saussure also altered the direction of the color progression from dark to light: from this point onwards, the lightest shade was defined as stage one. With this new version he undertook additional comparative measurements—at different times of day and at different angles between the horizon and the zenith—such as on the Col du Géant in the Mont Blanc massif.[17]

Yet how was de Saussure's instrument for measuring blue applied; what insights resulted from it for the history of methods and tools of scientific observation? Johann Samuel Ersch (1766–1828) and Johann Gottfried Gruber (1774–1851) describe this in the *Allgemeine(n) Encyclopädie der Wissenchaften und Künste* as follows:

> "[…] need the shade of the sky's blue be defined, then the instrument is to be held between the eye and the part of the sky being investigated and try [moving it] until no difference can be appreciated between the color on the field on the cyanometer and of the sky. But should the measurements at different times be comparable, then they must be undertaken in an open place, where the instrument can be illuminated by bright light; at a window the light reflecting from the sky off the walls might cause some disruption."[18]

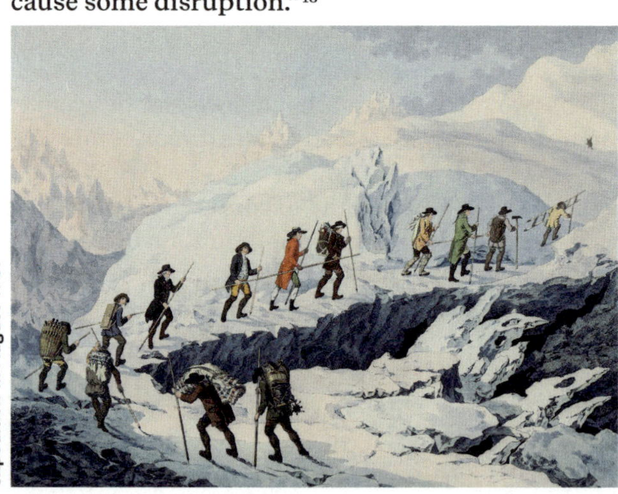

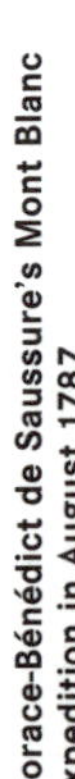

Ersch and Gruber additionally found it worth mentioning that de Saussure employed the pigment Berlin Blue in order to produce the cyanometer.[19] Berlin Blue was probably first produced in Berlin in 1706.[20] It is the first modern pigment that was synthesized and thus does not come from nature. The desire to make pigments in artificial processes accompanied the standardization of color that was gradually established in the eighteenth century. Berlin Blue spread quickly across Europe and was applied both in oil painting and in the production of watercolors.[21] Berlin Blue was not supplanted till the twentieth century by the even more modern phthalocyanine blue. This kind of (artificial) pigment yielded two advantages for de Saussure. Firstly, the pigment was of a consistently high quality.[22] Berlin Blue was known for its excellent color quality and also allowed good shading, even of darker tones. And secondly, Berlin Blue offered a relatively economical alternative to blue pigments from lapis lazuli or azurite. High quality lapis lazuli, for example, was very expensive as it had to be brought to Europe from Afghanistan.[23]

In any case, the instructions for constructing the instrument in de Saussure's article "Description d'un cyanomètre ou d'un appareil destiné à mesurer l'intensité de la couleur bleue du ciel" (Description of a cyanometer or a tool intended to measure the intensity of the color blue in the sky) are particularly interesting.[24] In an experiment in 2011, science historians Olaf Breidbach and André Karliczek tried to recreate the cyanometer.[25] For this they followed de Saussure's instructions precisely and employed the original Berlin Blue, ivory black and lead white pigments. De Saussure, however, gave no details about the shade differences on his cyanometer; he did not offer a pigment mixture as a starting recipe. Additionally, he did not fix the Berlin Blue at a particular level, but produced transparent mixtures each time. Subsequently, an individual reference distance has to be determined—which makes it clear that this was a subjective scale, dependent upon the discretion of the person constructing it. This reference distance served the purpose of differentiating between two different blue mixtures that had been applied to paper. If these mixtures could no longer be differentiated from the reference distance—but could be one step (30–50 centimeters) closer—then these were two blue shade increments that should be next to each other on the scale. This experiment clarified how much de Saussure's process was conditioned by the subjective setting of the scale increments—as well as by a trained sense of sight, on which the judgement of a blue ultimately also depended. With his measuring instrument de Saussure could only therefore create relative color tone references and not achieve a complete quantification of the "opaque vapours."

This combination—of a subjective measurement that through necessity became part of the production of the instrument, as well as the desire to quantify this opaque vapour—makes the cyanometer a significant object in the history of scientific observation. The development of the cyanometer took place at a time in which science and art were by no means as distinct from one another as they are today. The transformation only took place as the eighteenth century drew to a close, positioning science on the side of empiricism and objectivity, and art on the side of subjective imagination.[26] The idealized figure of a rational, enlightened researcher, exclusively interested in scientific insights, does not stand up to a perspective focused on observational practices, locating these in a societal context. Scientific research and discoveries were always, in practice, accompanied and driven by subjective wishes, hopes, expectations and promises. These by no means contradict scientific interests, but are productive elements of empiricism.[27] In de Saussure's work *Voyages dans les Alpes,* too, poetic landscape views and travel diaries are integrally interwoven between scientific observations and measurements:[28]

> "On the day I spent on Le Môle I clearly noticed a blue vapour which, excepting its density, was entirely like that which dominated in 1783. [...] I had observed this frequently prior to 1783 and according to my observations on the matter, spoken of it in my experiments in hygrometry. If this vapour is not opaque and one finds oneself within it, it can scarcely be differentiated; if one is however located above it and close to its surface, one can clearly differentiate it [...]."[29]

With the aid of the cyanometer de Saussure hoped to clearly reproduce his perceptions, allowing him to compare and further research the observations of vapour and sky color made at various altitudes. The cyanometer was to help him to establish his ideas of the connection between the amount of opaque vapour and the blue of the sky.

> His observations, which he collected (and quantified,) in order to exclude certain hypotheses, were initially central. With these he resorted to observational practices that were already applied in the sixteenth century in astronomy and meteorology: in the eighteenth century an essential means to knowledge developed from these. Nonetheless, de Saussure's faith in the potential of the cyanometer equally reflected (his) mistrust of the human senses. In the eighteenth century there was a vociferous debate about the deceptiveness of the senses.[30] This is reflected both in the attempts to chemically standardize colors and pigments

(such as Berlin Blue) and in the attempt to counteract the fallibility of the senses through the implementation of instruments.

Painting Sky Blue

Wednesday, April 4, 1979, Zollikon, in Ernst and Ursula Hiestand's studio.

Ursula comes to the studio door.

> Ursula: "Ernst, do you know where the Pantone color scale has gone?"

> Ernst: "No idea. Have a look if it's fallen behind the bureau again."

Pause for thought.

> Ernst: "Why didn't we actually include the cyanometer in the design for the twenty franc note?"

The cyanometer can be regarded as one of the first scientific color scales. Color scales can be classified as a specific form of color reference system and inasmuch are related to so-called color lexicons. The first scientific color lexicons came about mid-eighteenth century through classifying natural history, including over 4,000 color tones, recorded in color samples, color descriptions, and mixing formulae.[31] These were used to determine stones in mineralogy or plants and animals in biology. Color played an important part in placing these objects in the given classification systems.[32] During the course of the eighteenth century a scientific practice of classification using standardized color tables emerged.

> Unlike color tables, color scales were and indeed are not just used in order to reference the coloring of natural objects, but also as analytical measuring instruments: by locating them within a color scale, the particular quantities of a material in an object of investigation are measured.[33] Color scales thus extend beyond a purely descriptive practice of classification; the color value almost becomes a measured value of a natural phenomenon. The origin of this kind of color reference system is not to

be found in the sciences however, but in (artistic) craft: in the
seventeenth century there were already samples and standardized recipes for mixing colors for book painting or porcelain
manufacturing. And artists too, in particular landscape artists,
experimented with pigments and colors in order to achieve various effects. A practical engagement with pigments in craft
thus preceded scientific research, and indeed influenced the
latter.[34]

Look at landscape painting from Caspar Wolf (1735–1783), for
example, and the experimentation with blue tones as well as
the precise observation and recording of landscape impressions are striking. His Alpine works—around 200 paintings and
drawings—were created within a short period between 1774
and 1778. He painted the majority of these on commission from
the Bernese publisher Abraham Wagner.[35] Wagner used the
paintings for two of his projects: he exhibited the numerous
paintings as an alpine gallery in his home in Bern, and used
ten of them as watercolored engravings for the *Merkwürdige[n]
Prospekte aus den Schweizer-Gebürgen und derselben Beschreibung* (Remarkable Prospects from the Swiss Mountains and
Their Descriptions). [36, 37]

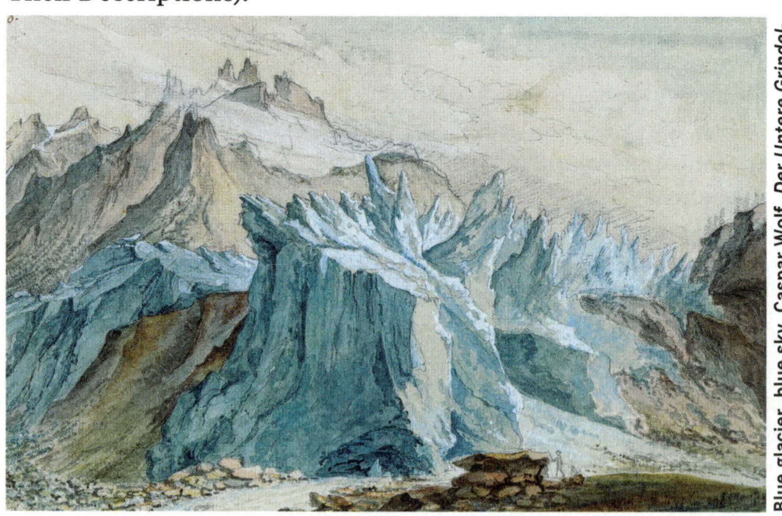

Blue glacier, blue sky. Caspar Wolf, *Der Untere Grindel-
waldgletscher mit kleinem Schreckhorn*, 1774–1777

Wagner's concept for the *Merkwürdige[n] Prospekte* was to
make the Alps appealing to a broader public: it was made up of
a mixture of reports from scientific expeditions and travel diaries. Looking at Wolf's engravings presented there, two things
are striking: for a start, geological details can be recognized,
such as the coloration of stone, which suggests mineralogical

composition or processes of erosion through falling water or glaciers. Wolf may have discussed these scientific details with his scientific companion Samuel Wyttenbach (1748–1830).[38] Secondly, it's notable that cloud landscapes and the sky's atmosphere are present everywhere—Wolf generated an almost comprehensive cross-section of meteorological phenomena. With this he covered a broad spectrum: from the dark mood of a winter sky to light cumulous clouds in high summer. In meteorology, too, the classification of cloud types was only nascent and Wolf's representations allow us to consider once again the significance of extensively studied observational processes.[39]

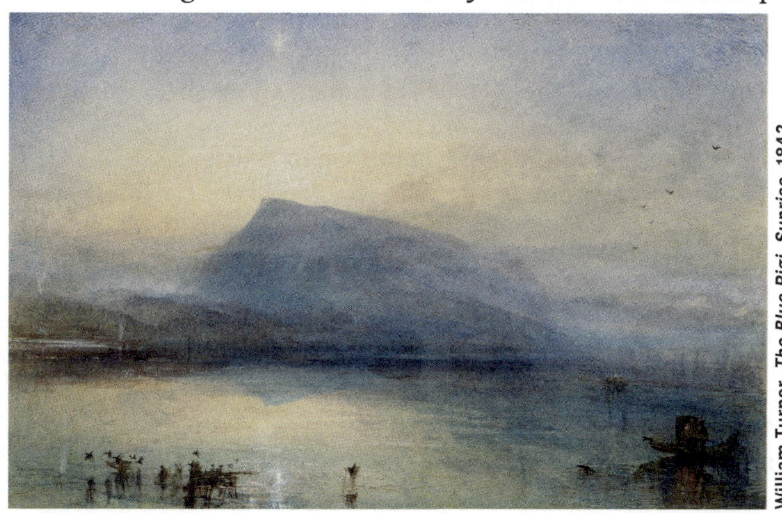

William Turner, The Blue Rigi, Sunrise, 1842

Landscape painters often developed their own techniques of color referencing, such as Caspar David Friedrich (1774–1840), who noted color number codes on sketches, or William Turner (1775–1851), who carried colored linen samples with him. Turner was a passionate traveller to the Alps and first came from London to Switzerland in 1802. British travelers could not travel to continental Europe after 1793 as a consequence of the French Revolution. The Treaty of Amiens in 1802 enabled artists and travelers from England to once more come to the continent. Although most traveled only as far as Paris, Turner was determined to visit the Alps.[40] His understanding of the Alps was marked by contemporary tourism and travel literature. His paintings, in turn, had a great influence on the image of the Alps in Britain. After his first travels to the Swiss Alps—and five further trips— he brought countless sketchbooks home.[41] These sketchbooks do not contain true to life illustrations of mountains and the atmospheric conditions in the sky, but pencil drawings and watercolors of alpine landscapes as Turner saw and experienced them. Here light and the atmosphere of the light at different times of day played an important part. A well-known example of this are the three watercolors *The Blue Rigi, The Red Rigi* and *The Dark Rigi*, which were made in 1841/2, a year after Turner had spent the summer in Lucerne. The changeable moods of mist and sunshine, color and light fascinated Turner so much that he obsessively observed and painted the view of the Rigi: in addition to the three main paintings, there exist countless sketches and studies.

> Even though half a century lies between Turner and de Saussure, it becomes clear from their artistic and scientific practices that both the art and the science is founded on what Lorraine Daston terms as "the same kind of healthy imagination."[42] What is more, both communicated, in art just as much as science, their passion for alpine travels as well as for the observation and recording of landscape impressions and natural phenomena in different ways. The descriptions of landscapes in *Voyages dans les Alpes* and Turner's alpine watercolors tempted a whole generation to travel to the Alps and see the grandeur of the mountains with their own eyes.

Blue, Bluer, Blueing

Although measurement of the sky above the Alps in the eighteenth and nineteenth centuries was always oriented also towards aesthetic criteria, in recent times, in the context of global environmental issues, this focus has shifted increasingly to another question: for contemporary scientists the blue in and of itself is of less interest than the absence of white, the missing clouds. Climate model calculations indicate that there will be fewer clouds due to global warming. De Saussure, meanwhile, saw in white merely the absence of blue: "[...] le blanc, ou l'absence totale du bleu [...]."[43] The climate scientists' perspective today turns this on its head, because the absence of white in turn also implies a blueness, which indicates environmental change beyond the blue. Sky blue has other connotations today than it did in de Saussure's time: then it did not suggest a threat, or doom, but was a facet of scientific curiosity and the aesthetic enjoyment of landscape.

Artificial blue, chemically manufactured color pigment, has a similar story: according to the official account from pharmaceutical giant Sandoz of the major fire in Warehouse 957 at the Schweizerhalle industrial area near Basel on November 1, 1986, careless handling of the highly flammable pigment Berlin Blue was the cause of one of the most severe environmental disasters of recent Swiss history. If this could still be recorded as an accident (and not, as according to more recent findings, as arson), sky blue—and with it the cyanometer—might obviously enjoy a renaissance today.

And so Swiss artist duo Christina Hemauer and Roman Keller, who have made performances and installations since 2003 that deal with the environment, energy, and cultural history, availed of the cyanometer in one of their artistic works. In the 2015 publication *Invent the Future with Elements of the Past* they proposed using the cyanometer again as an instrument with which to observe the sky and indeed the world: for a start, a decrease in the relative humidity in the atmosphere that is anticipated due to climate change.[44] Additionally, many predictions assume that in the future we will burn fewer fossil fuels and simultaneously enforce stricter emissions norms. This would lead to a decrease in particulates and aerosol (a heterogenous mix of solid or liquid particulate matter borne in the air). Climate modeling additionally predicts, as already mentioned, a decrease in clouds. The result of all these processes would be a change in the color of the sky—which Hemauer and Keller define as *Verblauung* (blueing). Measuring this with the aid of the cyanometer enables a visual approach to climate change that has scarcely been considered in contemporary climate research to date.

In any case, the idea that the sky is blueing fits neatly with the scenario that earth scientists from the Massachusetts Institute of Technology (MIT) have recently produced using their own model: according to their prognosis, which was published in *Nature Communications*, the color of the ocean will intensify in coming decades due to climate change. Its blue will become bluer and the greens greener, the study states.[45] This is because in regions such as the subtropics there will be fewer phytoplankton in future, which will render the already blue ocean still bluer. In the polar regions, however, where the ocean is green, growth in phytoplankton is forecast, leading to the impression that the sea is becoming greener. In an interview, however, scientist

Stephanie Dutkiewicz mentions that "the model suggests the changes won't appear huge to the naked eye."[46] Yet once upon a time the cyanometer was developed to measure this very kind of slight difference.

DR NINA BOOGEN is a researcher at the Center for Energy Policy and Economics at the ETH Zurich.

Annina Boogen: "Das Blau des Äthers," in: *Montan-Welten: Alpengeschichte abseits des Pfades (Æther 03)*, ed. Tina Asmussen (Zurich, 2019). See: www.aether.ethz.ch/ausgabe/montan-welten

1 See *documenta 5. Befragung der Realität – Bildwelten Heute* (ed. Documenta), exh. cat. (in folder form), vol. 1: Material; vol. 2: Exhibitors' List (Kassel, 1972).
2 See Michel de Rivaz, *Die schweizerische Banknote 1907–1997, Collection La mémoire de l'oeil* (Le Mont-sur-Lausanne, 1997), pp. 252–254.
3 Horace-Benédict de Saussure, *Voyages dans les Alpes, précédés d'un essai sur l'histoire naturelle des environs de Genève* (Neuchâtel, 1779–1796).
4 See André Karliczek, "Die Bemessung des Himmels: Das Cyanometer des Horace-Bénédict de Saussure," in *Ueber die Natur des Lichts. Die Farbe Blau in der Romantik*, ed. Olaf Breidbach (Wiederstedt, 2013), pp. 49–60.
5 Johann Samuel Ersch and Johann Gottfried Gruber, *Allgemeine Encyclopädie der Wissenschaften und Künste*, Section II (H–N), (Leipzig, 1831), p. 209.
6 See Pedro Lilienfeld, "A Blue Sky History," in: *Optics and Photonics News* 15/6 (2004), pp. 32–39.

7 Leonardo da Vinci, *Traktat von der Malerei*, transl. Heinrich Ludwig, ed. Marie Herzfeld (Jena, 1909), p. 110.

8 See Barbara Lafond-Kettlitz, "Die Alpen in Literatur und Malerei: Albrecht von Haller, Caspar Wolf, Ludwig Hohl, Ferdinand Hodler," in: *Études Germaniques* 256/4 (2009), pp. 933–953.

9 See Olaf Breidbach and André Karliczek, "Himmelblau – das Cyanometer des Horace-Bénédict de Saussure (1740–1799)," in: *Sudhoffs Archiv* 95/1 (2011), pp. 3–28, here p. 5.

10 Ibid., p. 23.

11 Ibid., p. 5.

12 Horace-Benédict de Saussure, "Schreiben des Herrn Professor von Saussure an den Herausgeber, seine Reise auf den Col du Géant betreffend," in: *Magazin für die Naturkunde Helvetiens* 4 (1789), pp. 471–524.

13 Ibid.

14 See Gabriele Busch-Salmen, Manfred Wenzel, Andreas Beyer, and Ernst Osterkamp, *Goethe-Handbuch Supplemente*, vol. 2, *Naturwissenschaften* (Stuttgart, 2016), p. 360.

15 See Breidbach and Karliczek, p. 6.

16 De Saussure describes the cyanometer and his experiments with the blue measure in various publications: Horace-Benédict de Saussure, *Relation abrégée d'un voyage à la Cime du Mont-Blanc* (Geneva, 1787); Horace-Bénédict de Saussure, "Description d'un cyanomètre ou d'un appareil destiné à mesurer l'intensité de la couleur bleue du ciel," in: *Mémoires de l'Académie Royale des Sciences de Turin 1788–1789* (Turin, *1790*), pp. 409–424; Horace-Benédict de Saussure, *Voyages dans les Alpes* (Neuchâtel, 1779–1796), vol. 4, § 2083-6.

17 See de Saussure, *Voyages dans les Alpes*, § 2083.

18 Ersch and Gruber, *Allgemeine Encyclopädie der Wissenschaften und Künste*, p. 209.

19 Ibid.

20 For a detailed description of the history of Berlin Blue, see Alexander Kraft, "Wege des Wissens: Berliner Blau, 1706–1726," in: *Gesellschaft Deutscher Chemiker*, ed. Fachgruppe Geschichte der Chemie, Mitteilungen 22 (2012).

21 See Michel Pastoureau, *Blau: Die Geschichte einer Farbe* (Berlin, 2013), pp. 106–108.

22 See André Karliczek, "Zur Herausbildung von Farbstandards in den frühen Wissenschaften des 18. Jahrhunderts," in: *Ferrum: Nachrichten aus der Eisenbibliothek* 90 (2018), pp. 36–49.

23 See Kraft, "Wege des Wissens: Berliner Blau, 1706–1726."

24 De Saussure, "Description d'un cyanomètre."

25 See Breidbach and Karliczek, "Himmelblau – das Cyanometer des Horace-Bénédict de Saussure (1740–1799)."

26 See Lorraine Daston, "Die kognitiven Leidenschaften: Staunen und Neugier im Europa der frühen Neuzeit," in: *Wunder, Beweise und Tatsachen: Zur Geschichte der Rationalität*, ed. Lorraine Daston (Frankfurt am Main, 2001), pp. 77–97.

27 See Susan James, *Passion and Action: The Emotions in Seventeenth-Century Philosophy* (New York, 1999).

28 See Claude Reichler, *Entdeckung einer Landschaft: Reisende, Schriftsteller, Künstler und ihre Alpen* (Zurich, 2005), pp. 81–82.

29 Horatius Benedictus von Saussure, *Reisen durch die Alpen: nebst einem Versuche über die Naturgeschichte der Gegenden von Genf*, vol. 4, trans. by J. S. Wyttenbach (Leipzig, 1781–1788), p. 376.

30 See Lorraine Daston, "The Empire of Observation, 1600–1800," in: *Histories of Observation*, ed. Lorraine Daston and Elizabeth Lunbeck (Chicago, 2011), pp. 81–113.

31 For a more detailed account of the history of color lexicons, see Friedrich Steinle, "Farben im 18. Jahrhundert: Praxisfelder und Systemversuche," in: *Ferrum: Nachrichten aus der Eisenbibliothek* 90 (2018), pp. 50–60.

32 See Klaus Hentschel, *Visual Cultures in Science and Technology: A Comparative History*, (Oxford, 2015), pp. 348–361.

33 See André Karliczek, "Zur Herausbildung von Farbstandards in den frühen Wissenschaften des 18. Jahrhunderts," in: *Ferrum: Nachrichten aus der Eisenbibliothek* 90 (2018), pp. 36–49, here pp. 44–45.

34 Ibid., pp. 41–42.

35 See Reichler, *Entdeckung einer Landschaft*, pp. 37–46.

36 Jacob Samuel Wyttenbach, Caspar Wolf, and Albrecht Haller, *Merkwürdige Prospekte aus den Schweizer-Gebürgen und derselben Beschreibung* (Bern, 1777).

37 See Konrad Bitterli, Andrea Lutz, and David Schmidhauser (eds), *Dutch mountains: Vom holländischen Flachland in die Alpen*, Kunst Museum Winterthur (Munich, 2018), pp. 44–63.

38 See Reichler, *Entdeckung einer Landschaft*, p. 48.

39 Ibid., p. 71.

40 See Monika Wagner, *William Turner* (Munich, 2011), pp. 24–44.

41 See David Blayney Brown, *J.M.W. Turner: Sketchbooks, Drawings and Watercolors* (London, 2012). The Tate Gallery homepage also offers detailed information on the collection of Turner's sketchbooks: see www.tate.org.uk/art/research-publications/jmw-turner

42 See Lorraine Daston, "Angst und Abscheu vor der Einbildungskraft in der Wissenschaft," in: *Wunder, Beweise und Tatsachen: Zur Geschichte der Rationalität*, ed. Lorraine Daston (Frankfurt am Main, 2001), pp. 99–125, here p. 105.

43 De Saussure, "Description d'un cyanomètre," p. 410.

44 Adrian Notz and Hans Ulrich Obrist (eds), *Invent the Future with Elements of the Past*, (Zurich, 2015).

45 See Stephanie Dutkiewicz et al., "Ocean colour signature of climate change," in: *Nature Communications* 10/578 (2019), pp. 1–13.

46 Ron Brackett, "Bluer Blues: Climate Change Will Alter the Colors of the Oceans, MIT Study Says," in: The Weather Channel, https://weather.com/news/news/2019-02-05-climate-change-oceans-colors-blue-green-phytoplankton (05.02.2019).

Must It Always Be the Mountains?

Reflections on gender roles seem
to come naturally in idyllic mountain
settings. In contemporary Swiss
literature this happens not infrequently
in a precarious manner.

Nadia Brügger

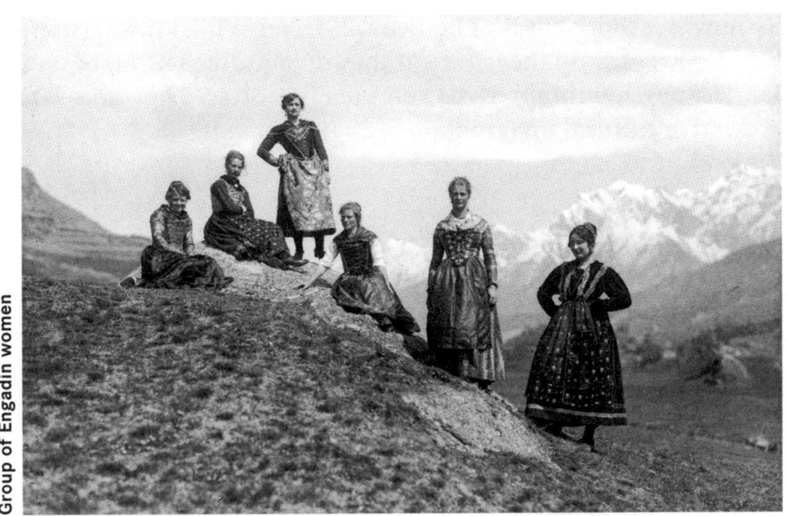

Literary reflections in and around idyllic conceptions of mount-ain landscapes are deeply connected with our ideas about gen-der. The idyll follows clear rules: it represents a limited space inhabited by only a few people and invokes the promise of happi-ness. This promise comes at a high price, however. The philo-sopher Sara Ahmed calls it "the happiness duty": the luring happiness refers the protagonists to designated places and thus has the power to regulate individuals and collectives, not infre-quently in a repressive way. The bourgeois family idyll is just one example. It has prevailed in Europe since the nineteenth century, superseding the Arcadian idyll with its shepherds and shepherdesses. In their place, the heterosexual couple and a common child, the nuclear family, form the affective center of the bourgeois idyll. Idylls are encoded in a gender-specific way. Women maintain that idyll, they even uphold it, but they lack a place of their own therein.

If we look at Swiss contemporary literature written by men dur-ing recent years, we might think at times that the fascination for this powerful narrative continues unabated: the narrative worlds displayed by Peter Stamm, Lukas Bärfuss, Jonas Lüscher and Lukas Holliger (to name but a few) are alike in the way they focus on a restrictive bourgeois environment. Men who leave are the all too familiar characters. In their effort to shape society towards more openness and diversity, the numerous feminisms of our time have created the potential for different fictional worlds. They wouldn't have to rely on the ordinary (family) man, whose character stands for a crisis of masculinity.

So how is it those kinds of heroes still arise? What kind of (literary) knowledge do they store in the surroundings of mountain landscapes, mountain idylls and village stories? How does our collective cultural imagination keep updating it?

Over the mountains to the male self

As Joan Didion has pointed out, we tell each other stories in order to live. The stories which are repeated ad infinitum sometimes strengthen an effective narrative. The Swiss mountains are also a "grand narrative" of this kind, that of the primeval landscape which defies all circumstances.

The gender researcher Franziska Schutzbach speaks of the mountains as a "spiritual foundation." They are the embodiment of a spirit of resistance, of masculinity and its self-reassurance. The Swiss mountains serve to constitute the identity of an entire nation: they are a space for memory; their barrenness is attributed to their inhabitants, and ultimately they also consolidate the gender relations which are found within the boundaries which they delineate.

Men are attributed with individuality. They stray; they leave their villages to make new discoveries; they climb mountains in order to battle against ice and snow and thus to confront themselves with their own fragile masculinity.

Women, on the other hand, wait. When male authors invent female characters, they are often shown to be dependent on male characters. Men go away and forget; women remain and remember.

Peter Stamm's *Weit über das Land* (To the Back of Beyond), is a good example. Published in 2016, the novel cites the tradition of the bourgeois idyll: it begins with a description of bushes which grow together into a wall of green as evening falls, clearly separating Astrid and Thomas's property from that of their neighbors. The family garden, initially a friendly place and a symbol of the idyll, tips over into the opposite and becomes a dark dungeon "from which there was no escape." Very swiftly, the reader lands in the restrictive world of detached houses.

Idyllic labor is female labor

The plot is told quickly: Astrid and Thomas's marriage functions in such a way that Thomas, sitting on the wooden bench in front of the house with a glass of wine, pictures how Astrid folds up the laundry, listens to the children's rustling noises in their beds and looks at herself in the mirror. Astrid bears sole responsibility for creating the idyll. This duty corresponds to the emotional labor, which in literary texts and in (Swiss) reality is traditionally devolved to women.

> And so it is this family space that Thomas leaves one evening without uttering a word. At the garden gate he smiles in amazement at his own audacity, and then he sets off, light of foot. It is here that his hiking trip to the mountains begins. It only functions because back at home Astrid continues to play "Happy Families," behaving as if Daddy had just left for work a little earlier than usual for once. For Astrid a new time reckoning begins ("It was their fourth breakfast without Thomas there"). She now has sufficient time to think about the relationship for which she is ultimately responsible—if she were to do anything else she would destroy the framework which she has been granted.

In the meantime, Thomas grapples with his very prototypical masculinity during the various stations of his journey: his cap pulled down well over his forehead, he can pretend to be incognito on the deserted country roads. His first conversation after his departure takes place in a hotel-like building that—like the family home—is surrounded by a tall hedge. The difference, however, is that behind it lies no monogamous marriage, but the workplace of sex workers. Here he can validate his own "desirability." His own physicality in surviving a fall into a rocky crevice, in testing himself against adverse nature—Stamm's protagonist combines dreams of a toxic masculinity, without being able to think of them in relation to his own vulnerability. Thomas reacts to the experience of being fragile only by imitation, for example of a flâneur or a mountaineer. He thus confronts himself with images and paradigms of masculinity. It fits this image that he is always present, unlike the wife who remembers him and who eventually sets out on a search for traces with the help of a policeman. Thomas feels as if he has neither a past nor a future. In the tone of the novel, this sounds like this:

> Thomas tried to think of home, his warm bed, Astrid and the kids. But the scenes escaped him, he saw mountains lit from within under a starless sky, he flew up never-ending sheer surfaces, so close to the rock that he could make out the tiniest details.

The attempt to remember fails because pictures of another idyll crowd in front of the pictures of the idyllic family place: images of glowing mountains which the runaway can fly up. This fantasy of the omnipotence of white masculinity heralds in advance the downfall of male hubris.

Thomas's return to the family nonetheless takes place simultaneously as a messianic luminous figure and as a man-child that can be certain of being welcomed back by the mother time and time again: Astrid has forgotten the slights and the pain. The novel closes with the idyllic feeling of happiness:

Just like her he had been awaiting this moment, this brief moment of happiness in which he would put out his hand and turn the doorknob. This moment of the door opening, when she would see his indistinct form in the dazzling noonday light.

Although it remains unclear whether the return really took place (the novel also permits the interpretation that Thomas did not survive the fall from the cliff but that the imagined projection is so strong that it takes on a life of its own and upholds itself beyond the death of the protagonist), the entry into domesticity promises a "brief moment of happiness" for both individuals, but is one which takes place under very different conditions. For the man it is the generous return from his hiking journey and hence personal fulfilment; for the woman his homecoming marks once more the start of the earlier time reckoning.

Thinking mountain spaces differently

The Swiss mountain world has served the self-staging of the male bourgeois subject not only since women were excluded from the Swiss Alpine Club in 1907. The cultural scientist Patricia Purtschert recently published a colonial history of white Switzerland which is based on two essential figures: the housewife and the mountaineer. They are both responsible for the development of the "Swiss identity," simply in different ways. The ideal Swiss as mountaineer and mountain guide stands for the conqueror of the highest peaks and discoverer of the nation and represents white hegemonic masculinity by ruling over women and non-white people.

The happy "mere housewife" exemplifies the bourgeois family situation as the head of a civilized and consumer-oriented domesticity but without the possibility of participation. In short: Switzerland with its two "idylls," the idyll of the bourgeois family under female administration and the male idyll of the mountain world.

It is due to authors like Noëmi Lerch, Yael Inokai, Anita Hanse-mann, Leta Semadeni and Annette Lory that in Swiss contemporary literature which focuses on mountain landscapes we can read not only texts which persist with the old tales. They present the mountains as spaces which are not really intended for women and which produce exclusions. To recast this mountain world and the associated idyllic concepts anew in literature is a feminist undertaking: to locate other gender relations within them, to reinterpret their restricted space and to make it into their own space for experimentation. Their approach is critical and invokes utopian spaces, rather than affirming existing concepts. This leads to a transformation by carrying forward a mighty narrative which will also mold us as readers and members of society. It is arduous work, and it will take time.

World's end behind the mountains

This is the task Noëmi Lerch takes on in her novel *Die Pürin*, published in 2015. The title of the novel plays on a double meaning: "Die Pürin" means "the farmer's wife" as well as "the female farmer." The protagonist says appositely: "I shall have to carry you away like a mountain." That is what we should do with stories which weigh us down and force life designs which differ from the norm into the background: carry them away like mountains.

Lerch's debut starts with the constraint of being—as a woman—a mere appendage:

> When die Pürin ("the farmer's wife," NB) wanted to become Pürin ("a farmer"), she was told it was against the law. Only a farmer's wife can be Pürin. And a Pürin without a husband, that was complicated enough. But die Pürin wanted to become a farmer alone, and as a woman.

The first sentence describes the assumption of not being able to become a subject because of a "law": The fact that for the nameless first-person narrator die Pürin is in any case die Pürin links the two figures together as accomplices from the beginning. Lerch's novel is set in the mountains as well. The relationship between two women builds its core.

> The first-person narrator works as a helper on the farm of die Pürin. They form a community together with fourteen cows, fourteen cattle, forty-seven hens and an old gray horse. The narrator documents life on the farm in writing; die Pürin takes

photographs: they each document each other. The narrator has come to this place because the old villa of her deceased grandmother is located here. It is increasingly falling into ruin: cracks appear in the house from which a black furry substance grows, as if the house were being carried on the back of an enormous bear. All the landscapes here are hazy and ramshackle, both inside and out. The fact that behind the crumbling mountains the world comes to an end, as the story suggests, makes the mountain world into a microcosm which is self-contained, in which both the narrator and die Pürin have free rein to do as they please. That there are no men here (even though they appear as past and lost ones) is not a new experimental situation.

Marlen Haushofer's novel *Die Wand* (The Wall), published in 1963, takes as its subject a radical recasting of idyllic concept. Alone in the world from one day to the next, cut off by an invisible wall from everything she knew before, the protagonist rediscovers the world. She documents her daily life in order to retain a feeling for time, or rather to find a new one by writing it herself. An encounter with a man who has strayed into what is actually a landscape without people ends badly (to put it mildly)—for the man. The protagonist—she, too, has no name—forms a family alliance with the handful of animals that belong to the remote hunting lodge in the mountains.

Tractors make better partners than men (says die Pürin)

Lerch also writes of a new type of relationship in a mountain setting: the fact that her female characters relate to each other in a radical manner opens up space for new possibilities and threatens the prevailing order. When the narrator meets die Pürin for the first time, she is sitting majestically on horseback—almost like a prince in a fairy tale. Lerch examines which forms of relationship prove to be liveable and legitimate, and which do not:

As a one-legged crow you sit in a box in my head. If only you could fly. I feed you with cake, think about you every day and forget that you cannot hear me. Sometimes I live with you in the box in my head. I ask you what we are going to do today. You don't answer, but the hens say they would like to come to me for supper. [...] The cocks want soup bowls instead of dishes and I mentally count the plates, dishes and bowls that I have.

The person addressed with the familiar form of "you" occurs regularly in the text and is linked with the sadness of loss. Also nameless and initially not defined as regards gender, through its "gaunt presence" and later the "man-of-the-world face" it evokes a person living as a man. Initially he becomes a one-legged crow sitting in a box in the protagonist's head: the box is tight and it is restricting—the crow cannot fly away. When the man-crow is addressed, the hens and cocks reply: The (heterosexual) partner relationship is recast with animals and the crow also exists in the text outside the box in the narrator's head: the narrator tends its injury and lays it in an urn when it dies. It is hard to say whether it might be possible to write more artistically about the process of burying a self-induced figment of the imagination.

Female freedom

In Lerch's work the mountain landscape becomes her protagonist's memory store. The insularity allows its contemplation. At the same time the narrator is permitted the freedom to forget:
> "What are you writing about," asks die Pürin, "all this time?"
> "The things I don't want to forget." "Well," says die Pürin, "so what will you forget, then?" "Everything, possibly," I say.

Forgetting everything, possibly, also means being able to possibly forget everything. And this opens up the opportunity to think about familiar things from a different perspective, to furnish them with different meanings. At the end, the nameless narrator leaves the crumbling mountains behind her. When she does so she has changed—and so has the mountain world.

NADIA BRÜGGER is a literary scholar and researcher at the University of Zurich.

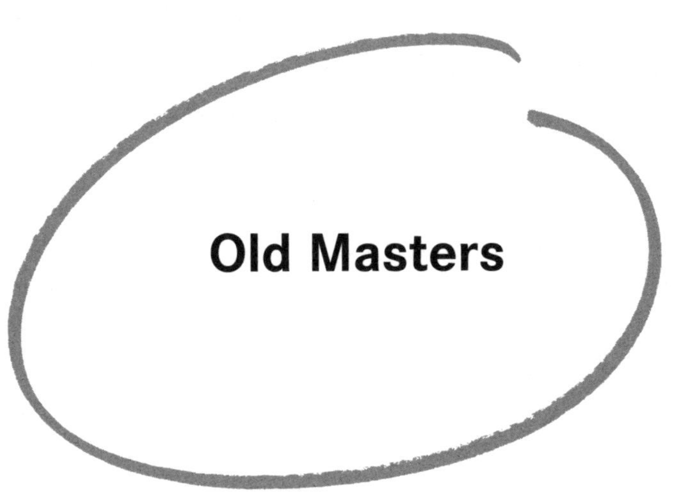

Old Masters

Why Do I Stay in the Provinces?
(1934)

On the steep slope of a wide mountain valley in the southern Black Forest, at an elevation of 1,150 meters, there stands a small ski hut. The floor plan measures six meters by seven. The low-hanging roof covers three rooms: the kitchen which is also the living room, a bedroom and a study.

Martin Heidegger

Scattered at wide intervals throughout the narrow base of the valley and on the equally steep slope opposite lie the farmhouses with their large overhanging roofs. Higher up the slope the meadows and pasture lands lead to the woods with its dark fir-trees, old and towering. Over everything there stands a clear summer sky, and in its radiant expanse two hawks glide around in wide circles.

This is my work-world—seen with the eye of an observer: the guest or summer vacationer. Strictly speaking I myself never observe the landscape. I experience its hourly changes, day and night, in the great comings and goings of the seasons. The gravity of the mountains and the hardness of their primeval rock, the slow and deliberate growth of the fir-trees, the brilliant, simple splendor of the meadows in bloom, the rush of the mountain brook in the long autumn night, the stern simplicity of the flatlands covered with snow—all of this moves and flows through and penetrates daily existence up there, and not in forced moments of "aesthetic" immersion or artificial empathy, but only when one's own existence stands in its work. It is the work alone that opens up space for the reality that is these mountains. The course of the work remains embedded in what happens in the region.

On a deep winter's night when a wild, pounding snowstorm rages around the cabin and veils and covers everything, that is the perfect time for philosophy. Then its questions must become simple and essential. Working through each thought can only be tough and rigorous. The struggle to mold something into language is like the resistance of the towering firs against the storm.

And this philosophical work does not take its course like the aloof studies of some eccentric. It belongs right in the middle of the peasants' work. When the young farmboy drags his heavy sled up the slope and guides it, piled high with beech logs, down the dangerous descent to his house, when the herdsman, lost in thought and slow of step, drives his cattle up the slope, when the farmer in his shed gets the countless shingles ready for his roof, my work is of the same sort. It is intimately rooted in and related to the life of the peasants.

A city-dweller thinks he has gone "out among the people" as soon as he condescends to have a long conversation with a peasant.

But in the evening during a work-break, when I sit with the peasants by the fire or at the table in the "Lord's Corner," we mostly say nothing at all. We smoke our pipes in silence. Now and again someone might say that the woodcutting in the forest is finishing up, that a marten broke into the hen-house last night, that one of the cows will probably calf in the morning, that someone's uncle suffered a stroke, that the weather will soon "turn." The inner relationship of my own work to the Black Forest and its people comes from a centuries-long and irreplaceable rootedness in the Alemannian-Swabian soil.

At most, a city-dweller gets "stimulated" by a so-called stay in the country. But my whole work is sustained and guided by the world of these mountains and their people. Lately from time to time my work up there is interrupted for long stretches by conferences, lecture trips, committee meetings and my teaching work down here in Freiburg. But as soon as I go back up there, even in the first few hours of being at the cabin, the whole world of previous questions forces itself upon me in the very form in which I left it. I simply am transported into the work's own kind of rhythm, and in a fundamental sense I am not at all in command of its hidden law. People in the city often wonder whether one gets lonely up in the mountains among the peasants for such long and monotonous periods of time. But it isn't loneliness, it is solitude. In large cities one can easily be as lonely as almost nowhere else. But one can never be in solitude there. Solitude has the peculiar and original power not of isolating us but of projecting our whole existence out into the vast nearness of the presence *(Wesen)* of all things.

In the public world one can be made a "celebrity" overnight by the newspapers and journals. That always remains the surest way to have one's innermost intentions misinterpreted and quickly and thoroughly forgotten.

In contrast, the memory of the peasant has its simple and sure fidelity which never forgets. Recently an old peasant woman up there was approaching death. She liked to chat with me frequently, and she told me many old stories of the village. In her robust language, full of images, she still preserved many old words and various sayings which have become unintelligible to the village youth today and hence are lost to the spoken language. Very often in the past year when I lived alone in the cabin for weeks on end, this peasant woman with her eighty-three years would still come climbing up the slope to visit me. She wanted to look in from time to time, as she put it, to see whether I was still there or whether "someone" had stolen me off unawares. She spent the night of her death in conversation with her family. Just an hour and a half before the end she sent her greetings to the "Professor." Such a memory is worth incomparably more than the most astute report by any international newspaper about my alleged philosophy.

The world of the city runs the risk of falling into a destructive error. A very loud and very active and very fashionable obtrusiveness often passes itself off as concern for the world and existence of the peasant. But this goes exactly contrary to the one and only thing that now needs to be done, namely, to keep one's distance from the life of the peasant, to leave their existence more than ever to its own law, to keep hands off lest it be dragged into the literati's dishonest chatter about "folk-character" and "rootedness in the soil." The peasant doesn't need and doesn't want this citified officiousness. What he needs and wants is quiet reserve with regard to his own way of being and its independence. But nowadays many people from the city, the kind who know their way around and not least of all the skiers, often behave in the village or at a farmer's house in the same way they "have fun" at their recreation centers in the city. Such goings-on destroy more in one evening than centuries of scholarly teaching about folk-character and folklore could ever hope to promote.

Let us stop all this condescending familiarity and sham concern for "folk-character" and let us learn to take seriously that simple, rough existence up there. Only then will it speak to us once more.

Recently I got a second invitation to teach at the University of Berlin. On that occasion I left Freiburg and withdrew to the cabin. I listened to what the mountains and the forest and the farmlands were saying, and I went to see an old friend of mine, a seventy-five-year-old farmer. He had read about the call to Berlin in the newspapers. What would he say? Slowly he fixed the sure gaze of his clear eyes on mine, and keeping his mouth tightly shut, he thoughtfully put his faithful hand on my shoulder. Ever so slightly he shook his head. That meant: absolutely no!

Translated by Thomas Sheehan

Rock Crystal
(1845, excerpt)

Among the high mountains of our
fatherland there lies a little village with
a small but very pointed church-tower
which emerges with red shingles from
the green of many fruit-trees, and
by reason of its red color is to be seen
far and away amid the misty bluish
distances of the mountains.

Adalbert Stifter

The village lies right in the center of a rather broad valley which has about the shape of a longish circle. Besides the church it contains a school, a townhall, and several other houses of no mean appearance, which form a square on which stand four linden-trees surrounding a stone cross. These buildings are not mere farms but house within them those handicrafts which are indispensable to the human race and furnish the mountaineers with all the products of industry which they require. In the valley and along the mountainsides many other huts and cots are scattered, as is very often the case in mountain regions. These habitations belong to the parish and school-district and pay tribute to the artisans we mentioned by purchasing their wares. Still other more distant huts belong to the village, but are so deeply ensconced in the recesses of the mountains that one cannot see them at all from the valley. Those who live in them rarely come down to their fellow-parishioners and in winter frequently must keep their dead until after the snows have melted away in order to give them a burial. The greatest personage whom the villagers get to see in the course of the year is the priest.

They greatly honor him, and usually he himself through a longer sojourn becomes so accustomed to the solitude of the valley that he not unwillingly stays and simply lives on there. At least, it has not happened in the memory of man that the priest of the village had been a man hankering to get away from or unworthy of his vocation.

No roads lead through the valley. People use their double-track cart-paths upon which they bring in the products of their fields in carts drawn by one horse. Hence, few people come into the valley, among them sometimes a solitary pedestrian who is a lover of nature and dwells for some little time in the upper room of the inn and admires the mountains; or perhaps a painter who sketches the small, pointed spire of the church and the beautiful summits of the rocky peaks. For this reason the villagers form a world by themselves. They all know each other by name and their several histories down from the time of grandfather and great-grandfather; they all mourn when one of them dies; know what name the new-born will receive; they have a language differing from that of the plains; they have their quarrels, which they settle among themselves; they assist one another and flock together when something extraordinary has happened.

They are conservative and things are left to remain as they were. Whenever a stone drops out of a wall, the same stone is put back again, the new houses are built like the old ones, the dilapidated roofs are repaired with the same kind of shingles, and if there happen to be brindled cows on a farm, calves of the same color are raised always, so that the color stays on the farm.

To the south of the village one sees a snow-mountain which seems to lift up its shining peaks right above the roofs of the houses. Yet it is not quite so near. Summer and winter it dominates the valley with its beetling crags and snowy sides. Being the most remarkable object in the landscape, this mountain is of main interest to the inhabitants and has become the central feature of many a story.

There is not a young man or graybeard in the village but can tell of the crags and crests of the mountain, of its crevasses and caves, of its torrents and screes, whether now he knows it from his own experience or from hearsay. The mountain is the boast of the villagers as if it were a work of theirs and one is not so sure, however highly one may esteem the plain-spokenness and reputation for truth-telling of the natives, whether they do not fib, now and then, to the honor and glory of their mountain. Besides being the wonder of the valley, the mountain affords actual profit; for whenever a company of tourists arrives to ascend the mountain the natives serve as guides; and to have been a guide, to have experienced this or that, to know this or that spot, is a distinction every one likes to gain for himself. The mountain often is the object of their conversation at the inn, when they sit together and tell of their feats and wonderful experiences; nor do they omit to relate what this or that traveler had said and what reward they had received from him for their labor. Furthermore, the snowy sides of the mountain feed a lake among its heavily forested recesses, from which a merry brook runs through the valley, drives the saw-mill and the flour-mill, cleanses the village and waters the cattle. The forests of the mountain furnish timber and form a bulwark against the avalanches.

The annual history of the mountain is as follows: In winter, the two pinnacles of its summit, which they call horns, are snow-white and, when visible on bright days, tower up into the blackish blue of the sky in dazzling splendor, and all its shoulders are white, too, and all slopes. Even the perpendicular precipices, called walls by the natives, are covered with white frost delicately laid on, or with thin ice adhering to them like varnish, so that the whole mass looms up like an enchanted castle from out of the hoary gray of the forests which lie spread out heavily about its base. In summer, when the sun and warm winds melt the snow from their steep sides, the peaks soar up black into the sky and have only beautiful veins and specks of white on their flanks—as the natives say. But the fact is, the peaks are of a delicate, distant blue, and what they call veins and specks is not white, but has the lovely milk-blue color of distant snow against the darker blue of the rocks. When the weather is hot, the more elevated slopes about the peaks do not lose their covering of eternal snow. On the contrary it then gleams with double resplendence down upon the green of the trees in the valley; but the winter's snow is melted off their lower parts. Then becomes visible the bluish or greenish iridescence of the glaciers which are bared and gleam down upon the valley below. At the edge of this iridescence, there where it seems from the distance like a fringe of gems, a nearer view reveals confused masses of wild and monstrous boulders, slabs, and fragments piled up in chaotic fashion. In very hot and long summers, the ice-fields are denuded even in the higher regions, and then a much greater amount of blue-green glacier-ice glances down into the valley, many knobs and depressions are laid bare which one otherwise sees only covered with white, the muddy edge of the ice comes to view with its deposit of rocks, silt, and slime, and far greater volumes of water than usual rush into the valley. This continues until it gradually becomes autumn again, the waters grow less, and one day a gray continuous gentle rain spreads over all the valley. Then, after the mists have dispersed about the summits, the mountain is seen to have draped itself again in its soft robe of snow, and all crags, cones, and pinnacles are vested in white. Thus it goes on, year after year, with but slight divergences, and thus it will go on so long as nature remains the same, and there is snow upon the heights and people live in the valleys. But to the natives these changes seem great, they pay much attention to them and calculate the progress of the seasons by them.

The ascent of the mountain is made from our valley. One follows a fine road which leads south to another valley over a so-called "neck." Neck they call a moderately high mountain-ridge which connects two mountain-ranges of considerable magnitude and over which one can pass from one valley to another between the mountains. The neck which connects our snow-mountain with another great mountain-mass is altogether covered with pine-forests. At its greatest elevation, where the road begins gradually to descend into the valley beyond, there stands a post erected to commemorate a calamity. Once upon a time a baker carrying bread in a basket slung around his neck was found dead on that spot. They painted a picture of the dead baker with his basket and the pine-trees round about, and beneath it an explanation with a request for prayer from the passer-by, and this picture they fastened to a wooden post painted red, and erected it at the spot where the accident occurred. At this post, then, one leaves the road and continues along the ridge of the "neck" instead of crossing it and descending into the valley beyond. There is an opening among the pine-trees at that spot, as if there were a road between them. In fact, a path is sometimes made in that direction which then serves to bring down timber from the higher regions, but which is afterward overgrown again with grass. Proceeding along this way, which gently ascends, one arrives at last at a bare, treeless region. It is barren heath where grows nothing but heather, mosses, and lichens. It grows ever steeper, the further one ascends; but one always follows a gully resembling a rounded out ditch which is convenient, as one cannot then miss one's way in this extensive, treeless, monotonous region. After a while, rocks as large as churches rise out of the grassy soil, between whose walls one climbs up still farther. Then there are again bleak ridges, with hardly any vegetation, which reach up into the thinner air of higher altitudes and lead straight to the ice. At both sides of this path, steep ledges plunge down, and by this natural causeway the snow-mountain is joined to the "neck." In order to surmount the ice one skirts it for some distance where it is surrounded by rock-walls, until one comes to the old hard snow which bridges the crevasses and at most seasons of the year bears the weight of the climber.

From the highest point of this snowfield, two peaks tower up, of which the one is higher and, therefore, the summit of the mountain. These pinnacles are very hard to climb. As they are surrounded by a chasm of varying width—the *bergschrund*—which one must leap over, and as their precipitous escarpments afford but small footholds, most of the tourists climbing the mountain content themselves with reaching the bergschrund and from there enjoy the panorama. Those who mean to climb to the top must use climbing-irons, ropes, and, iron spikes.

Besides this mountain there are still others south of the valley, but none as high. Even if the snow begins to lie on them early in fall and stays till late in spring, midsummer always removes it, and then the rocks gleam pleasantly in the sunlight, and the forests at their base have their soft green intersected by the broad blue shadows of these peaks which are so beautiful that one never tires of looking at them.

On the opposite, northern, eastern, and western sides of the valley the mountains rise in long ridges and are of lower elevation: scattered fields and meadows climb up along their sides till rather high up, and above them one sees clearings, chalets, and the like, until at their edge they are silhouetted against the sky with their delicately serrated forest—which is indicative of their inconsiderable height—whereas the mountains toward the south, though also magnificently wooded, cut off the shining horizon with entirely smooth lines.

When one stands about in the center of the valley it would seem as if there were no way out or into the basin; but people who have often been in the mountains are familiar with this illusion: the fact is, diverse roads lead through the folds of the mountains to the plains to the north, some of them with hardly a rise; and to the south where the valley seems shut in by precipitous mountain-walls, a road leads over the "neck" mentioned above.

Translated by Dr Lee M. Hollander

Gravity and Grace
(1947, excerpt)

All the *natural* movements of the soul are controlled by laws analogous to those of physical gravity. Grace is the only exception.

We must always expect things to happen in conformity with the laws of gravity unless there is supernatural intervention.

Simone Weil

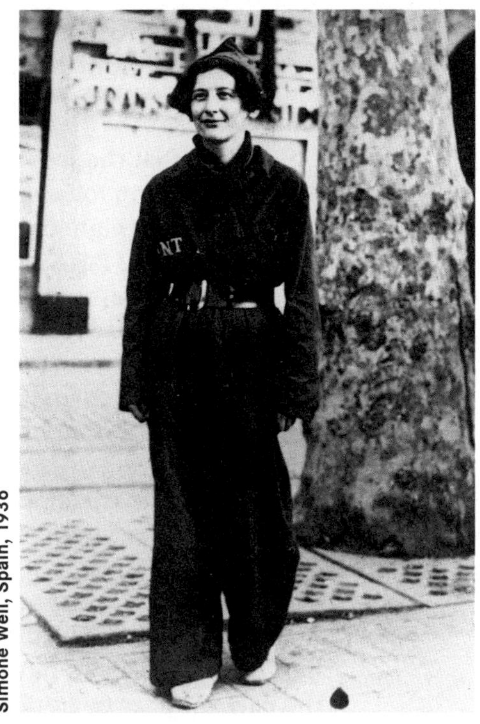

Simone Weil, Spain, 1936

Two forces rule the universe: light and gravity.

Gravity. Generally what we expect of others depends on the effect of gravity upon ourselves, what we receive from them depends on the effect of gravity upon them. Sometimes (by chance) the two coincide, often they do not.

What is the reason that as soon as one human being shows he needs another (no matter whether his need be slight or great) the latter draws back from him? Gravity.

Lear, a tragedy of gravity. Everything we call base is a phenomenon due to gravity. Moreover the word baseness is an indication of this fact.

The object of an action and the level of the energy by which it is carried out are distinct from each other. A certain thing *must* be done. But where is the energy to be drawn for its accomplishment? A virtuous action can lower a man if there is not enough energy available on the same level.

What is base and what is superficial are on the same level. "His love is violent but base": a possible sentence. "His love is deep but base": an impossible one.

If it be true that the same suffering is much harder to bear for a high motive than for a base one (the people who stood, motionless, from one to eight o'clock in the morning for the sake of having an egg would have found it very difficult to do so in order to save a human life), a base form of virtue is perhaps in some respects better able to stand the test of difficulties, temptations and misfortunes than a noble one. Napoleon's soldiers. Hence the use of cruelty in order to sustain or raise the morale of soldiers. Something not to be forgotten in connection with moral weakness.

This is a particular example of the law which generally puts force on the side of baseness. Gravity is, as it were, a symbol of it.

Queueing for food. The same action is easier if the motive is base than if it is noble. Base motives have in them more energy than noble ones. Problem: In what way can the energy belonging to the base motives be transferred to the noble ones?

I must not forget that at certain times when my headaches were raging I had an intense longing to make another human being suffer by hitting him in exactly the same part of his forehead.

Analogous desires—very frequent in human beings.

When in this state, I have several times succumbed to the temptation at least to say words which cause pain. Obedience to the force of gravity. The greatest sin. Thus we corrupt the function of language, which is to express the relationship between things.

Attitude of supplication: I must necessarily turn to something other than myself since it is a question of being delivered from self.

Any attempt to gain this deliverance by means of my own energy would be like the efforts of a cow which pulls at its hobble and so falls onto its knees.

In making it one liberates a certain amount of energy in oneself by a violence which serves to degrade more energy. Compensation as in thermodynamics; a vicious circle from which one can be delivered only from on high.

The source of man's moral energy is outside him, like that of his physical energy (food, air, etc). He generally finds it, and that is why he has the illusion—as on the physical plane—that his being carries the principle of its preservation within itself. Privation alone makes him feel his need. And, in the event of privation, he cannot help turning to *anything whatever* that is edible.

There is only one remedy for that: a chlorophyll conferring the faculty of feeding on light.

Not to judge. All faults are the same. There is only one fault: incapacity to feed upon light, for where capacity to do this has been lost all faults are possible.

"My meat is to do the will of Him that sent me." There is no good apart from this capacity.

To come down by a movement in which gravity plays no part. [...] Gravity makes things come down, wings make them rise. What wings raised to the second power can make things come down without weight?

Creation is composed of the descending movement of gravity, the ascending movement of grace and the descending movement of the second degree of grace.

Grace is the law of the descending movement.

To lower oneself is to rise in the domain of moral gravity. Moral gravity makes us fall towards the heights.

Too great an affliction places a human being beneath pity: it arouses disgust, horror and scorn.

Pity goes down to a certain level but not below it. What does charity do in order to descend lower?

Have those who have fallen so low pity on themselves?

The Blackbird
(1929)

The two men of whom I must speak—in order to tell three brief stories, for which the choice of a narrator is a matter of some importance—had been childhood friends; let's call them Aone and Atwo.

Robert Musil

For such friendships become in principle all the more extraordinary the older one grows. One is transformed in the course of these years from head to foot and from the tips of the hairs to the depths of the heart, but the relationship to the other remains curiously the same and changes as little as the bond that every man sustains to the various gentlemen whom he addresses, one after the other, as I. The question is not whether one still experiences things in the same way as the little boy with the broad face and blond hair who once posed for his photograph; no, one can not even say that one has a fond feeling for that silly little me-ish monster. And in the same way one is not in full accord with one's best friends, or even satisfied with them; indeed, many friends can hardly stand each other. These are even, in a certain sense, the deepest and best friendships and capture the elusive inner essence without any superfluous additions.

The youth which bound the two friends Aone and Atwo together had been nothing less than a religious one. They had been brought up together in an Institution which flattered itself that it attached a proper importance to religious principles, while its pupils staked their honor on ignoring them. The church belonging to the Institution, for example, was a large, lovely, proper church with a stone tower, reserved for the use of the school. Because no one from outside ever entered it, a few groups of schoolboys could, while the others in the front benches alternately stood and kneeled as the holy customs demanded, play cards behind the confessionals, smoke cigarettes on the organ stairs, or remove themselves to the tower, which supported, under its peaked roof, a stone balcony like a candle-holder, upon whose dizzying surface acrobatics could be performed of a sort which might have cost even less sin-laden youths their necks.

One of these challenges from God involved pulling oneself up onto one's hands on the platform using a slow pressure of the muscles and remaining there swaying back and forth while gazing downwards. Anyone who has tried this stunt on the flat ground will know how much self-confidence, expertise, and luck it requires to repeat the trick on a foot-wide strip of stone at the top of a tower. Indeed many bold and agile lads never dared to try it, even when they were able to troll about in their hands on level ground. Aone, for example, did not. Atwo, however, and this may well serve to introduce him as a narrator, had been the inventor of this character test in his boyhood. It was hard to find another body like his. He did not lug around the usual sport-induced muscles, but seemed to have been simply and effortlessly garnished with musculature by nature herself. A narrow, rather small head sat on the top, with eyes which were like lightning wrapped in velvet, and teeth that recalled the gleam of a hunting animal more readily than they suggested the gentleness of a mystic.

Later, in their college days, the two friends fell under the enchantment of a materialistic philosophy, which explained human beings as physiological or economic machines—which perhaps they really are—without recourse to the soul or God; though it never occurred to them that the charm of this philosophy resided less in its truth than in its demonic, pessimistic, threatening character. Already they stood to one another as friends of youth. For Atwo was studying forestry and talked about moving far away—to Russia or to Asia—as a forest-engineer, as soon as his studies were over, while his friend had chosen a more down-to-earth enthusiasm in the place of this boyish one, and was active in the up-and-coming labor movement. When they ran into each other again just before the Great War, Atwo had already put his Russian adventures behind him and did not care to talk about them. He was employed in the offices of some large firm and seemed to have suffered considerable setbacks, although he was comfortable in a middle-class way. His friend, on the other hand, had developed from a combatant in the class struggle into the editor of a newspaper which printed a good deal on the theme of social stability and was owned by a stockbroker. The two scorned each other mutually and inseparably afterwards, but they lost track of one another again; and, as they finally came together once more, Atwo recounted what follows in the way in which one shakes out a sack of memories in front of a friend in order to go on with a blank canvas. Under these circumstances, it doesn't much matter what the other answered, and the conversation can be reported almost as a monologue. It is more important to try to describe exactly how Atwo looked at the time, for the immediate impression he made is not entirely irrelevant to the meaning of his words. But this is difficult. At best one might say that he resembled a sharp, slim, nervy, riding whip, which, resting its soft tip, leans against a wall; in such a half-standing, half-collapsed position he seemed to be completely comfortable.

Some of the most curious places in the world—said Atwo—are those Berlin courtyards, where two, three or four houses show their backsides to one another, and cooks sit between their walls in four-cornered dens and sing. You can tell from the look of the red copper cutlery on the shelves how loudly it rattles. A man's voice far below growls abuses to a girl above, or heavy wooden shoes crash against the ringing plaster back and forth. Slow. Hard. Tireless. Pointless. Always. Is it that way or not?

The kitchens and bedrooms look out on this side and that; they lie adjacent to each other, like love and digestion in the human body. The marriage beds are piled up in layers; for all the bedrooms in the building have the same location, and the window, bathroom and closet walls determine the place of the bed almost exactly to a half-meter. The dining rooms are heaped up on top of one another, just like the bathrooms with their white tiles and the balconies with their red lampshades. Love, sleep, birth, digestion, unexpected reunions, troubled and convivial evenings, are stacked up in these houses like columns of breadrolls in an automat. One's personal fate is decided the moment one moves into one of these middle-class dwellings. You will admit that human freedom lies mainly in where and when a person does something, for what people do is almost always the same. So it bodes ill when everything runs according to the same basic plan. Once I climbed up a wardrobe just to exploit the vertical for a change, and I can testify that the unpleasant conversation which I was forced to have as a result looked very different from up there.

Atwo laughed over the recollection and filled his glass. Aone was thinking that they were sitting on a balcony with a red lampshade that belonged to his own dwelling, but he said nothing, knowing too well what objection he could have made.

Even today I still admit—Atwo conceded on his own—that there is something impressive in this monotony, and at the time I believed I perceived something of the desert or the ocean in this atmosphere of crowded dullness. A slaughterhouse in Chicago, although the idea of it turns my stomach, is at any rate something different from a flowerpot! The strange thing was, however, that just at the time in which I lived in this flat I thought extraordinarily often about my parents. You remember that I had lost almost all connection with them, but a sentence now came into my head: They gave you the gift of life; and this odd sentence kept coming back to me time after time, like a fly which refuses to be shooed away. I have nothing more to say about this artificially-pious way of talking, which gets imprinted on us as children. But when I looked at my flat, I used to tell myself: Look, now you have bought your life, for so-and-so many marks yearly rent! Maybe I even told myself: Now you've made a life by your own exertions! That life lay in the middle, as it were, between department store, insurance-policy, and pride. And so it seemed to me incredibly strange, indeed even a mystery, that something had been given to me whether I wanted it or not, and that that thing was the foundation of everything beyond it. The sentence concealed, I think, a treasure of irregularity and unpredictability which I myself had buried. And just then the thing happened with the nightingale.

It began with an evening like many others. I had stayed at home and was sitting up in the smoking-room after my wife had gone to bed; the only difference between this and similar evenings was perhaps that I had not taken up a book—or anything at all; but even that had happened before. After one o'clock, the streets begin to grow more peaceful and conversations come to seem out of place; it is pleasant to follow with one's ears the progress of the night. By two o'clock the noise and laughter below are clearly nothing more than drunkenness and loitering. I became aware that I was waiting for something, but I had no idea what it was. At about three o'clock—it was in May—the sky began to grow lighter; I felt my way through the dark apartment to the bedroom and laid myself silently in bed. I was now expecting nothing more than sleep followed by a day like all the rest. Soon I no longer knew whether I was awake or asleep. A dark green gushed between the curtains and the gaps in the shutters; narrow foaming bands of morning light snaked their way through. It could have been my last waking impression, or else a peaceful dream-image. Then I was fully awakened by something coming nearer: sounds. Once, twice, drunk with sleep, I made certain. The sounds settled on the roof of the neighbouring house and from there sprang into the air like dolphins. I could also have said, like balls of light at a fireworks display, for the impression of balls of light stayed with me. As they fell to earth they exploded softly on the windowpanes and sank like great silver stars into the depths below. I now experienced something magical; I lay in my bed like a stone figure in a sarcophagus, awake, but awake in a different way than by day. It is difficult to describe, but when I reflect on it it was as though something had turned me inside out: I was no longer a statue in relief but something sunken beneath the surface. And the space of the room was not hollow and empty, but filled with some material which does not exist among the materials of day, a black-transparent substance, which I could feel through only darkly, and which I too seemed to be made of. Time ran in quick, fever-small pulsebeats. Why shouldn't something happen now that would not happen otherwise?—It is a nightingale singing!—I said to myself half-aloud.

Now perhaps there are indeed in Berlin—Atwo continued—more nightingales than I had thought. At the time I believed that in this stony wilderness there were none, and that this one had flown to me from afar. To me!!—I felt and sat up smiling—A bird from heaven! Such things exist! In such a moment you see one is ready in the most natural way to believe in the supernatural, as though one's childhood had been spent in a magic realm. I thought straight away: I will follow the nightingale! Farewell, my dear!—I thought—Farewell, my dear, farewell house, farewell city…! But before I was out of bed, and before I had determined precisely whether I should climb out to the nightingale on the roof or follow it through the streets, the bird had grown silent and seemed to have flown away.

Now it sang on another roof, for another sleeper.—Atwo reflected.—You will assume that the story is now over?—It was only now beginning, and I hardly know how it should end!

I was abandoned, left behind with a burden of deep discontent. It was no nightingale, it was a blackbird, I told myself, just as you want to say. These blackbirds imitate other birds, as everybody knows. Now I was fully awake and the silence oppressed me. I lit a candle and studied the woman who lay next to me. Her body looked a pale brick color. The white edge of the blanket lay against her skin like a strip of snow. Broad shadow-lines, whose origin was difficult to determine although they must of course have had to do with the candle and with the position of my arms, curved around her body.—What's the difference—I thought—if it was really only a blackbird! Oh, on the contrary;

it's just the fact that it was only a plain old blackbird which could bring on this madness: that makes it count for much more! You know how one weeps only at a small disappointment; with one twice as great one brings out a smile. And meanwhile, I kept looking at my wife. Everything hung together, though I don't know how. For years I have loved you, I thought, like nothing else in the world, and now you lie there like a burned-out husk of love. You have become a stranger to me: I've come out on the other side of love. Was it disgust? I don't remember ever having felt disgust. I can only describe it in this way, as though a feeling could bore through the heart like a mountain, on whose other side there lies another world, with the same valley, the same houses and little bridges. But I didn't know what it was at all. Today I still don't know. Perhaps it is wrong to tell you this story in connection with the two which follow. I can only tell you how it struck me as I was experiencing it. A signal from somewhere had reached me—that was my impression.

I laid my head against her body, which slept on innocent and unaware. Her breast seemed to rise and fall in an exaggerated manner, and the walls of the room slapped gently up and down against her sleeping figure, like the high seas against a ship which is already far out onto the water. I probably never would have succeeded in taking leave, but it occurred to me that if I left then I would be like a little boat abandoned in loneliness and run over carelessly by a large, secure ship. I kissed the sleeper; she showed no reaction. I whispered something in her ear, perhaps so carefully that she did not hear it. Then I ridiculed myself and made fun of the nightingale, but I furtively got dressed. I think that I sobbed while doing so, but then I really went. It was breathtakingly simple, though I tried to tell myself that no upright man would behave in this way. I remember I was like a drunken man who scolds the street on which he is walking in order to assure himself of his sobriety.

Naturally, I have often thought of going back; at times I would have crossed half the world to do so. But I never did. She had become, in brief, untouchable for me; I don't know if you understand: Someone who experiences the depths of an injustice can never again make it right. I don't want, incidentally, your forgiveness. I want to tell my stories in order to determine whether or not they are true; I haven't been able to express myself freely to anyone for years, and, if I were to hear myself talking to myself aloud, I would, to tell you the truth, find myself a little uncanny.

Take it for granted then that my reason won't give an inch to your scepticism.

But two years later I found myself in an end zone, the blind corner of a battleline in the South Tyrol, which turned back from the bloody graves of Cimi di Vezzena to Lake Caldonazzo. The line lay deep in the valley, like a sunny wave over two hills with charming names, and rose up again on the other side, only to lose itself in the quiet mountains. It was in October. The almost unoccupied trenches were sunk in dead leaves, the lake burned noiselessly in blue, the hills lay there like huge faded wreaths; like grave-wreaths, I often thought, though without a trace of fear. Hesitant and unsteady, the valley flowed around them; but on the other side of the border we held it left this sweet diffusiveness behind and drove like a trumpet-blast, brown, broad, and heroic, into the hostile distance.

At nights we moved forward into it to occupy a new position. We lay so open in the valley that the enemy could have slaughtered just by throwing stones from above, but we were treated only to slow artillery-fire. Even so, on the morning after such a night we all wore strange expressions which did not vanish for hours: our eyes had widened, and the heads on many shoulders were held up irregularly, like a trampled lawn. But in every one of those nights I lifted my head many times above the edge of the trench and looked cautiously over my shoulder like a lover. Then I saw the Brenta massif, light sky-blue, folded stiffly as out of glass, standing in the dark. And in these nights the stars were huge, punched out of gold foil, and glistened as though baked out of a rich dough. Even at night the heavens were still blue; the thin, maidenly sickle-moon, all golden or silver, lay on its back in the middle and swam in enchantment. You must try to imagine how beautiful it all was; nothing is so beautiful when life is secure. Then I couldn't hold myself back and crept out, compelled by happiness and longing, to take a walk as far as the gold-green black trees, standing between them upright in the night like a little brown-green feather in the plumage of the quietly sitting, sharp-beaked bird, Death; a bird so magically colorful and black, you can't imagine it.

Daytimes, back in the base camp, one could, on the other hand, even go out riding. In places where there is time both to reflect and to panic one learns for the first time to comprehend the danger. Every day claims its victims, a fixed weekly average, such-and-such percent, and the general command of the division takes charge of the figures with all the impersonality of an insurance agency. So did we all. Instinctively, one knows what one's chances are and feels assured of them, even when the conditions are not exactly favourable. That is the remarkable peace in which one lives when constantly under fire. I must emphasize this, in case you get the wrong impression of my circumstances. So it may happen that one suddenly feels driven to seek out a certain familiar face which one has seen a few days before; but it is no longer there. Such a face can unsettle us more that is reasonable and remains suspended in the air like a candle-shimmer. One is less frightened of death than ordinarily but open to all sorts of excitements. It is as though the fear of the end which always seems to lie on men like a stone were suddenly rolled away, and there now bloomed, in the indefinite region of death, a strange freedom.

Once, during this time, an enemy plane came over our quiet camp. This did not happen frequently, for the mountains with their narrow troughs between the armed peaks had to be flown over at a height. We stood directly on one of the grave-wreaths, and, in a moment, the sky was dotted with white shrapnel clouds of the bomber as though from a nimble powder-puff. It looked cheerful and almost friendly. The sun shone through the tri-colored wings of the plane as though through a church window or colored silk-paper as it flew over our heads; all that was missing was the music of Mozart. The thought went through my head that we were standing there like a group of race-watchers and that we made an ideal target. And indeed someone said: Better get down! But no one had the desire to dive like a field-mouse into its hole. At that moment, I heard a light ringing which came closer ro my fascinated upstaring face. Of course it could have happened in reverse, so that I first heard the ringing and then grasped the approach of danger; but in the same moment I knew: it was an airstave. These were sharp iron spears no thicker than a carpenter's pencil which planes used to let drop; and if one hit your skull it went straight through to the soles of your feet, but they hardly ever hit, and they were soon given up. For this reason it was my first airstave; but bombs and machine-gun fire have their own sound, and I knew immediately with what I had to do. I was tense with expectation, and, in the next second, I had the strange improbable sensation: it's going to hit!

And do you know how it was? Not like a terrible realization, but like an unexpected happiness! At first I wondered how it was that only I had heard the ringing. Then I thought that the noise would disappear again, but it did not. It came closer to me, though still in the distance, and grew perspectively greater. I looked cautiously at the faces around me, but no one else seemed to register it. And in that moment, when I became convinced that I alone heard this faint song, something came up out of me against it, a ray of life just as unlimited as the death coming towards me from above. I am not inventing this; I am trying to describe it as simply as possible. I am convinced that I have expressed myself in an exact and sober manner, though I realize that it is to a certain extent as it is in dreams, where one imagines oneself to be speaking with perfect clarity and what comes out is a pure nonsense.

This went on for a long time, during which only I heard the event approaching. It was a thin, singing, simple, high sound, as when the rim of a glass is made to whine, but there was something unreal to it. You have never heard such a thing, I said to myself. And this sound was directed to me. I was bound up with this sound and never doubted in the least that something decisive was moving forward and taking me with it. Not a single one of my thoughts was of the sort that ought to come in the moment of departure from life: everything I felt was directed towards the future; and I must simply say that I was certain in the next minute of feeling God's nearness near to my body. That is no small thing in a man who has not believed in God since his eighth year.

Meanwhile, the sound from above had assumed a solider form; it swelled and threatened. I had asked myself a few times whether I should give the alarm, but whether I or another was going to be hit, I didn't want to do it! Perhaps God is nothing more than the way in which we poor beggars, in the confines of our existence, boast to ourselves of having a rich relative in heaven. I don't know. But it was plain that the air had now begun to ring for the others as well; I observed spots of agitation flitting over their faces, and, you see,—not one of them let a word escape either. I looked again at their faces: these lads, in whose minds nothing could have been further than these thoughts, were standing there without knowing it like a group of disciples who are waiting for a message. And suddenly the singing became an earthly sound, ten feet, a hundred feet over us, and died. It, the thing, was there. In the middle between us but nearest to me, something had lost its voice and been swallowed up by the earth and had burst into an unreal noiselessness. My heart beat broadly and peacefully; I cannot have been shocked for more than a fraction of a second; I never lost the smallest fraction of time in my life. But what I first became aware of was that they were all staring at me. I stood on the same spot, but my body had been violently dragged to the side and had carried out a deep, half-circle bend. I felt as though I were awaking out of stupor and did not know how long I had been absent. Nobody addressed me. Finally someone said: An airstave! and everybody wanted to go after it, but it was stuck meter-deep in the earth. At that moment a warm feeling of gratitude came over me, and I think that I flushed all over. If someone had said that God had entered into my body, I would not have laughed. But I would not have believed it either. I would not have believed that I had carried away the smallest sliver of God in my body. And still, every time I think of it, I long to experience once again more clearly something of the same sort!

And I did experience it again, by the way, only not more clearly. So Atwo began his last story. He seemed to be growing less certain of himself, but one could see nevertheless that for that very reason he was burning to hear himself tell this story.

It had to do with his mother, who had not possessed much of Atwo's love, though he maintained it had not actually been so at all.—On the face of it,—he said—we didn't suit each other, and that is after all to be expected when an old lady has lived decades in the same little town and has a son, who, to her way of thinking, has accomplished nothing in the wider world. In her company I was as uncomfortable as with a mirror which slightly distorts the width of everything, and I grieved her by refusing to visit home for years on end. But every month she wrote me a worried letter full of questions, and although I ordinarily did not answer it, there was still something strangely privileged about our relations, and despite everything I was deeply attached to her, as later became apparent.

Perhaps she had passionately impressend on herself decades ago the image of a little boy, in whom she may have set God knows what hopes, which could not be erased later; and because I myself was this long-lost boy, her love hung on me as if all the set suns still wavered somewhere between light and darkness. Here again you will ascribe to me a kind of secret vanity, but it is not that. For I can testify that I don't pass the time with myself well. What so many people do when they look complacently at photographs which represent them in their younger days, or when they think back happily on what they did there and then, this Bank-of-Myself system, is entirely incomprehensible to me. I am not particularly moody, nor do I live only for the moment, but when something is over, then it's over with me, and when I remember in a certain street that I often took this route in the past, or when I see a house in which I used to live, I feel automatic, instinctive repulsion, like a pain, as though I were thinking of something shameful. What has happened flows away as one changes; and it seems to me that, however much one changes, one would not really do so if the one left behind were really so unobjectionable. But precisely because I usually feel that way, it was wonderful to learn that at least one human being had held fast to a certain picture of me throughout my whole life; probably a picture which never corresponded to what I was, but which was, nevertheless, in a certain sense, my fiat of creation and my authentication. Do you understand me when I say that my mother had, in this figurative sense, the nature of a lion shut up in the person of an in many ways limited woman? She was not clever according to ordinary standards; she was unable to ignore anything, but her mind didn't range very far either. When I think of my childhood, I cannot say that she could be called good, for she was impetuous and subject to nerves, and you can imagine what results from the union of passion with a narrow perspective. But I should like to maintain that there is a greatness, a character, that unites itself even now in a mysterious way with the incarnation in which a person ordinarily presents himself to our eyes, just as in fairy-tales the gods took on the forms of snakes and fish.

Shortly after the event of the airstave, I landed in a Russian prison camp as a result of a military encounter and later took part in the great transformation. I did not return so quickly, for that new life agreed with me for a long time. I am still full of admiration;

but one day I discovered that I could no longer pronounce a few statements of necessary dogma without yawning, and to escape the associated danger to life, I sought refuge in Germany, where individualism was in an inflationary boon. I got involved in dubious business enterprises of various sorts, partly out of need, partly out of pleasure of being in an old country again where one can do wrong without having to be ashamed of it. It did not go well, and sometimes it went very badly. My parents were not in good shape either. A few times my mother wrote: We can't help you now, but if I could help you with the little bit which you will one day inherit, I would wish my own death. That's what she wrote, even though I hadn't visited her for years, or given her any sign of affection. I must confess that I held it only as an exaggerated form of speech and ascribed to it no real importance, when, at the same time, I never doubted the sincerity of the feeling which expressed itself so sentimentally. But now something thoroughly strange happened. My mother really did fall sick, and one could well believe that she had taken my father, whom she tended to dominate, with her.

Atwo thought for a moment.—She died of an illness which she must have suffered for a long time without anyone's knowing of it. One could naturally give the coincidence many natural explanations, and I'm afraid you will judge me harshly if I don't. But the astonishing thing was again the surrounding circumstances. She did not want to die. I know that she tried to defend herself against an early death, and she complained vigorously. Her instinct for self-preservation, her resolve, her wishes, were all directed against the outcome. One cannot say that a decision of character won out over the inclination of the moment; for she could have thought earlier of suicide or elective poverty, which she did not. She was entirely a victim. But have you never observed that your body has another will than your own? I believe that what we call will, and all of our feelings, impressions and thoughts, which apparently have dominion over us, do so only as representatives of a kind of limited authority, and that in times of serious illness and recovery, in uncertain battles, and in all shifts of fortune, there is a form of ultimate decision on the part of the body, which ultimately holds power and truth in its own possession. But let that be as it may, what is certain is that I was convinced that there was something entirely voluntary in the death of my mother, and if you think that is only my imagination, let me just state that, in the moment in which I received the news that my mother was sick, even though there was no reason to be worried, I was entirely changed, and that in a striking way. A hardness which had enclosed me melted away for a moment, and I can say no more than that the situation in which I found myself from then on had much in common with waking up on the night in which I left my house, and with waiting for the singing arrow from above. I wanted to travel to my mother immediately, but she kept me away with all sorts of excuses. First it was that she would be delighted to see me, but I should wait until her trivial illness was over so that she could receive me in a state of health; later she communicated to me that my visit would be too much excitement for her just then; finally, when I insisted, she said she was just at the turning point: I should only be patient a little longer. It looked as though she was afraid that seeing me again would make her uncertain. And then everything was decided so quickly that I came just in time for the funeral.

I found my father sick too, and, as I told you, I could soon do nothing more than help him die. He had been a good man, but in these weeks he was strangely stubborn and moody, as though he held a lot against me and was angry about my being there. After his funeral I had to settle the household affairs, and that also took several weeks: I was in no hurry. People from the town visited me now and then out of established habit and showed me in which chair my father used to sit in the living-room, and in which my mother, and where they themselves had sat. They inspected everything and offered to buy this or that piece from me. They are so thorough, these people in the provinces, and once one of them said to me, after he had examined everything closely: It's a terrible thing indeed when a whole family dies out within a few weeks!—nobody counted me. When I was by myself I sat quietly and read children's books. I had found a large carton of them in the attic. They were dusty and covered with soot, some of them dried out, some of them damaged by moisture, and if you knocked on them they expelled black velvet clouds. The marbled end-pages had come loose from the covers and left only groups of jagged islands. But when I slipped into the pages, I triumphantly absorbed the contents like a mariner steering between dangers, and once I made a singular discovery. I noticed that the black on the top, where one turned the pages, and on the bottom edge was, in a faintly visible way, different from that left by mildew, and then I found all kinds of indescribable spots, and finally wild, faded, pencil traces on the title-pages; and all of a sudden the recognition overwhelmed me that the marks of these passionate grippings, these pencil scratches and hastily-planted spots, were the traces of a child's fingers, my own child-fingers, preserved for thirty years in the attic and forgotten by all the world! Now, I tell you, for other people there is nothing special about these memories of themselves, but for me it was as though the last had become first. I had found another room which, thirty and more years ago, had been my nursery; later it was used for linen-storage and the like, but essentially it had been left as it was when I sat there at the spruce-table under the petroleum lamp with its three dolphins who carried its pulls in their mouths. There I sat again hour after hour and read, like a child whose feet do not yet touch the floor. Our heads, you see, are unstoppable or tower into nothingness; we get used to it because we have something solid underfoot; but childhood is the state of being insecure at both ends and having, in place of the rugged tongs of later, hands of tender flannel. One sits in front of a book as though sailing through the room on a little leaf over precipices. I tell you, I really no longer reached under the table to the floor.

I set up a bed in this room and slept there. And then the blackbird came again. Once, after midnight I was aroused by a wonderful heavenly song. I did not wake up immediately but first listened to it for a long time in my sleep. It was the song of a nightingale, but the bird was not sitting in the garden bushes but on the roof of a neighboring house. I began to sleep with open eyes. There are no nightingales here—I thought—, it is a blackbird.

You don't have to suspect that I have told you this story once already today! But you should know how I thought: There are no nightingales here; it is the blackbird! I awoke, it was four o'clock in the morning, day was returning to my eyes, sleep fell away of a wave; and there, in front of the light which was a delicate woollen cloth, sat a blackbird in the open window! It sat there as truly as I am sitting here now.

I am your blackbird,—it said,—don't you remember me?

I really did not remember at first, but I felt supremely happy when the bird spoke to me.

Once before I sat on this window ledge, don't you remember?—
it went on, and now I answered: Yes, once you sat there, where
you are sitting now, and I quickly shut the window.
I am your mother—she said.

Well—perhaps I dreamed that part. But I didn't dream the bird;
it sat there, then flew into the room, and I quickly shut the window. I went up to the attic and looked for a big wooden cage,
which I had in mind, for the blackbird had been there before, in
my childhood, as I just said. First she had sat on the window
ledge and then she had flown into the room, and I had brought
a cage, but she quickly grew tame and I did not need to keep her
locked up; she lived at large in my room and flew in and out.
And one day she left again and did not return, and now she was
finally there again. I had no desire to make difficulties for myself and to worry about whether it was the same blackbird or
not; I found the cage and a new box of books too, and I can only
say to you: I was never so good a man as from that day on when
I took in the blackbird. But I probably can't tell you what it is to
be a good man.

Did she often speak to you after that?—Aone asked slyly.

No,—Atwo answered—She never spoke. But I had to find blackbird feed for her, and worms. It was a little difficult, as you can
see, that she ate worms and that was I supposed to think of her
as my mother—; but it went all right; it's all a matter of what one
is accustomed to, I can assure you, and we have to get used to
more commonplace things as well! Ever since I have kept her
near me, and I can tell you no more; that is the third story, and
how it will end, I don't know.

But you are implying,—Aone tried discreetly to assure himself—
that all of this added up to something?

Good heavens!—Atwo contradicted him—it all just happened
that way, and if I knew what it all added up to, I would hardly
need to tell you the stories. But it is like hearing a sound without being able to tell; is it a whisper or just rustling?

Translated by Catherine Wilson

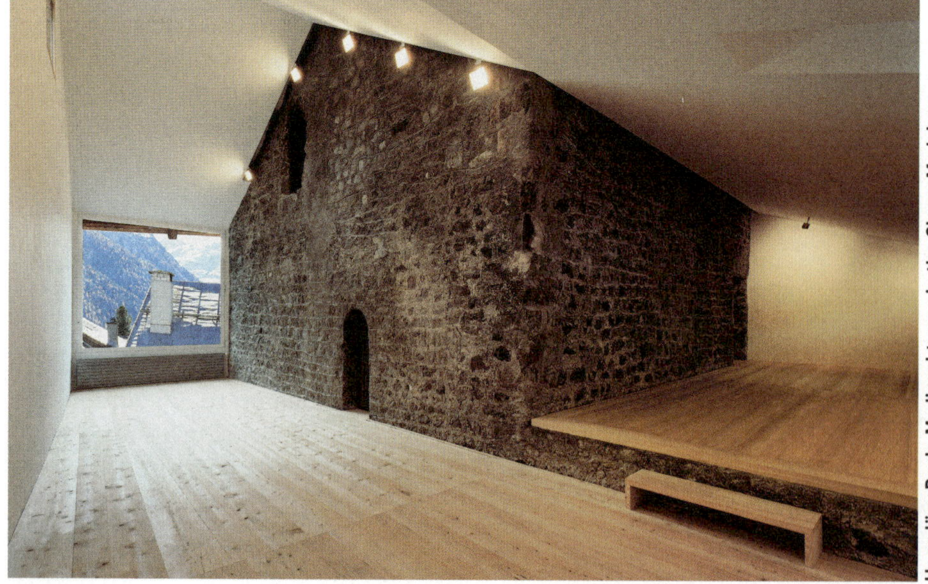

Hans Jörg Ruch, Medieval tower in the Chesa Madalena

Postcard   Hamish Fulton

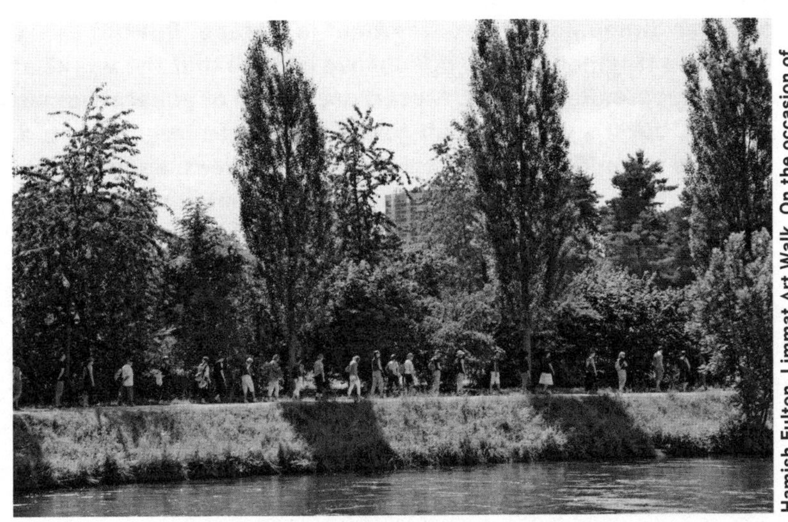

Hamish Fulton, Limmat Art Walk, On the occasion of Art and the City in Zurich, 2012

"A 21-day walking journey on pavements, bicycle paths, tracks, footpaths, rocks and snow, starting by encircling Obersee and Zurichsee. So then I walked around the two lakes there, and then I walked from there to the Engadin and then I walked up and down seven small mountains, including Piz Julier and Piz Err, for example. And then I returned to the Zurich region and I walked again, going to the other way around two lakes, to sort of complete the walk."

Postcard Giorgio Griffa

Typical human traces are signatures with dates written on walls, but also photos, marks, drawings, memos, as well as the instructions to cook rice. Other traces are present and are also alive: works of art, a Matisse painting, la Divina Commedia, a Beethoven concert. This is the point. Artworks continue to live after their own time, remain alive in other cultures after the period of their birth. And I cannot know if the traces made by my brush will be alive or not. I can only hope. Fragments are part of something larger that may be lost or living in another dimension. Every fragment is a trace. But not every trace is a fragment. In my opinion we can tell that the works of Shakespeare, Rembrandt, Mozart are traces of general human history, but it's very difficult to tell if they are fragments too. Perhaps it could be said that they are borderless, endless fragments. But that would mean they are fragments no more. Fragments are generally materials that have the characteristics of traces: they move from their physical world to our mental world, from their time to our time. Both traces and fragments may have a hierarchy when they fix the first sign, a figure or a word. However, in the same way there may be no hierarchy when they are in an indeterminate, generic context; for instance, a footprint on the sand is quite different from that footprint on the moon.

A sign that represents an apple or a rectangle establishes a hierarchy: it places the apple or the rectangle at the front. Instead a sign that only represents the trace, the mark of the brush, does not have a fixed hierarchy. We can bring forward whatever we want, the emotion of color, a memory of nature, the action of tracing, the quality of matter, the definition of space, or the temporal confusion that may lead to Stendhal syndrome, general equilibrium, hidden memories, the fascination of the unknown.

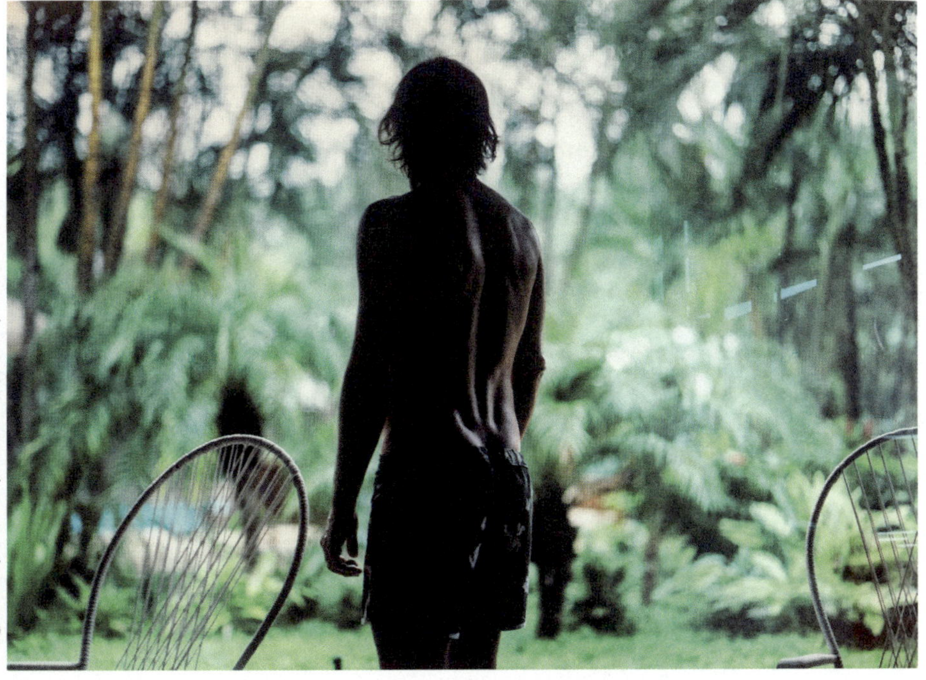

Doug Aitken, *Island II*, Ink Tree Editions, 2009

E.A.T.
Fresh
Stimulating
Striking Engadin
Inspiring
Childhood memories,
Zuoz!
Luminosity
Beatrix & Hans Ulrich
Cosmopolitan
Attention-grabbing
Cristina's soul
The cool Castell
Different
Thought-provoking
A mountain breeze
Family
I love you
Bon appetit
Happy birthday!
Thank you!

Postcard — Andrea Deplazes

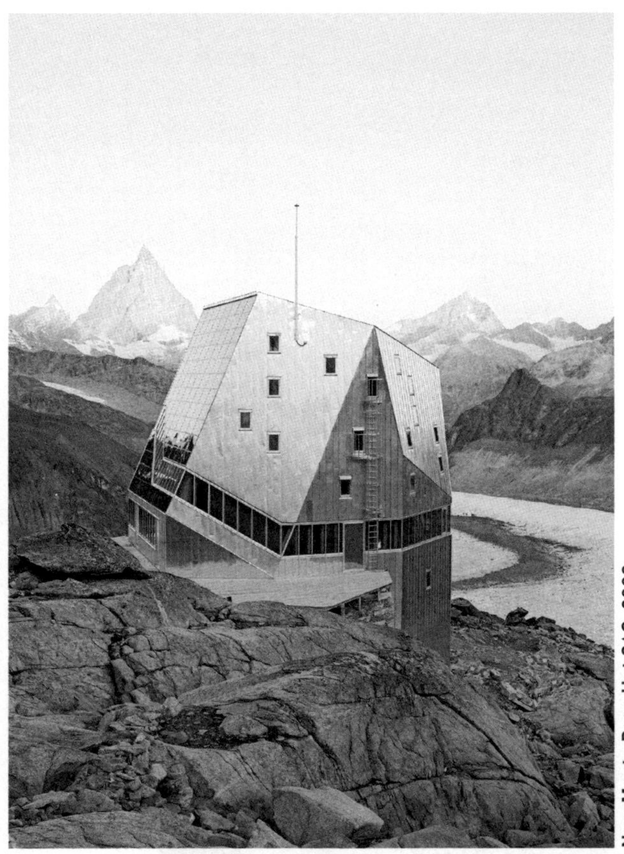

New Monte Rosa Hut SAC, 2009

The Monte Rosa Hut is one in which hikers and climbers stay overnight. The building site is located at an attitude of 2,883 meters in an extremely remote mountainous area, the Monte Rosa massif. That's where you'll find the highest peak on Swiss territory, the Dufourspitze–or Dufour peak–and if you want to climb this peak, you'll need a "pit stop station," so to speak. Not far away, with an impressive infrastructure, are Zermatt and the famous Matterhorn, which attract many tourists from all over the world. But high in the mountains near the Dufour peak, you're in a completely secluded place: there is snow and a glacier, but nothing else.

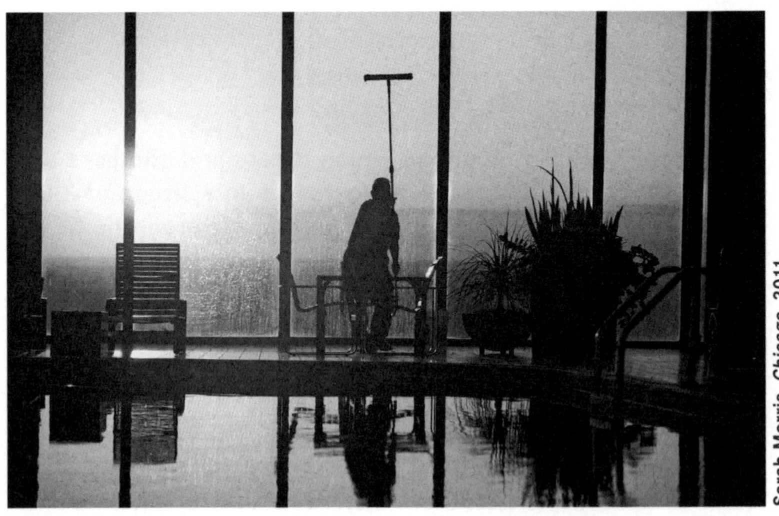

Sarah Morris, *Chicago*, 2011

It was in the eighties that I once had lunch in Vienna with Hans Hollein and Walter Pichler at the legendary restaurant Koranda. We spoke about the fact that Pichler and I were born a few miles away and how, just because I was Italian and Pichler German-speaking, I ended up studying in Florence and he in Vienna. Hollein had married a woman from Innsbruck, and Ettore Sottsass was also from Mother Innsbruck. In short, a certain geographical area connected us, namely the Alpine region. It had not only influenced our generation but also the generation of such people as Matteo Thun and many other architects and designers.

> The Engadin Art Talks deepened the conversation that had begun in Vienna. A decade of E.A.T. means a decade of regular, in-depth analysis of everything that the human mind can produce, in image, language, philosophy, and architecture. And all in the presence of the strong nature of the Alps. So in Zuoz it happens that critics, theorists, historians, artists, and architects confront each other and compare the products of their thoughts and the subsequent physicalizations.

My conversations with Hans Ulrich Obrist, Lawrence Weiner, and Peter Zumthor were exciting, as were the contents and contributions of the other invited speakers. Everything had a consequence for me. All my works made in the USA in the early seventies suddenly appeared to me as a way of building an alphabet that derived from the Dolomite mountains of my childhood. An alphabet that for me had to become architecture, just like the Rocky Mountains became significant places for Native Americans in their nomadic wanderings.

> As a consequence, I started to photograph mountains again while returning from Zuoz, where the Art Talks took place, to Moane in the Val di Fassa. So I finally managed to close a chapter of my creative work that had started many years earlier in my Dolomites and matured during my wanderings in the Rockies. In November 2012, the exhibition *Vienna and Surroundings* took place in the Galleria Giovanni Bonelli in Milan. Works by Abraham, Hollein, Peintner, Pichler, Sottsass and myself were shown, accompanied by a text by Thomas Bernhard. All we artists have one thing in common: the nature of the mountains has strongly influenced us and our works.

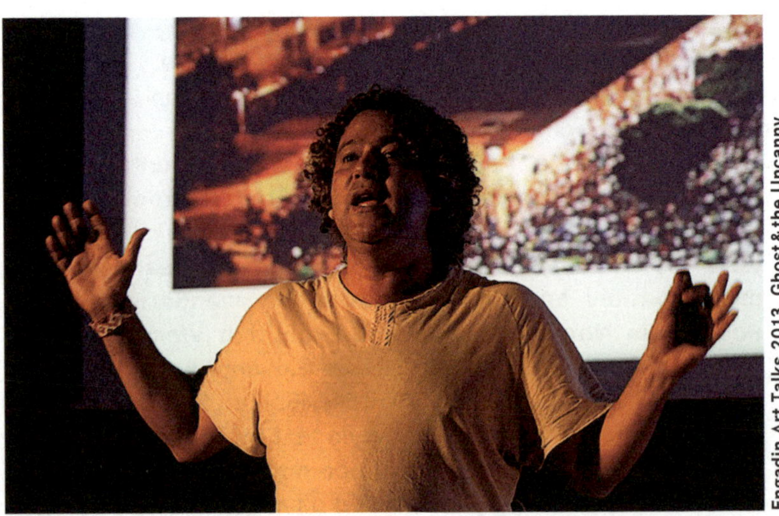

Engadin Art Talks 2013, Ghost & the Uncanny

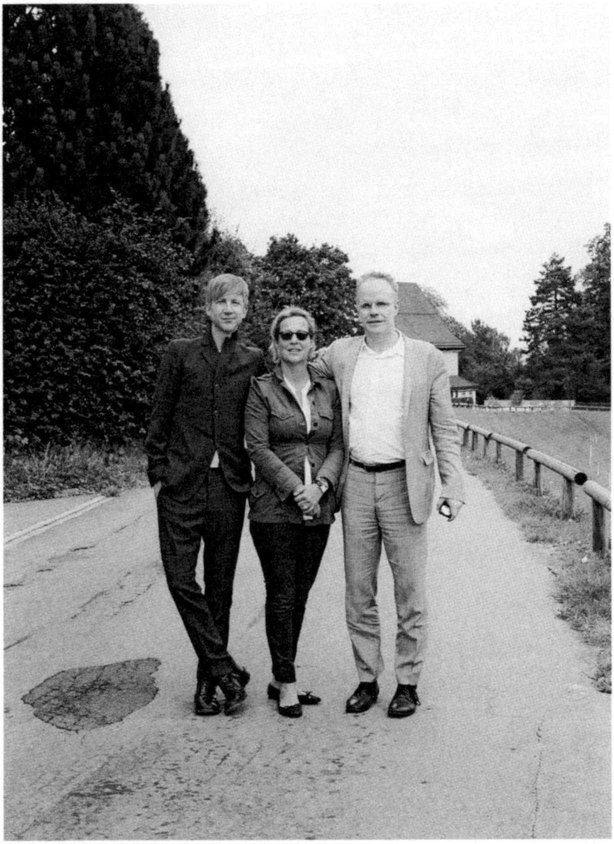

Jefferson Hack, Cristina Bechtler and Hans Ulrich Obrist on the Robert Walser Sprint, 2012

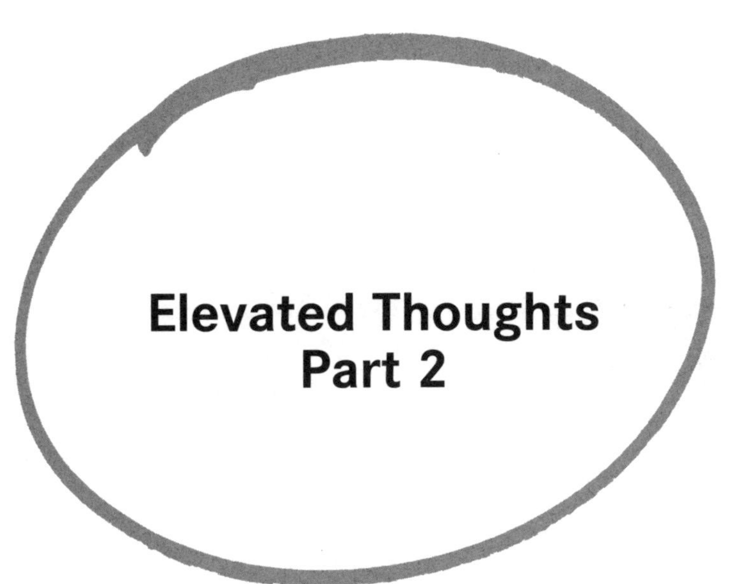

Elevated Thoughts
Part 2

Hans Ulrich Obrist

Making The Invisible Visible:
Art Meets AI

Ian Cheng, 2019

As a curator, my daily work is to bring together different works of art and to connect different cultures. Since the early 1990s, I have also started to organize conversations and meetings to practitioners from different disciplines in order to go beyond the fear of pooling knowledge.

Marshall McLuhan has noted the ability of art to "anticipate the future." In the foreword to his book *Understanding Media* he calls art "an early alarm system," which is pointing us to new developments in times ahead and allowing us "to prepare to cope with them". He says: "Art as a radar environment takes on the function of indispensable perceptual training." In 1964, when his book was first published, the artist Nam June Paik was just building his robot "K-456" to experiment with the technologies that subsequently would start to influence society. He had worked with television earlier, challenging its usual way of consuming, and later made art with global live satellite broadcasts to use the new media less for entertainment but to point us to their poetic and intercultural capacities (which are still mostly unused today).

The reason to look closely at AI is that it is one of the most important questions of today, how capacious Artificial Intelligence will become and what dangers may arise from it. There is a lot of basic research being done at the moment, and there are as well first applications that already influence our everyday lives in a more or less recognizable way.

Many of the contemporary artists are following these developments closely at the moment. They are articulating different doubts on the promises of AI and remind us not to associate the term "Artificial Intelligence" solely with positive notions. To the current discussions about AI the artists contribute their specific perspective and notably their focus on questions of image-making, creativity and programming as artistic tools.

The deep connections between science and art were already noted by the late Heinz von Foerster, one of the architects of cybernetics, who worked with Wiener from the mid-1940s, and, in the 1960s, founded the field of second-order cybernetics, in which the observer is understood as part of the system itself and not an external position. I had known Foerster well, and in one of our many conversations, he said about his views on relation between art and science: "I've always perceived art and science as complementary fields. One shouldn't forget that a scientist is in some respect also an artist. He invents a new technique and he describes it. He uses language like a poet, or the author of a detective novel, and describes his findings. In my view, a scientist must work in an artistic way if he wants to communicate his research. He obviously wants to communicate and talk to others. A scientist invents new objects, and the question is, how to describe them. In all of these aspects, science is not very different from art."

When I asked him how he defines cybernetics, von Foerster answered: "The substance of what we have learned from cybernetics is to think in circles: A leads to B, B to C, but C can return to A. Such kinds of arguments are not linear but circular. The significant contribution of cybernetics to our thinking is to accept circular arguments. This means that we have to look at circular processes and understand, under which circumstances an equilibrium and thus a stable structure emerges." So, what do contemporary artists have to say about Artificial Intelligence?

"Artificial Stupidity"

Hito Steyerl, an artist who works with documentary and experimental film, considers two key aspects that we should keep in mind when reflecting on the implications of AI for society. First, the expectations of so-called Artificial Intelligence, she says, are often overrated and the noun "intelligence" misleading. To counter that she uses the term "artificial stupidity." Secondly, she points out that programmers are now making invisible software algorithms visible through images, but to understand and interpret these images better, we should apply the expertise of artists.

Steyerl has worked with computer technology for many years and her recent artworks have explored surveillance techniques, robots and computer games, as in *How Not to Be Seen* (2013) on digital image technologies, or *HellYeahWeFuckDie* (2017) about the training of robots with the still difficult task of keeping the balance. But to explain her notion of "artificial stupidity," Steyerl refers to a more general phenomenon such as the now widespread use of Twitter bots. She says: "It was and still is a very popular tool in elections to deploy Twitter-armies to sway public opinions and deflect popular hashtags and so on. This is an Artificial Intelligence of a very, very low grade. It's two or maybe three lines of script. It's nothing very sophisticated at all. Yet the social implications of this kind of artificial stupidity, as I call it, are already monumental in global politics."

Visible/Invisible

The artist Paul Klee often talked about art as 'making the invisible visible.' In computer technology, most algorithms work invisibly in the background; they remain inaccessible in the systems we use daily. But lately, there has been a very interesting comeback of visuality in machine learning. The ways that self-learning algorithms of AI are processing data have been made visible through applications such as Google's *DeepDream,* in which the process of computerized pattern-recognition is visualized in real-time. The application shows how the algorithm tries to match animal forms with any given input. There are of course many more AI-visualization programs. These in their way also 'make the invisible visible.' The difficultly in the general perception of such images is in Steyerl's view that these visual patterns are viewed uncritically as realistic and objective representation of the machine process. She says about the aesthetics of such visualizations:

> "For me this proves that science has become a sub-genre of art history. [...] We now have lots of abstract computer patterns that might look like a Paul Klee painting, or a Mark Rothko, or all sorts of other abstractions that we know from art history. The only difference, I think, is that in current scientific thought they're perceived as representations of reality, almost like documentary images, whereas in art history there's a very nuanced understanding of different kinds of abstraction."

Thus, what she seeks is a more profound understanding of these computer-generated images, and the different aesthetic forms that they use more or less consciously. It is obvious that these images are not generated with the explicit goal of following a certain aesthetic tradition. In a conversation with Steyerl, the computer engineer Mike Tyka explained the functions of these images:

> "Deep-learning systems, especially the visual ones, are really inspired by the need to know what's going on in the black-box. Their goal is to project these processes back into the real world."

But nevertheless, they have also aesthetic implications and values which have to be taken into account. One could say that while the programmers use these images to better understand the algorithms, we need the knowledge of artists to better understand the aesthetic forms of AI. As Steyerl has pointed out, such visualizations are sometimes understood as 'true' representations of processes, but we should pay attention to their respective aesthetics and their implications, which have to be viewed in a critical and analytical way.

> In 2017, the artist Trevor Paglen created a project to make these invisible AI algorithms visible. In "Sight Machine," he filmed a live performance of the Kronos Quartet and processed the resulting images with various computer software programs used for face detection, object identification and even missile guidance. He projected the outcome of these algorithms in real time back to screens above the stage. By demonstrating how the different kinds of programs interpreted the images of the musicians, Paglen showed that AI algorithms are always determined by sets of values and interests, which they then manifest and reiterate, and thus must be critically questioned. The significant contrast between algorithms and music also brought into question the relationships between technical and human perception.

Computers as a Tool for Creativity That Can't
Replace the Artist

Rachel Rose, a video artist who thinks about the questions posed by AI, employs computer technology in the creation of her works. Her films create for the viewer an experience of materiality through the moving image. She uses collaging and layering of the material to manipulate sound and image, and the editing process is perhaps the most important aspect of her work. She also talks about the importance of decision-making in her work. For her, her artistic process does not follow a rational pattern. She explained this by means of a story by the theater director Peter Brook from his 1968 book *The Empty Space.* When Brook designed the set for his play *The Tempest* in the late 1960s, he started by making a Japanese garden, but then the design evolved, becoming a white box, a black box, a realistic set and so on. But in the end, he returned to his original idea. Brook writes that he was shocked by working for months only to end at the beginning. But this shows that the creative artistic process is done in a succession where each step builds on the next and in the end, it comes to a conclusion which is unpredictable. It is not a logical or rational succession but a process that mostly has to do with the artist's feelings in reaction to the previous result. Rose said about her own artistic decision-making:

> "It to me is distinctively different from machine learning because at each decision there's this core feeling that comes from a human being that has to do with empathy, that has to do with communication, that has to do with questions about our own mortality that only a human could ask."

This last point underlines the fundamental difference between any human artistic production and so-called computer creativity. Rose sees AI more as a possibility to create better tools for humans:

> "A place I can imagine machine learning working for an artist would be not in developing an independent subjectivity like writing a poem or making an image, but actually in filling in gaps that are to do with labor, like the way that Photoshop works with different tools that you can use."

And though such tools may not seem spectacular, she says, "they might have a larger influence on art" because they provide artists with further possibilities in their creative work.

The engineer Kenric McDowell in a conversation with Rachel Rose at the Google Cultural Institute added that he also believes that there are false expectations around AI. "I've observed," he says, "that there's a sort of magical quality to the idea of a computer that does all the things that we do." He continues: "There's almost this kind of demonic mirror that we look into, and we want it to write a novel, we want it to make a film, we want to give that away somehow." He himself is instead working on projects where the humans are collaborating with the machine. One of the main aspects of research into AI is now in this way to find new means of interaction between humans and software. And art, one could say, needs to play a key role in that discussion, since it focuses on our subjectivity and essential human aspects like empathy and mortality.

Cybernetics/Art

Suzanne Treister is an artist whose work from 2009 to 2011 serves as an example of what is happening at the intersection of our current technologies, the arts, and cybernetics. Treister has been a pioneer in digital art since the 1990s, inventing for example imaginary video games and painting "screenshots" from them. In her project *Hexen 2.0* she looked back at the famous "Macy" conferences on cybernetics, that were organized in New York by engineers and social scientists between 1946 and 1953 to unite the sciences and develop a universal theory of the workings of the mind.

In her project, she created thirty photo-text works about the conference attendees such as Wiener and von Foerster; she invented tarot cards; and she made a video based on photomontage of a "cybernetic séance" in which the conference participants are seen sitting at a round table as if in a spiritualistic séance and certain of their statements on cybernetics are heard in an audio-collage, thus combining rational and irrational forms of knowledge. Treister also pointed out that some of the participating scientists in fact worked for the military; thus the application of cybernetics could be seen in an ambivalent way even back then, between knowledge and its application in state control and power.

If one looks at Treister's work about the participants, one also sees that there was no visual artist included. This dialogue is obviously needed for future discussions. And it is a bit astonishing that it wasn't realized then, given von Foerster's keen interest in art, who recounts how his relation to the field dates back to his childhood:

> "I grew up as a child in an artistic family. We often had visits from poets, philosophers, painters and sculptors. Art was a part of my life. Later, I got into physics, as I was talented in this subject. But I always remained conscious of the importance of art for science. There wasn't a great difference for me. For me, both aspects of life have always been very much alike, and accessible too. We should see them as one. An artist also has to reflect on his work. He has to think about his grammar and his language. A painter must know how to handle his colors. Just think of how intensively oil colors were researched during the Renaissance. They wanted to know how a certain pigment could be mixed with others to get a certain tone of red or blue. Chemists and painters collaborated very closely. I think the artificial division between science and art is wrong."

Though for von Foerster the relation between art and science was always clear, for our own society this connection remains to be made. There are many reasons to multiply the links. The critical thinking of artists would be beneficial in respect to the dangers of AI, as they point our attention and awareness to the different questions that they consider as essential from their specific perspective. With the advent of machine learning, new tools are available to artists for their work. And as the algorithms of AI are made visible through artificial images in new ways, artists' critical visual knowledge and expertise will be harnessed. As many of the key questions of AI are philosophical in nature, and can only be answered from a holistic point of view, the way things play out among the adventurous artists will be worth following.

Simulating Worlds

For the most part, the works of contemporary artists have been embodied ruminations on AI's impact on existential questions of the self and our future interaction with non-human entities. Few, though, have taken the technologies and innovations of AI as the underlying materials of their work and sculpted them to their own vision. An exception is the artist

Ian Cheng, who has gone as far as to construct entire worlds
of artificial beings with varying degrees of sentience and intelligence. He refers to these worlds as "live simulations." His
Emissaries trilogy (2015–2017) is set in a fictional post-apoca-
lyptic flora and fauna, in which AI-driven animals and creatures explore the landscape and interact with each other.
Cheng uses advanced graphics but has them programmed
with a lot of glitches and imperfections, creating a simultaneously futuristic and anachronistic atmosphere. Through his
Emissaries series, which charts a history of consciousness,
he asks the question: "What is a simulation?"

> While the majority of artistic works that utilize recent devel-
> opments in AI specifically draw on the field of machine learning,
> Cheng's live simulations take a separate route. The protago-
> nists and plot lines that are interlaced in each episodic simu-
> lation of *Emissaries* utilize the complex logic systems and
> rules of AI.

What is profound about Cheng's continually evolving scenes
is that complexity arises not through the desire/actions of any
single actor or artificial godhead, but instead through their constellation, collision and constant evolution in symbiosis with
one another. This gives rise to unexpected outcomes and un-
ending, unknowable situations—you can never experience the
exact same moment in successive viewings of his work.

> Cheng also had a discussion with the programmer Richard
> Evans, who recently designed "versu," an AI-based platform
> for interactive storytelling games. His work lays the focus on
> the social interaction of the characters in the game, reacting
> in a spectrum of possible behaviors to the choices made by
> the human players. In their conversation, Evans said that a
> starting point for his newest project was that most earlier
> simulation video games such as "The Sims" did not sufficiently
> take into account the importance of social practices. Simu-
> lated protagonists in games would often act in ways that did
> not correspond well with real human behavior. Knowing social
> practices limits the possibilities of action, but is necessary
> to understand the meaning of our actions. This is what inter-
> ests Cheng for his own simulations. The more parameters of
> actions in certain circumstances are determined in a com-
> puter simulation, the more interesting it is for Cheng to ex-
> periment with individual and very specific changes. He said:
> "I gather that if we had AI with more ability to respond to

social contexts, tweaking one thing you would get something quite artistic and beautiful."

In that way, Cheng sees the work of programmers and AI simulations also as creating new and sophisticated tools for experimenting with the parameters of our daily social practices. In this way, the involvement of artists in AI will lead to new kinds of open experiments in Art. Nevertheless, such possibilities are, as more AI capabilities in general, still in the future. Recognizing that this is an experimental technology in its infancy, very far from apocalyptic visions of a super-intelligent AI takeover, his simulations occupy prosaic avatars such as strange microbial globules, dogs and the undead.

Such discussions between artists and engineers—like the ones mentioned above—of course are not totally new. In the US during the 1960s, the engineer Billy Klüver brought artists together with engineers in a series of events, and in 1967 he founded the *Experiments in Art and Technology* program with Robert Rauschenberg and others. In London, at around the same time, Barbara Steveni and John Latham, with the Artist Placement Group, took this a step further by asserting that there should be artists in residence in every company and every government. Today, these inspiring historical models can be applied to the field of AI.

As AI comes to inhabit more and more of our everyday lives, the creation of a space that is non-deterministic and non-utilitarian in its plurality of perspectives and diversity of understandings will undoubtedly be essential.

Philip Ursprung

What Cities Know:
Kashef Chowdhury in Dhaka

Is there such a thing as an urban knowledge? By urban knowledge I mean less the issue of a knowledge about the city, for example *about* the history and theory of the urban. I mean the question of whether we can locate a knowledge that is, as it were, spatially and temporally embodied in the city, manifested in the facades and squares, the people and things, the movements and atmospheres, the noises and rhythms. It would be a knowledge which cannot be defined in the form of concepts or data, that is to say, in terms of language or statistics, but in actions and spaces, movements and images, affects, and sensory impressions. It would be a knowledge that articulates historical changes before they are grasped theoretically or historiographically.

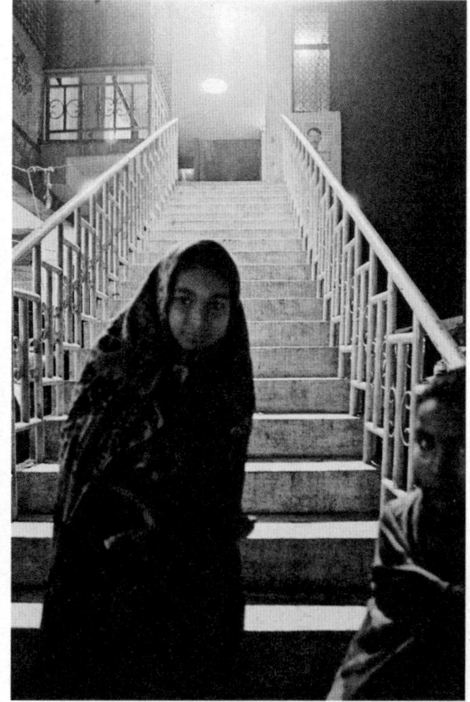

Such an urban knowledge, I would argue, manifests itself in the connection between Kashef Chowdhury's photographs and Dhaka. He depicts the urban in a set of miniatures, as if he would propose a series of scenes for a movie, or chapters in a novel. He shot the photographs assembled in the book *Dhaka: Memories or Lost* around the time of the Millennium, between the late 1990s and the early 2000s. During those years, Dhaka was rapidly transforming to become what is now "ranked" as one of the most densely populated and largest cities in the world. As a professional photographer and architect he was obviously very well aware of the rapid change and densification of the garden city located within the world's largest delta. But he does not reproduce the stereotypes of urban change, such as scenes of demolition and construction, traffic jams, polluting smokestacks, misery and inequality. Chowdhury did not document the change of the built environment from a distance, forensically. He did not represent the city as a series of deserted "scenes of crime" as Walter Benjamin described the images taken in the empty streets of Paris around 1900 by Eugène Atget in his essay *The Work of Art in the Age of Mechanical Reproduction* (1936). Rather than focusing on the scenery of the built environment, he concentrates on the *witnesses* of the change.

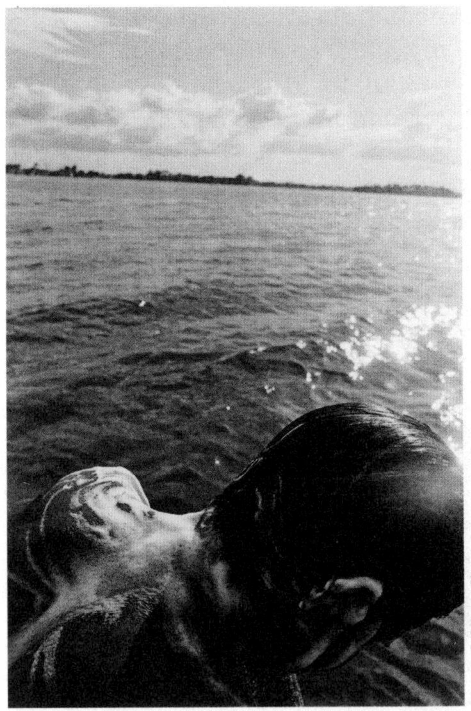
Kashef Chowdhury

As readers of the book we can follow the transformation of the urban space indirectly, by means of those who are present. There is a melancholic atmosphere in his images, halfway between the nostalgia for what is disappearing and the excitement of things to come. I was struck by the image of two young girls at the bottom of a generous stair leading to a brightly lit interior space. The future, so I interpret the image, lies ahead of them, the path is clearly defined. Yet they turn their backs to it and stand in the dark, looking towards the bottom of the stair as if they were hesitant about where to go and what to expect. On another page, there is the image of a young man washing his hair in the river. The immense space of the river opens up to a wide open space, the morning sunlight reflected in the moving water. The man's face is turned away from the camera. The mythical figure of Atlas comes to my mind, carrying the weight of the world on his shoulders in the same way that this young man, with remnants of shampoo on his back, seems to carry the weight of the river. The spectacular environment symbolizes both a chance and a burden, both the future and the past. On another page, there is the image of a man carrying suitcases on a platform where a train is about to depart. The long shadow must stem from the morning sun; the person has probably just arrived, perhaps from the countryside. The composition of the image with its oblique shapes and hard contrasts recalls the Bauhaus photography of the 1920s. It is about speed, dynamism and new beginnings. But the man's posture is everything but heroic. He looks tired and worried. Is this progress or decline?

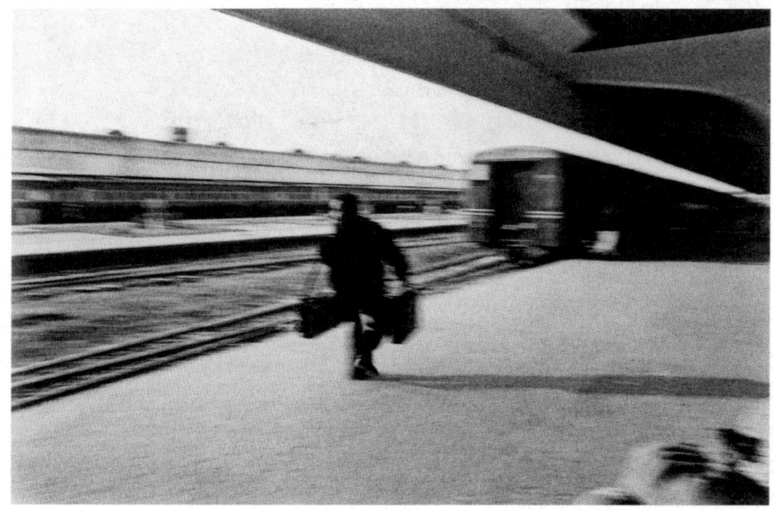

Kashef Chowdhury

In Chowdhury's images, knowledge is embodied in people as well as in things. The image of a tree in a park at night, illuminated by floodlights, tells the viewer about the quality of life in a city that has been famous for its gardens for centuries. One can well imagine strolling amongst the trees and relaxing after the heat of the day. The photograph has an ornamental quality, as if it were a woven texture that welcomes the visitors. But the tree also seems to foresee that this balance might change. It seems to know that the demand for green space by an ever-growing population will change the environment. How long will the parks remain open to the public, how long will they resist the pressure on open building terrain? Another image depicts a wooden formwork, perhaps for a concrete pillar, towering towards the sky. It tells about the process of construction, yet it is unclear what is being built. The formwork looks as if it has been assembled entirely by hand, without machinery. It outlines the future as if it would prefigure a skyline yet to come. And finally there is the strange image of a sidelight of a truck, protected by a cage of wires. The handmade structure that resembles a tiny bird-cage protects the valuable accessory from being crushed or stolen. The simple detail could also be the beginning of a movie about the infrastructure in Dhaka. More than any statistics could, it illustrates the care that is taken for objects, the scarcity of spare parts and the changes taking place in traffic.

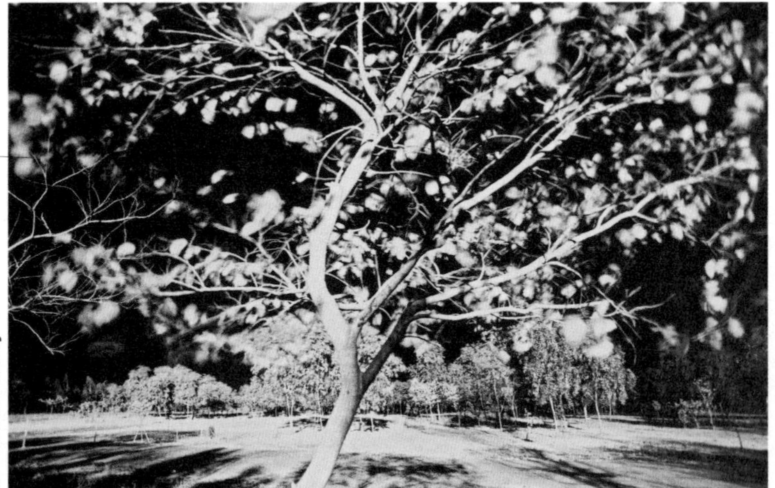

In Chowdhury's photographs people and objects are more than figures in front of the backdrop of the city. They constitute the urban, they perform urban living, they produce, day after day, the very texture of the urban space. The human, the man-made, and the non-human intertwine, the concrete and the imagined blur. It is telling of Chowdhury's attitude that water is present in many of his images. In guise of the delta and the monsoon rain, water is omnipresent in the city. But it is also an element that connects the material with the imagined, the reality with dreams, the past with the present and the future. A programmatic image is the photograph of the blurred window of a vehicle, probably a car or bus. I assume that a large street opens up, but the dimension is difficult to grasp. The heavy rain has literally washed the central perspective out of focus. I face a grainy, blurred surface, as if I have been moved back in time to an early age of photography. Even as a viewer, I feel protected behind the window, but I can sense that the photograph was taken from within a vehicle and that the photographer is only temporarily sheltered from the immense forces of the rain. The pedestrian walking in the rain featuring in another photograph prefigures what the photographer behind the camera will probably do himself in a moment, namely to get soaking wet. And it reminds me as an observer what has happened to me during comparable rainstorms elsewhere.

Chowdhury used a 35 mm Contax camera with a Zeiss lens and black-and-white film. The prints show the original frame, and the negatives are not manipulated. The Millennium was a time when digital cameras were still the exception. The urban transition of Dhaka happened in parallel with the technological shift in photography. The camera space between the lens and the negative that captures the images relate to the urban spaces defined by the people and object. The normal and wide-angle lenses imply a proximity between the photographer and his subjects. The persons were certainly aware of the presence of the photographer, who moves around the city day and night on foot or by public transportation. The spaces depicted are neither the protected private space where the viewer takes on the role of the voyeur, nor the controlled public space, where the viewers are in the role of monitoring. They are common spaces that are accessible to all and where the common goods such as water, light, and air, along with language, images, memories, and hopes, are shared. It is in these spaces where the urban knowledge is formed. Thanks to the images of Kashef Chowdbury, we can access them.

See: Kashef Chowdhury, *Dhaka: Memories or Lost*
(Scheidegger & Spiess, 2017)

Helene Romakin

Peter Zumthor in the Landscape of South Devon

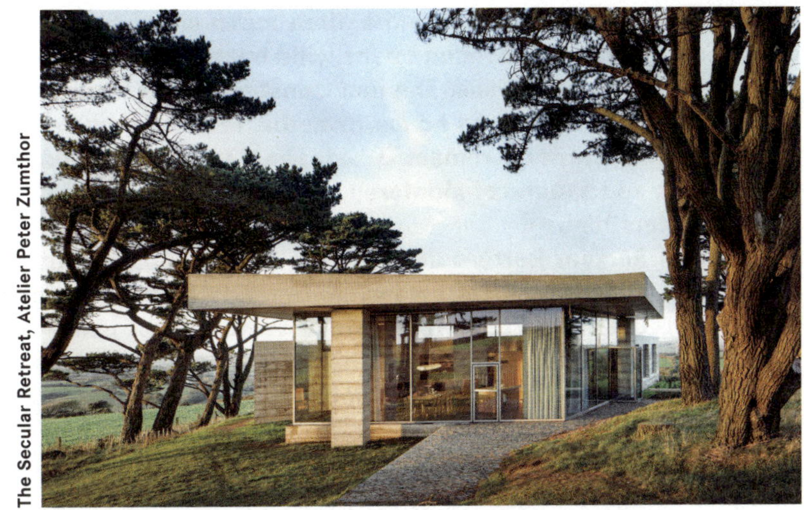

Peter Zumthor's Secular Retreat is located on a hill in South Devon, near the village of Chivelstone, just a mile from the coast, between the resorts of Salcombe and Hallsands. A two-hour train trip from London's Paddington Station to Totnes is followed by a forty-minute car ride flanked by traditional English hedgerows, which wind their way across the rolling countryside, curve after curve. This journey with its succession of short intermezzos is the England imagined by tourists: friendly and picturesque. When the hedges are trimmed back and the scenery is not completely obstructed, the passing vistas might afford a glimpse of the coast or—like something out of the mythic world of J.R.R. Tolkien—the Dartmoor nature reserve on the side opposite.

This elusive encounter with the landscape continues in the inconspicuous entrance to the property, which first leads to a parking lot rimmed by hedges. The building itself initially remains out of view. Following my visit, the landscape architect Charlotte Rathbone who worked on the project explained that the intended effect was inspired by eighteenth-century estates and their avenues, in which the full extent of the property was only incrementally revealed upon approach. Situated on a lower level within the grounds, the one-story structure makes a modest impression in the landscape. With its horizontal orientation, the building does not sit enthroned on the hill, but seems to reflect the surrounding context. This effect is underscored by the reinstated hedges and artificially raised garden at the front of the house.

The building is fully exposed to the often harsh weather conditions of Devon, as evidenced by the wind-beaten shrubs and sea-salt deposits in the soil. The new construction is located on the site of a demolished house from the 1940s. A few details of the old property remain: a hexagonal veranda behind the kitchen, and a stand of Monterey pines that are now some twenty meters high.

Secular Retreat—like all Zumthor buildings—is an exercise in superlative craftsmanship. Every detail has been conceived to utmost perfection. A defining feature is the use of layered concrete, hand-tamped and mixed from local materials: a technique that the architect previously employed in the internationally acclaimed Bruder Klaus Chapel in the Eifel region of Germany. The rammed concrete walls are constructed in layers, with each line marking a single day's work. The roughness of the material is transcended in favor of its haptic qualities. The notion that the structure could have been fashioned with one's own hands gives it a feeling of intimate familiarity. The resulting strength and solidity of the walls might feel constrictive were it not for the subtly incorporated shadow gaps along the top edge. These imbue the solid concrete with lightness while the heavy roof, itself a technical masterpiece, seems to float. Through such details, Zumthor creates a safe and secure place of refuge, protected from the winds coming off the sea. The limestone floors were based on a bespoke pattern, painstakingly adapted stone by stone to the exact dimensions of each slab from the local quarry. If a slab were to break, it would have required a rework and redesign of the potential templates.

The house features a very simple layout arranged on a single level. There are two wings, one with two bedrooms, the other with three, each containing its own bathroom. The two wings lead into a large living space with an open kitchen, a colorfully furnished lounge with fireplace, and a number of more private seating areas. Even if the furnishings may be a matter of debate—they are cheerful, but perilously close to kitsch in some cases—guests wishing to indulge in seclusion or escape from everyday life with family or friends will find nothing lacking.

Peter Zumthor dedicated himself early on to the atmospheric aspects in his works, which have consistently divided the architectural world into two camps: the enthusiastic phenomenologists and the critical intellectuals. Zumthor deftly presents himself in the media and in his self-published monographs as an architect of the senses. Indeed, this positioning has paid off, and once you have experienced his projects in person, you realize there could very well be some truth to it. Zumthor is the epitome of a sensitive practitioner with a perceptual affinity for spaces, an ability for which he is celebrated worldwide. Critics, on the other hand, accuse this sensual architecture of perpetuating an anti-modern and romanticized image that impedes intellectual and differentiated discussions. When Zumthor speaks of atmospheres as an architectural quality, this implies metaphorical, sense-oriented and transcendental meanings in which architecture becomes a direct experience.

Zumthor remains a master of the media game—perhaps it is his strategy to use his special status to carve out greater freedom for himself, and perhaps this has also proven itself over the years as a successful method for the implementation of his ideas. "It has become rare to be able to sit in a house and look out at a beautiful landscape where no trace of another building interrupts the lines of the rolling hills. Quietness, contemplation, pure luxury. I could not resist to try to create this house," Zumthor is quoted as saying in the Secular Retreat press release. Abstraction from the world, romanticism, devotional spaces, an architectural safe haven—these are the images most people associate with Zumthor. The fact that they can also take on lives of their own and reduce the complexity in the perception of Zumthor's work can be seen in the marketing strategy of the project sponsor.

I am a cultural studies specialist more than an architectural historian or theorist. Perhaps that explains my desire to regard architecture in the context of its political, economic and ecological landscape. Only when looking at a building in connection with its surroundings do I feel like I have gotten to the true nature of the structure with its walls, windows, doors and roofs. After my visit to Secular Retreat, I asked myself: What did I actually experience there and what has remained in my memory? What are the similarities to other projects by the architect? What does Zumthor's architecture seek to achieve, and what does it demand from the viewer or user? For me, it is clear that Zumthor's keen attention to material culture, topography, site specificity and global economy is thoroughly reflected in his architecture. He creates far more than just an atmosphere. Through his architecture, Zumthor sensitizes viewers to the surrounding context.

Das Raumschiff Erde hat keinen Notausgang (Spaceship Earth Has No Emergency Exit) is the name of a collection of essays published in response to the nuclear disaster in Fukushima with texts by contributors such as Paul J.Crutzen and Peter Sloterdijk. The title alludes to Buckminster Fuller's metaphor of planet Earth as a spaceship. In the late 1960s, Fuller wrote about utopian and visionary models that would enable an ecologically sustainable human existence on Earth. Fifty years later, climate change has become a tangible reality. The urgency of the associated political questions not only dominates news coverage in the media, but also defines transnational relations and the image of Western society. Meanwhile, even many of the most skeptical hold-outs are coming to recognize the reality of climate change and rapidly altering ecosystems and their permanent impact on living conditions across the globe. All the more interesting is Zumthor's commentary on the longing for an experience of nature with no human traces whatsoever. The anthropocentric image of nature has undergone a transformation: today there is no such thing as untouched nature or an innocent landscape.

> We can no longer escape from our present-day surroundings— not even when on holiday. The expansive windows of Secular Retreat might not reveal any other buildings—just as Zumthor envisioned ten years ago at the outset of the project—but a wind turbine has now come into view, along with several other traces of human interference. Devon is a political landscape marked by agricultural production, which has taken shape over the decades and centuries at the hands of hard-working local farmers. The visible nature has been tamed, the result of crop growing and livestock cultivation.

In this project, Zumthor communicated the desire to provide nature with a framework. Nature sometimes needs a "human addition" to be truly beautiful, he is quoted as saying in *The Guardian.* Zumthor understands architecture as a tool or method for seeing things or drawing attention to things that otherwise remain unseen. It seems as if the architect is engaging in a mindfulness exercise when designing and building. He sharpens his senses not only for himself and the participating team, but also for those who later use, visit or experience the building. The underlying idea is based on the creation of new perspectives and images by emphasizing certain views and infusing them with associations and memories. Sometimes it resurrects history or rediscovers historical references to a place. I would argue that this combination of facilitating a contemplative experience and a conscious perception of the context reveals much of the essential quality of Zumthor's architecture.

Ultimately, it is the Monterey pines that serve as the emblematic summation of Secular Retreat. In a personal conversation, Peter Zumthor told me that he had insisted on retaining the Monterey pines, which were originally imported from Canada. He explained that there is no "otherness" today because the "other" is already integrated into the landscape. For him, the pines constitute part of the history and landscape of Chivelstone, on a par with the historically formed hedges. With his solicitous interest in the pine trees, the architect adds to the international canon of stories about trees, even if such an affiliation is likely unintended. More recently in this category, the 2018 novel *The Overstory* by the American writer Richard Powers presents trees as the real protagonists and shows their profound influence on human lives.

The Hidden Life of Trees (2015) by Peter Wohlleben is another example among many that depict trees as sentient beings with feelings. A potential quintessence of these projects is that humans should no longer occupy the center of our worldview. One strategy for engaging with the current conception of the world and humanity's role therein is to examine the history of places, spaces and topographies. In his latest publication A *Feeling of History,* Zumthor called it a process of "emotional reconstruction." It is these moments of re-enactment and reconstruction of history, the rediscovery of the original landscape or the use of nature, that shape our understanding of the environment. Walter Benjamin once stated in his so-called "thought-image" *Excavation and Memory:* "He who seeks to approach his own buried past must conduct himself like a man digging. Above all, he must not be afraid to return again and again to the same matter; to scatter it as one scatters earth, to turn it over as one turns over soil." In *A Feeling of History,* Peter Zumthor expresses the desire that his buildings communicate with their surroundings. Secular Retreat is a successful example of this.

Helene Romakin is a PhD student at the ETH Zürich.

Erling Kagge and Finn Canonica

A Short Walk in Oslo

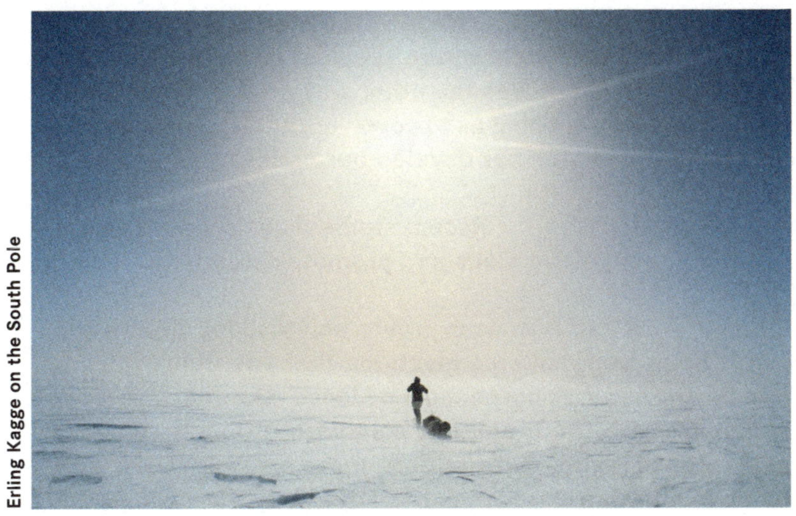

Erling Kagge is well known for accomplishing what no other human in history has done. In the 1990s, he ventured to both the North and South Poles and scaled the heights of Mount Everest. Since then he has kept up his addiction to extraordinary experiences, whether it be walking across LA on foot, sailing across the Atlantic twice, hiking through the sewers of New York, you name it. He is what some would call a Renaissance man. A lawyer by training, he studied philosophy after exploring the far reaches of the globe, starting his own publishing house, becoming a renowned collector of contemporary art, and authoring slim but thought-provoking tomes.

Finn Canonica   Erling, you have written three books on the defining themes of your life: walking, silence and collecting art. I think these three themes are interconnected. That's what I want to talk to you about. We are here in the center of Oslo. It's still summer, but cooler winds have already set in. Where should we go on our walk?

Erling Kagge   My suggestion would be to walk toward the harbor. It will be nice with water and we can see where things take us from there.

Finn   Why are you so fond of walking?

Erling   Simply because I can. It has an intrinsic value for me. I don't just walk to get from point A to point B—though that is certainly part of it. Walking is a core activity of my life. But isn't that true for our entire species? Homo sapiens didn't invent bipedalism. It was the other way around. The ability to walk on two legs enabled us to cover longer distances, discover new territory and further develop our brains.

> Finn   Recent studies have shown that walking increases cognitive skills and promotes creativity.

Erling   It has even been proven how walking affects thinking. It helps you make connections that you didn't have before. Memories are sharpened, and ideas take shape. We don't just think with the brain, but also with the body. When we move, our thoughts and emotions move as well. You're surely familiar with this experience from everyday life—if something isn't going well, you feel an urge to get up and move about.

> Finn   It's crazy, but I often can't think properly in my office. I can get a lot of things done, but I'm seldom able to come up with fresh new ideas. I lack clarity when I'm sitting.

Erling   It's the same for me. It's actually strange how rarely people just go for a walk. We would all benefit from it. I even think the political scene would be different if politicians did more walking.

> Finn   You have surely already contemplated how so many major cultural figures throughout history were passionate walkers. Once you start thinking about it, the list of names gets longer and longer. Aristotle strolled about and lectured in the colonnades of the Lyceum. The students of this school were called Peripatetics, from the Greek *peripatos:* covered walk. Immanuel Kant took a daily walk in Königsberg. Dorothy Wordsworth was a walker, as was Virginia Woolf, and Rebecca Solnit, whom I greatly admire, wrote a whole book about walking.

Erling   Nietzsche remarked that he had little confidence in his own thoughts if they were not conceived outdoors in the fresh air, while walking, although I believe he was not that keen on walking. Kierkegaard was a walking street philosopher. I recently found a passage in *Slowness* by Milan Kundera where he describes how we walk slower or faster, depending on the kind

of thoughts and feelings we are having at that particular moment. When I walk at a fast pace it feels like many emotions
are held at a distance and when I slow down they are returning.

Finn   You mention Kundera. In your books on walking
and silence, you create an essayistic lightness reminiscent of
Kundera.

Erling   Thank you for the compliment—I'll happily take it.
Lightness is very important to me. Not only on expeditions
but whenever I'm on the move, I always try to be as lightweight
as possible.

Finn   Perhaps we ourselves become lighter when we're
walking and our thoughts are flowing. In any case, it is fascinating how our thinking changes depending on the kind of
movements we are making. If we're trying to juggle several
balls or balance on a narrow beam, it's impossible to think of
anything else. The frontal lobes of the brain are working too
hard. We can take advantage of that when we're being tor-
mented by negative thoughts. As soon as we engage in any
sort of complicated physical movement, like fighting our way
through the undergrowth in a forest, our worries subside.

Erling   What's even better is when you don't think anything at all while walking. This usually only happens after you're
been at it for a few hours. Then it feels almost meditative, and
afterwards your mind is completely refreshed.

Finn   The main reason many people don't walk places
is to save time. By bus, bicycle or car, it's faster, the thinking
goes. Is it true that you always walk when you go to work at
your publishing house?

Erling   Often, but not always. The rationale about saving
time sometimes seems like nonsense. Time saved for what?
To stare at your mobile phone? I think most people generally
have much more time than they admit to themselves. So much
in our lives is fast-paced. While walking, time stretches out,
independent of minutes and hours. And this is precisely the
secret held by all those who go by foot: life is prolonged when
you walk. Walking expands time rather than collapses it.

Finn   I usually ride my bike because I can't drive a car. But whenever I do walk to work, I discover something new that I never noticed from the bike, because it goes by too fast and you have to focus on the traffic.

Erling   A normal walking pace is ideal for taking in our surroundings. I often study trees, people, weather, and building facades on my walks through Oslo. I am always seeing something new, not much, every day.

Finn   Having a conversation while walking is one of the best things. When I'm in motion, entirely different things come to mind. I feel bolder, looser, and I'm also much better at processing what my conversation partner is saying.

Erling   Thoughts should be allowed to hang there and float. They don't need to be fully formed from one second to the next. Motion, emotion. Sometimes these incipient thoughts might lead to something useful, other times not. If you go walking together, it's also easier to handle when the other person is silent.

Finn   You said you like looking at buildings when you walk through town. I like to look at the sky. For example, now I'm noticing how incredibly big the seagulls are in Norway. Walks are a kind of school of seeing. The English Romantics recommended nighttime walks because you're forced to look and observe even more attentively. Did walking help you develop your taste in art?

Erling   I don't know if there's such a direct connection. I would have to think about it. By moving, I move my mind. Walking makes me feel calmer and better able to concentrate. It keeps me from being constantly distracted. That's certainly useful when you're trying to figure out whether a work of art appeals to you. I think the ongoing flow of information that we voluntarily subject ourselves to is not good for us. We look at the screen and time passes. We absorb information, but we don't experience it, and that ends up changing us over time. That's the problem with these potent technologies. Technology is not simply a means of achieving goals. Technology always goes hand in hand with an altered perception of the world. That's the opinion of Martin Heidegger who has also written on the topic, and it has always made sense to me.

FC   Your book is called *Silence: In the Age of Noise.* If I understood it correctly, silence is a kind of inner space for you, one you create and return to again and again.

Erling   Yes, exactly. I'm fascinated by the objective silence I experienced walking to the South Pole alone; for me, silence in nature is of the highest value. That's where I feel most at home. Still, if I hadn't been able to experience stillness amid city life, my longing for silence would be too great and I would have needed to return to nature more often. I believe it's possible for everyone to discover this silence within themselves. It is there all the time, waiting for us, even when we are surrounded by distracting sounds, lights and images, and as one's own fleeting thoughts. We lose a bit of ourselves along the way. I am not only thinking of how exhausting it can be to process so many impressions. This is off course true, but there's more to it than that. Noise is addictive, and that is why we need silence.

Finn   In Thomas Mann's *Magic Mountain,* there's a chapter about the essence of time. For the protagonist Hand Castorp, the first two weeks pass by incredibly slowly because everything is new. Then he gets used to the strict daily routine in the sanatorium, and before he knows it, seven years have gone by.

Erling   Habits are sometimes good, but they are also among the biggest factors limiting and diminishing our lives. You have to fight against them, try something new, take calculable risks and make life more complicated than necessary.

Finn   But not everyone can venture to the South Pole, or climb Mount Everest just to make their life more varied and perhaps a little more dangerous.

Erling   No, you're right. And if you live in Sudan there is no reason to. But most Norwegian and Swiss people would benefit from walking across Hardangervidda or Zurich, or around the port of Oslo, like we're doing now.

Finn   In Los Angeles, you went from one end of the city
to the other and it took four days.

Erling   Yes, Angelinos and tourists are seeing LA through
car windows; we wanted to experience the city from a different angle, from the pavement, in slow motion. By the way, it's
an adventure I recommend to everyone.

Finn   And then you once crawled through the New York
sewer system, which I wouldn't necessarily recommend for
imitation. You said everyone is an explorer. Did you mean that
in this context?

Erling   Yes, sure, why not do something totally surprising?
As you get older, this urge notably drops off, which is actually
a pity.

Finn   But you know yourself that raising children is an
incredible adventure that takes a lot of energy.

Erling   Yes, true. That's the Fourth Pole. The easiest to
achieve but by far the most demanding afterwards.

Finn   You once said that basically anyone could go to
the South Pole.

Erling   You reach the South Pole not just with your feet,
but first and foremost with your head. It's a mental challenge.
But what I meant was that people can achieve more than they
believe is possible. I'm not necessarily talking about professional careers. I think many people don't manage to realize
their potential. They could see and experience much more. But
they have to want it, to live it to the maximum, and they need
to become more fearless. That's what it's all about. If you live
in Norway or in Switzerland, there's a tendency to become
comfortable. Many things are made easy for you. But I firmly
believe that you should voluntarily choose to make life a little
difficult for yourself.

Finn   Does that also apply to your taste in art? You have
a great collection—in part because you like more difficult
artists who don't produce works that aim to please.

Erling   Yes, I sometimes find it difficult to understand what is great art and what is not, and then I have to act ahead of my own taste and intellectual capacity. Buying art I like at first glance would be too easy for me, and a poor basis for a collection.

Finn   Why?

Erling   Works of art with instantaneous and obvious aesthetic appeal too often end up boring me.

Finn   What exactly do you look for in a work?

Erling   A good work of art seems like a thinking machine that reflects the artist's ideas, hopes, lovesickness, failures, intuitions and other experiences and emotions. I often stay silent when I consider buying because I cannot find the relevant words and because I feel that I am separated from so much every single day. There's a lot I don't understand, that I can't move beyond, and art reminds me of that. I become more honest, more alive in what I am doing, and it makes me shut the world out. Then I can no longer separate myself from what I am doing.

Finn   Perhaps we should ask ourselves these questions more often, including about personal acquaintances or whether we should attend this or that event. There is this great biography of Goethe by Rüdiger Safransky in which the author describes the German poet as the type of person who continually asked himself these kinds of questions. And that is precisely why he was able to create a work of art out of his life. But specifically: you collect Klara Lidén, a Swedish artist. Do her works exemplify what's important to you in art?

Erling   Yes, it's a good example of art you have to work for a little. First of all, you're a bit confused by the dented trash cans, the objects that look like junk, her strange videos in which she wanders and does acrobatics through urban environments. As I tend to frequent so-called non-places in cities, I was initially attracted by her interest in tunnels, bridges and buildings. Then as I explored her work in more detail, I realized she could draw me more and more into her world.

Finn   In my opinion, your book *A Poor Collector's Guide to Buying Great Art* is a book with rules that can also be applied to life in general, even if you don't collect art.

Erling   How do you mean?

Finn   You describe collecting as a process in which you have to continually push yourself to your limits, both aesthetically and financially. You have to know when to decide quickly and when to take your time. To build a collection that is interesting yet remains personal, you say that a person needs to be obsessed, have a strong will, sometimes be a little crazy, not look too much at what others are doing. That sounds like a guide to life.

Erling   Yes, I'm certainly all for passion and following your own path.

Finn   That's a romantic definition of life.

Erling   I'm a romantic, without a doubt. I'm interested in big ideas and big emotions. Collecting art should be a matter of the heart, and my heart is often an adventurous one. I think the same thing about artists. Either they are, or they're not. No one can only be half an artist—then they're simply not one.

Finn   We talked about silence. Above all, you mean the ability to separate oneself from the noise of the world. But the art world is a pretty noisy place inhabited by people who like to make noise in their own self-interest. How can you find calm and quiet amidst this noise and navigate your own path?

Erling   It's difficult because you have to talk to people when you collect. You collect with eyes, ears and nose and it's not easy to shut yourself off. Sometimes you make mistakes, but odd works belong in every good collection. So that is okay.

Finn   If you were starting a collection today, how would you go about it?

Erling   The world is fair in the sense that everybody who would like to build an interesting collection has to see a lot of art, live with art, read, listen, make decisions and worry about how to pay invoices on time. I am not aware of any short cuts.

Finn		How did you start collecting anyway?

Erling		It was a lithograph by a Norwegian artist, influenced by Edvard Munch. It shows a dark-haired woman floating and languishing in front of three male figures. It was obviously about jealousy. My girlfriend had just left me and I was lovesick.

Finn		What does art collecting have in common with polar expeditions?

Erling		You're only asking that question because of my personal biography. But they actually do have a lot in common. For an explorer as for a collector, a lot of things boil down to wonder. It is one of the purest forms of joy that I can imagine. I often wonder, I do it almost everywhere. You also have to be very well prepared for both activities. Preparation is actually everything. I did not reach the South Pole because I'm in better shape than others, but in large part because I was well prepared. If you want to buy art, the same thing applies.

Finn		How did you become a polar explorer?

Erling		I simply set off one day and put one foot in front of the other.

Finn		It can't have been that easy.

Erling		Ah, I almost forgot to mention–I always ate a lot of porridge.

Bice Curiger

Water is for Everyone: Oscar Tuazon

"I grew up on Suquamish land near the Port Madison reservation in Washington State, and in my teens, I studied the Lushootseed language. I haven't been so deeply involved in politics, but this issue [Native American water rights] was something that really spoke to me; it was very clear that something should be done. I think about the camp at Standing Rock as this laboratory of architecture, combining traditional forms with improvization and technology. It was amazing. Every object had a function—there was a total economy of purpose." Oscar Tuazon

Infrastructure is a word from the language of public officials,
but here we are dealing instead with an artist who asks existential questions such as: Where does water come from, and
how, when it flows out of the tap? Or—in places of urban drear-
iness, concrete and steel deserts—can unexpected signs of life
be imagined there? Can a new, raw poetry emerge from them?

> The sculptures of Oscar Tuazon contain more than it seems at
> first glance. They are intelligent, wild creatures that immedi-
> ately involve us physically, and surprise us. We walk around
> them, cross them, want to find out whether they have a frontal
> view or not. We can get involved in the meanings radiated by
> their materials, products of heavy industry, with their traces
> of use, their "normality," their intrusive yet repressed omni-
> presence. The sculptures also play with statics and balance,
> or contain references to recent art history. But all of this
> would be too little for Tuazon were it not for the fact that a
> utility value is often included: an offer to a community still to
> be found that could use and enliven the objects or structures.
> In 2011, he built a concrete platform as a stage, complete
> with spotlights, connected to an unstable "house of cards"—
> with thick gray walls leaning against each other (as a "para-
> pavilion," at the 54th Venice Biennale), or with a public fireplace
> (Sculpture Projects Münster 2017).

Oscar Tuazon's lecture at E.A.T. on the topic of "Snow & Desert"
dealt with his personal engagement in the protests against the
planned Dakota Access oil pipeline, which will be laid through
the Sioux Indian reserve in North Dakota. With touching empathy, Tuazon described the beauty and fragility of the tribal
way of life, how it is exposed to political and economic forces,
and what is at stake: the pollution of their water, the destruction
of a holy tomb, as well as the threat to an important cultural
form. With an engaging intensity, Tuazon turned his lecture into
an impressive performance that broke with the usual time limits.

> The watercolors depicted here, painted by Oscar Tuazon in his
> hotel room during his stay in Zuoz, radiate a special calm, nour-
> ished by meditation on water, its states of aggregation and
> potentials that extend into spaces of time and cosmic events.

WASSER IST FÜR ALLE DA…
Bice Curiger

"Infrastruktur" ist ein Wort aus der Beamtensprache – hier aber haben wir es mit einem Künstler zu tun, der so existenzielle Fragen stellt wie: Woher und wie kommt das Wasser zu uns, wenn es aus dem Wasserhahn fliesst? Oder: Die Orte urbaner Tristesse, die Beton- und Stahlwüsten – lassen sich in ihnen unerwartete Lebenszeichen imaginieren, kann aus ihnen eine neue, rohe Poesie entstehen?

In den Skulpturen von Oscar Tuazon (*1975 in Seattle) steckt mehr, als es auf Anhieb den Anschein hat. Natürlich sind es intelligente, wilde Gebilde, die einen sofort körperlich einbeziehen und überraschen. Wir gehen um sie herum, durchqueren sie, wollen herausfinden, ob sie eine Frontalansicht besitzen oder eher nicht. Wir können uns auf die Bedeutungen einlassen, welche ihre vorgefundenen Materialien ausstrahlen. Produkte der Schwerindustrie, mit ihren Gebrauchsspuren, ihrer "Normalität", ihrer aufdringlichen und doch verdrängten Allgegenwart. Die Skulpturen spielen auch mit Statik und Balance oder enthalten Verweise auf die neuere Kunstgeschichte. Aber all das wäre für Tuazon zu wenig, wäre nicht oft auch ein Gebrauchswert mitgeliefert, ein Angebot an eine noch zu findende Community, welche das Objekt oder die Strukturen benutzen und beleben könnte.

So baute er 2011 eine Betonplattform als Bühne mit Scheinwerfern, verbunden mit einem labilen "Kartenhaus", mit dicken, aneinander gelehnten grauen Wänden (als "Parapavillion an der 54. Biennale di Venezia), oder eine öffentliche Feuerstelle (Skulpturprojekte Münster 2017).

Der Vortrag, den Oscar anlässlich des EAT zum Thema „Schnee & Wüste" hielt, drehte sich um sein persönliches Engagement bei den Protesten gegen die geplante „Dakota Access"- Ölpipeline, die durch das Reservat der Sioux- Indianer in North Dakota führen soll. Mit berührender Einfühlung schilderte Tuazon die Schönheit und Fragilität des Lebensform der Stammesbevölkerung, wie sie den politischen und ökonomischen Kräften ausgesetzt ist, und was auf dem Spiel steht: Die Verschmutzung ihres

Wassers, die Zerstörung einer heiligen Grabstätte, sowie die Bedrohung einer wichtigen Kulturform. Mit einnehmender Intensität liess Tuazon in einer zeitliche Grenzen sprengenden Performance den Vortrag zum eindrücklichsten Erlebnis werden.

Die hier abgebildeten Aquarelle (<u>Wasser</u>farbe!) — Oscar Tuazon hat sie während seines Aufenthalts in Zuoz vor dem Fenster seines Hotelzimmers gemalt — strahlen eine besondere Ruhe aus, genährt aus der Meditation über das Wasser, seine Aggregatzustände und Potentiale, die in die grossen Zeiträume und das kosmische Geschehen ausgreifen.

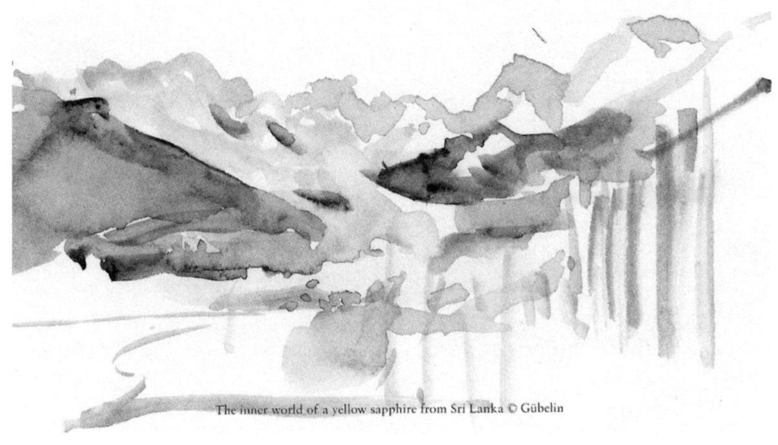

The inner world of a yellow sapphire from Sri Lanka © Gübelin

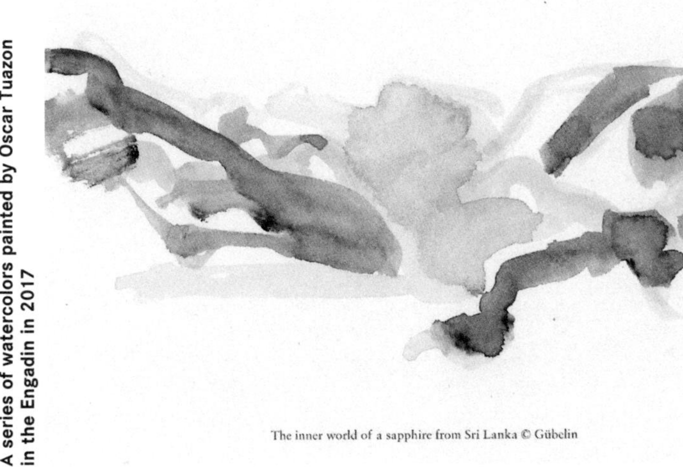

The inner world of a sapphire from Sri Lanka © Gübelin

A series of watercolors painted by Oscar Tuazon in the Engadin in 2017

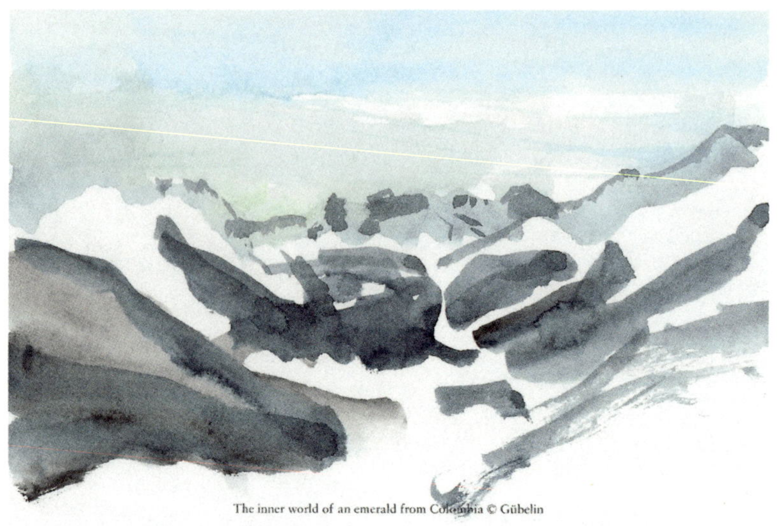

The inner world of an emerald from Colombia © Gübelin

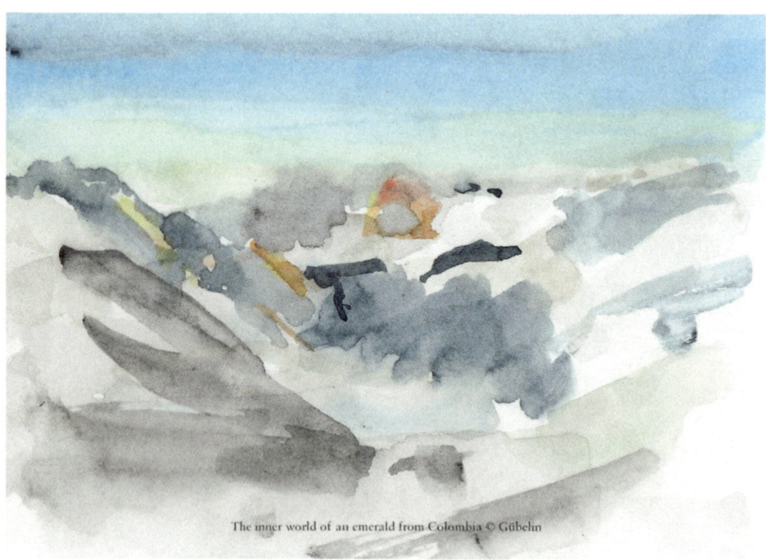

The inner world of an emerald from Colombia © Gübelin

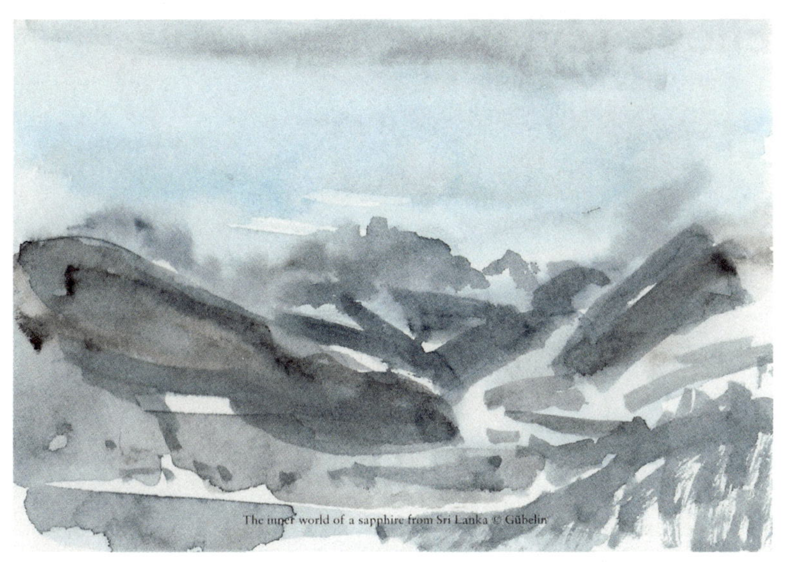

The inner world of a sapphire from Sri Lanka © Gübelin

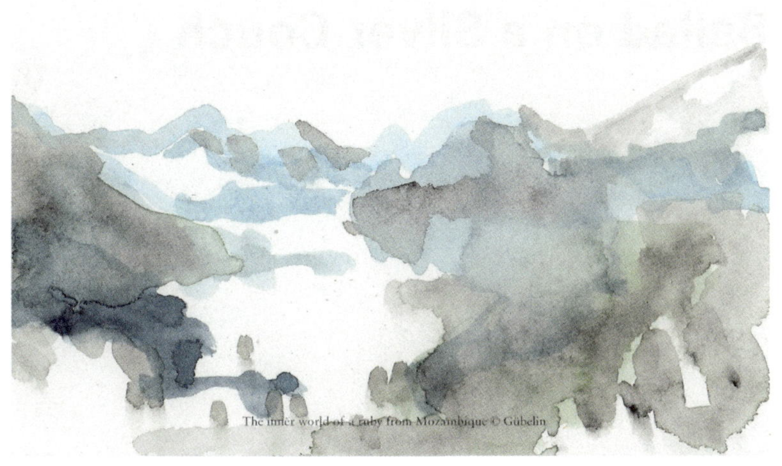

The inner world of a ruby from Mozambique © Gübelin

Eileen Myles

Ballad on a Silver Couch

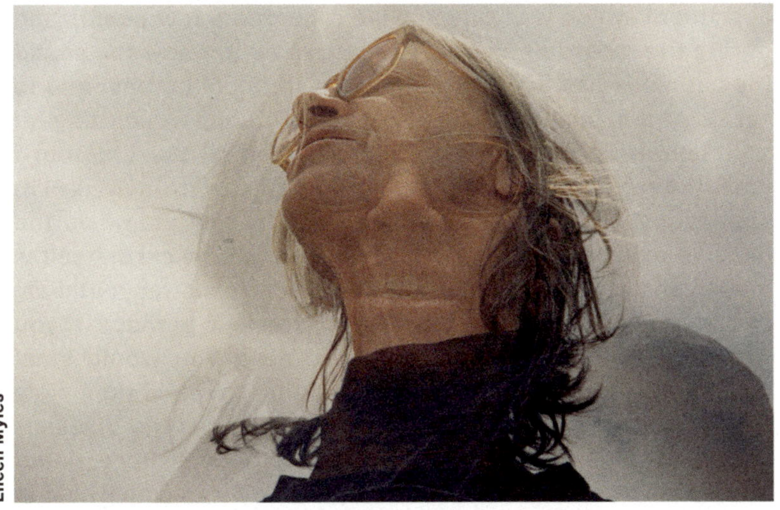

I can't separate the snow & the desert from the sky & the stars. They remain like ambient furniture—the sea, the dirt and all the apparatus . . . my number 10 pen. On this 23rd day of January let this ballad begin.

[long silence]

I live some of the time in Marfa . . . apparently it does snow there though I haven't seen it and Marfa is desert—high desert which means mountainous. It's interesting people don't immediately conclude that. I didn't. They wait for some other explanation—high desert means high noon or high time. Like an emotional pitch rather than a literal relationship to land mass and gradation. Like high desert is just singing its heart out. And in a way . . . like when I first saw what sound looks like on a computer—a composer I know Elliot Sharp had a whole recording set up in his Brazil-like—not Brazil the country but the film—his Brazil-like apartment. I never liked that film at all but it exhibited a defining moment in sci-fi that you always see now like some guy and increasingly a woman lives in a rough sometimes small sometimes cavernous but never cozy never bourgeois space that has all the high end technology you might want but in a raw punky way. It's almost cute—a profusion of wires and big genius hair explodes from the head of the subject as they are leaning out of a partially opened door or they're wearing a hoodie like Mr. Robot, lots of takeout coffee cups around, but Elliot Sharp had this set up in his apartment which was tiny and we recorded a few poems and during the recording the cat jumped. I saw it—I saw the sound the cat made like a mountain range a series of bumps—and to get rid of that sound he just eliminated that blip like cutting off a mountain tip which we do in the States all the time but I could never imagine Switzerland doing but I'm inviting—I'm suggesting here that you might think of "mountain" as the desert's expressiveness, not lungs but when the earth itself is molten and happening and it splashes volcanic matter youthfully and mountains form. When the desert 'comes' perhaps. If you were making a model of this phenomena you would start small—like drops of water or milk and film that and then blow it up thousands of times so the lizard becomes the dinosaur and the splash in the cup made the mountain range huge. Henry Miller who was very important to me when I was young said in his book about America, *The Air-Conditioned Nightmare*, that the desert was the only place he found on his cross-country trip across America that felt genuinely evil. I quoted that in my twenties as experience dark experience but I didn't know the desert then. Since then we've met. I somewhat live in the desert now. Some of the time. But I also know the desert through cross-country trips 2002 passing through Barstow with a cat and two dogs and another human, my then girlfriend. I feel compelled to say that that girlfriend has since transitioned which I relate to snow. I went through menopause when everyone else was beginning to transition and the snowflake operated for me like a symbol for that category of magical change maybe also resisting the inevitable thought that the unfertile female is a desert. We'll leave that for a while. Though I think she's the world. We drove through Death Valley. It was so hot and we pulled into a motel that had strong AC which Americans love. We love ice and we love AC. What I chiefly remember about staying in the motel in Barstow is getting tons of local very good jerky. It was fruity, some was actually vegetarian and lots of it was hot but chiefly it was dried meat that we ate in our car and later on in our room. Really delicious but we were eating the dead. There they were with their outstretched arm dying.

[lifts her arm sort of pathetically at 90 degrees]

Like a left-over angle from a Disney cartoon. It's like you didn't want to ever fail in the desert, an LA feeling, obviously we see

that cartoon hand and arm outstretched like this coming into
the shot of somebody's failure out there. Someone who is no
one. From an older part of history. Not part of the story but
part of the landscape. How it chills us. I can't think of the desert
without thinking about immigration and the word coyotes for
those who ferry immigrants. I had to really resist including
the word illegal right there.

> Meaning that I've been hypnotized, media and language works
> that way. Illegal. It's an emotional word but this is not an ani-
> mated version of the world. I mean I'm borrowing from its
> power. Isn't animation inherently propaganda. I realize how
> much snow stands in for feeling. How delightful—fat flakes
> might pour down on someone who had died in the desert in
> order to change the subject. And this [the extended arm] would
> form a cactus and then the snow would thicken and magically
> we would just go somewhere else. In the white way not the
> immigrant way. Isn't the desert just brown. About ten million
> people enter the US illegally at this time in history. We mostly
> have that rather than refugees. In the mythic version the desert
> exists as a kind of test. If you can perform this labor, surviving
> our hinterlands, then you can begin to be American. But the
> reality is more if you don't die of thirst you might still wind up
> on the side of the road with the border patrol and then be in
> a camp/jail for months even years and then get thrown back
> to your home in Mexico or Central America, South America or
> somewhere else. And most often you then turn around and
> start walking again. In a way it's just the scale of one guy's
> story repeated millions of times, his family is here (America,
> the national studio I write from) and so no matter how many
> times you capture him and send him back there is nothing for
> him to do but return which is to say he starts walking again.
> Which is as dramatic as the splashes in the small bowl being
> banged up to movie scale. And that's the fear. The thirst is
> coming north. And btw—in buying up all the water rights in
> America Nestle is pre-deserting the continent of North America.
> Water rights are not human rights the CEO of Nestle famously
> says and now I'll return to my local desert in Marfa.

You probably know that Marfa is the name of a character in
Crime and Punishment. Or it might be the name of a character
from Jules Verne. Both stories raise their heads from time to
time. The station-master's wife was a serious reader though
let's reverse that instead. There was a serious reader, a woman,

whose husband was the station-master. I think that would be true. Most of us in this room are professional readers much more I think than station-masters. I like reading more than I like writing and I do it more but when I rattle off the history of the desert I nearly repeat the tale that she is the wife of him who did something. Who's he. Yet we know something about her a moment that splashed up from her life of reading. She named the town. Her reading named the town. Previously I think it had been called Pump Town because in the desert conditions of land, a basin surrounded by a crown of mountains, a depression under which was a lot of water often determines a name. Surely it had an indigenous name. Trains in the 19th century would stop in Pump Town because they were fueled by steam and had to load up and get water from this place. So the place was only known as that, somewhere you would pump from. A pit stop. But that's not enough she said. It needs a name. It's funny that I think of the train as the sound of the west. There's so much space and the horn approaches and dies down like a total performance in that openness. The West didn't want those trains, the animals didn't, the native Americans didn't. I hear that crying sound that extends across the land and I think the West. But that's cause I am from Boston. I romance the sound of colonialism.

> Apparently a kid who didn't come from here (Marfa) was visiting his cousin and he was walking along the tracks with his headphones on and he didn't hear it. The engineer kept blowing and blowing his horn and the kid missed his own assassin. There's flowers along the side of the tracks. I don't mind bringing in a snowflake here. From the head of the flower comes a many headed shower of uncanny blossoms. That's corny. When I said flower I wasn't thinking real snow. I was thinking symbolic snow, large like in Christmas decorations. So much of snow is the idea and then the real snow comes and it's up there with rainbows or coming upon a waterfall in terms of natural miracle. I'm a kid. I'm hitch-hiking. The truck driver stops the truck and makes me & the friend I'm hitch-hiking with look out. In another setting my dog starts jouncing. It's an abstraction, like things go alkaline or salty, but it's snow, kicking a whole other involuntary system on when you least expect it. And you can see it in the sky too. It's a cold gray but kind of bluish. It's somehow flat. But you feel that there's something behind it. But not the ache of rain. It's spikey. It's interesting that snow is all change

at least the first one in your life or of a season or in a place you're passing through and that place is marked forever even as something shared with another person—remember the snow. Omigod yes . . . whereas the desert is . . . well Rumi says life is like wearing tight shoes in the desert. I guess I just flipped it. And I know he says something else somewhere absolutely how could he not about the desert but unfortunately I am on a train and I scanned all my Rumi quotes onto my phone and I left the book in Nottingham leaning against my silver rolling bag. I am thumbing through and I don't see the other desert quote anywhere but I'm sure that Rumi thought the desert was the world. Or the world is the desert. And I could say that's because he lived in Syria and Turkey and Baghdad. So of course he thought the desert was the world. But it's the constant isn't it and the snow is not. The desert seems to be what we return to. Before the World Trade towers were taken down all you had to do to get to America at least from the south was cross a river. The Rio Grande. And that was not always its name. But it's important that the name now is Spanish. Theirs. Make America Mexico again was the best joke of the campaign. You could pay a guy a quarter to get across the river and you'd sit in a rubber inner tube and he'd push you across the Rio Grande. I didn't need that ride but my friend Debbie wanted me to experience this in 1992 when I was a presidential candidate because at least part of my candidacy was experiencing things that no other candidate would dare think or feel. Now I would have to walk across the desert and soon I will have to scale a wall. No. You would simply have to experience a wall. That's what the wall wants. The wall seems as abstract as a snowflake.

> There's two lumps in your neck that you can simply feel. I mean right in front. I'm jiggling it. I picture a neck as almost spinal and one of those two things hurts, I have a sore throat and I'm hoping that won't still be true in the moment I'm reading this talk. I'm changing the subject.

In my beatitude I want to tell you about my couch. It seems like forever but last night I dreamed of a silvery leatherette couch, a battered couch, very large and cool that I bought in the Southern Hemisphere place where this gathering we are now at was happening in my dream. I had purchased the couch cheaply and was so excited and had it moved here to the large barn slash loft I occupy in my head. I was intending

245

for you all to come there for my talk and I would sit on my couch. And I still think that. That we should think about where we are. That's all we can do.

> But in the dream when I was about to give this talk the couch had been turned around, a different way and I began to wake in the dream and know that there was no way I could get the couch to Texas or New York and it would be difficult to get you guys to come to the talk there. In my barn. I was letting go and it felt good and I was no longer worried about what I would say right now. There's two ways of looking at snowflakes. I mean there's four actual categories which are needle, column, plate and rime. But existentially speaking there's two. I'll say it. It's real and fake. Fake is the large shiny cardboard snow-flake that hangs in a store window and the snowflake, I remember, hanging across a street in Los Angeles or San Diego, these snowflakes are really ideas unlike the snowfall that comes down suddenly pleasing me and my dog and providing a transition in a movie or a story. The snow falls.

Certainly the wall is an idea in the head of the man 'Prump' who is posing as the president of the United States these days. Yet a puppet can kill as we also know from movies which increasingly we are living in. The truest achievement of virtual reality was to prepare the world for fascism. Is it true. One person whirls around in Oculus Rift meaning the world does. We're fucked. Rachal who I had dinner with tonight in Nottingham told me that as the female MP was being stabbed the man who as it turns out is in the maximum security prison where her partner currently works, this man repeated as he stood on the steps stabbing the woman, Britain first, Britain first. Desert or Snow, that's chilling. Rachal's point was that the media did not make enough of that. Yes she was murdered because she was a woman because a woman is an inferior holder of ideas and that is of course as stupid and unreal as the cardboard snowflake, and Hillary Clinton was surely deposed because she was a woman. But Rachal's point is that he was killing her for England and that is a new idea. New since World War I. Or is it Malcolm Gladwell new. That one not so tiny lethal gesture needs to be looked at carefully for its meaning because many are also making that gesture. She did not die alone. He did not kill alone. The single murder is equivalent to the wall. It was terrorism. And it was lethal to all of us to not call it that. We just keep the money here. We keep the desert there. And when Prump stood at his obscene inaugural event he gave a speech in which he said three times America first, America first, America first. It's easy to say that he is a murderer too. He's kind of for it, leaving the Chihuahan desert on this side and the Sonoran desert on that side and the people with no place to go. And the animals are stuck too. Our money can't flow. Our work can't flow. I mean the world's. It's not a wall it's a dam. I mean a certain amount of Mexico's wealth is up here wouldn't you say. I'm thinking of the water being pumped into the trains in the 19th century, and I haven't even mentioned the big deals getting made in Texas.

Not far from me is a town called Balmorhea and it's a little like Austin in that it's got a spring fed public pool. Really large and warm because it's hot springs water so you can swim there all year round and the water comes from an aquifer that is under Balmorhea. There's caves and crevices and arcades, they have tried for years to measure how deep it is and literally nobody knows. It goes down and down, it seems endless. The measuring project has not begun nor has it been completed. Close by at MacDonald Observatory there are events called Star Parties in which you sit outside on benches and the astronomer who idly makes jokes about his wife (I'm barely touching that war) says that if you look at that little tiny faint star right up there and he has a laser to point out things in the night and this star that you can barely see is actually in another galaxy. Suddenly a little hole opens up and you're out of here and in there. But the expanse of the aquifer at Balmorhea feels that way. I think it's why I feel at least out there in Texas that these things the sky and the desert and the night and the water under the ground that nothing is all that separate. And the mountains here on the train. Blazingly real. Always part of the argument. Why is Switzerland safe.

I could stop right there. Let it snow let it snow let it snow.

So there's two things going on. A man named Carlos Slim who used to be the second richest man in the world but now he's like fourth wanted to build a pipe from Mexico to somewhere up above Texas, I don't even know how far and in this excitement a lot of other "alternative energy" projects began to crop up because the pipeline from Mexico I think was not about oil but natural gas and the people on the border (this side) in a very poor town called Presidio (meaning fort) were convinced by the big guys that they would get a really good deal on natural gas if they said yes to this project and they aren't rich so they said yes, the poor say yes it's like being choked or the dehydration is hinted at—I could turn the spout on or I can turn it off—but in the town of Balmorhea they were invited to welcome fracking. Just think. They have one of the deepest aquifers in the entire southwest. No one knows how far and wide it goes. Balmorhea said yes.

So I don't probably need to go on right there. We're all making jokes in Marfa that we ought to go for one more clean swim in Balmorea before we're all just little incandescent beings swimming around in that pool that tank of flaming methane gas. It's like we're living at the end of the world or the edge. Maybe worrying about this is like wearing tight shoes in the desert. It would be great to think that in a way. Rumi called his funeral the wedding party. He was always making fun of the wrong thing. If you asked him who was better or holier or righter he would always say you. I remember my friend in Miami telling me that the people who decided to pound the earth like a bitch and take everything they wanted and drive big cars actually believe in global warming but their response is to have fun and pump and take take—that party rather than being like those of us who want it to slow down like the world of the aquifer like earth time we don't know how deep or wide it is, we want more time in the plural are we just missing the fact of death the inevitably of the desert being everywhere on both sides of the wall which is just a symbol for taking. It's a dam and there's just a lot of stateless people dying of dehydration in the desert and on flimsy boats in the ocean, drowning, and in camps like cages on earth and increasingly nations are becoming banks isn't that the British plan that's what I heard last week Britain's gonna become offshore like a big secret checking account and America's just gonna make a deal—maybe Carlos and Kelsey Warren and the Nestle CEO are like the partiers at one long day of the dead doing the skeleton [extends her arm] at the rest of the world maybe they are the spiritual masters, they are Rumi and not me, and they know that when dying

the bats of the sense fly into the sunset
while the pearl of your soul rolls to sunrise

But that feels like a snow job to me.

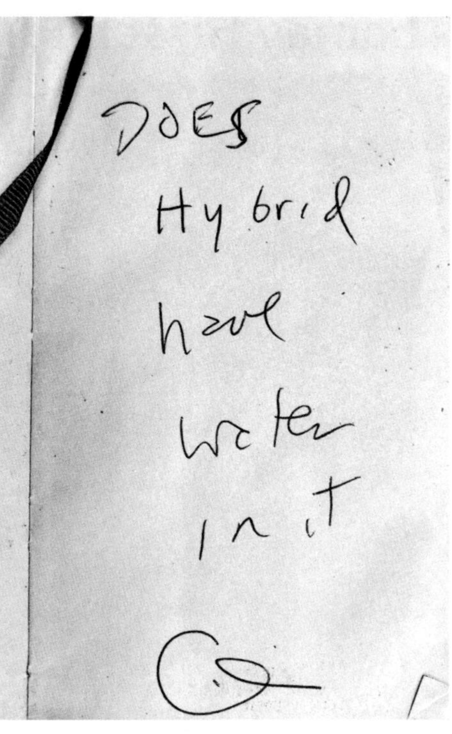

A note from Eileen Myles in Finn's diary

Thomas Hirschhorn

Some Moments of Grace (in My Work):
A Tribute To Simone Weil

The notion of "Grace" is meaningful to me and significant in my work. I want to and always will create openings for Grace. Therefore I would like to share with you some examples of moments of Grace that have appeared in some of my works.

> I want to work, and I want to fight for Grace, for Moments of Grace–in my Art and throughout my Art. This means I must lose myself in my Artwork and give my sense of self up in doing so. I must lose myself and give myself up so completely that, as such, this becomes the competence to do my work. Losing one's self and giving one's self up means working within the difficulty, the precariousness, the chaos, the emptiness and even the senselessness of doing an Artwork today. It means facing those problematics in a conscious Headlessness. Losing myself in Art and giving myself up in doing my work of Art is the opposite of doing nothing or not loving Art. Because losing myself and giving myself up in and throughout my work must be my unique and only competence to do Art.

Grace draws itself on Art. Art as such can generate "Moments of Grace." These moments are evidence that Art is a transformational act. Grace offers itself–it appears without being planned, calculated, or provoked. If I want to perceive and be in touch with Grace, I must be awake, alert, and attentive, and accept those Moments of Grace in their precariousness and uncertainty. I need to acknowledge that Grace cannot be measured, pinned down, or documented, and can't count as a result. Grace is not definable by success or failure; I need to acknowledge that there can be Grace even in failure. Moments of Grace can arise when everything seems in vain and all seems lost.

> Therefore, even if I can and want to share memories of some Moments of Grace (in my work), I must be aware of Simone Weil's statement: "Grace fills empty spaces but it can only enter where there is a void to receive it, and it is grace itself which makes this void."* → p. 168

→ p. 168

---

* "La grâce comble, mais elle ne peut entrer que là où il y a un vide pour la recevoir, et c'est elle qui fait ce vide." (Simone Weil, *La Pesanteur et la Grâce,* chapitre "Accepter le vide")

Niklas Maak

Are There Signs of Life
in the Ruins of Late Capitalism?

Dawn of the dinosaur: Are we the last generation to see
the big city as a promise?

At first sight, the city looks okay. If you believe in the language
of tourism, urban life is as attractive as ever. The website
"Germany Travel" celebrates a "glamorous, vibrant, never
sleeping Berlin," a "city of unlimited possibilities": "Wherever
you go, you can experience the pulsating life."

On Culturetrip.com, "the unyielding tempo of the Big Apple at
night, bright lights, eclectic nightlife," "twirling street per-
formers" and "fine cuisine at 3 am" make "the city that never
sleeps certainly lives up to its name."

The rhetorics of the city's unquestioned attractiveness are
reminiscent of Petula Clark's 1964 song "Downtown," where
the dissatisfied suburban listener just had to go where "The
lights are much brighter" and "listen to the music of the traffic
in the city, linger on the sidewalk where the neon signs are
pretty," to forget all his or her troubles and cares.

But is that still the case? Thanks to E-Mobility, the "music of the
traffic" will be soon reduced to the modest howling of tires,
and the *bright lights* dimmed by an eco-responsible AI. The ex-
uberant aesthetics of the "bright lights, big city" Metropolis,
the mise-en-scene of the urban as the only desirable lifestyle,
were made possible with an unprecedented waste of energy.
Today, everything about the lyrics seems wrong. The brighter
lights, the open world, the columns of glittering, confidently-
humming road cruisers, the wild mix of people and cultures in
the middle of the city…the downtown I live nearby has none
of that. What you find instead are empty shopping streets. A
tour bus. Horse-drawn carriages, beer bikes, gridded sand-
stone facades. Expensive boutiques. Unaffordable apartments
with ambitious Anglophone names ("The Upper East").

Could it be that we're the last generation to see the big city as
a promise? Could it be that the contemporary big city center
appeals mostly to wealthy retirees and tourists?

The urban aesthetic augurs an end. New luxury condos and
skyscrapers writhe and have holes and torsions like a person
standing awkwardly in the corner and shrinking away. The
promise of sovereignty, confidence, and power is gone. What
they offer instead is security and comfort, and sometimes
colorful Instagrammable slapstick culture for tourists and pen-
sioners, like Anish Kapoor's silly and highly elaborate London

observation tower, or Thomas Heatherwick's "Vessel" in Manhattan. They basically define the ideal city inhabitant not as an alert, critical citizen but as a consumer of attractions and city furniture that has been erected to be climbed upon and from which to enjoy views and make selfies (after the death of shopping, this might become the main reason to visit cities). City furniture occupies formerly empty public squares that had been able to host skaters, political demonstrations, protest marches. The gentle labyrinth of Parisian park chairs, ice cream stands, protected bicycle lanes, hedged playgrounds, wooden lounge chairs, hailed as "city improvements," are also barricades, fortifications against the occupation of public space by dissatisfied, politicized masses and chaotic subjects. Things that look like street lights are actually surveillance cameras; city furniture with embedded charging stations actually collect important amounts of data from those enjoying a sunny moment.

The city does not even look like that promise of congestion and condensation, intensity, danger and opportunity anymore.

Metropolitan centers have become ruralized. Cafés run by bearded men in flannel are cobbled together with raw wood, as if they were surrounded not by a big city and Google but by a forest full of grizzly bears.

The economic and social development of the city centers fulfills all the negative criteria attributed to villages: a homogenous demographic structure, xenophobia (refugees are always sent to the suburbs), narrow streets, deceleration, and an aesthetics of the idyll.

As everything in the cities grows smaller and more rural—as one-way streets become children's play zones and latte macchiatos are served on self-chopped wooden boards, as the city becomes addicted to the decelerated, idyllic, and homemade—large-scale things are happening in the country. Large structures are frowned upon in cities like Paris and Munich and skyscrapers are forbidden, but gargantuan distribution and logistics centers and server farms are built outside of the city limits, lying around the countryside like toppled high-rises.

Claims issued under the banner of humanism, stating that nothing could replace the vibrant atmosphere of the modern metropolis, sound increasingly questionable. This might be the case for a wealthy, privileged urban bohemia or bourgeoisie, but it is definitely not true for a lower-middle-class commuter who struggles to pay his or her rent in a social housing complex in the banlieues of Paris—not to mention people living in the outskirts of Nairobi or Mumbai. It's not an anthropological given to see the big city as a promise.

Future of the Village: The Riace-Camini Case

But there has always been something depressing about heading to the countryside—like an admission of being overwhelmed by the noise, speed, complexity, and modernity of metropolises. The country was for wannabe aristocrats in green corduroy trousers who were horrified by the city's mirrored glass facades, to whom country magazines at train station newsstands promised idyllic half-timbered houses, sunflowers, and horses galloping in the sunset. In other words, the countryside was projection, a kind of pre-modern relaxation zone for big-city dwellers who tried to enjoy the countryside without getting in trouble with what they framed as the "basket of deplorables" (Hillary Clinton), i.e. the actual population, tourmented by economic structural change.

A journey to the countryside has often been misunderstood as an act of de-politicization or a retreat into the private and nostalgic. This has always been wrong. Anyone who has laid eyes on the futuristic paintings of Benedetta Cappa or John Berger's books, like *A Seventh Man,* or has visited the village of Tarnac, an experimental village of Altermondialistes in the heart of France, knows that the countryside can also be a respite from the slowness and torpor and museum-like atmosphere of the city, an space of hopeful acceleration and politicization.

If cities are becoming increasingly overpriced, overly controlled, tourist-friendly Potemkin villages alluding only formally to the long gone glory of the chaotic, lively, dangerous beauty of the metropolis, and offering security and comfort only at the price of a loss of self-determination: could the actual rural village become a space of freedom, experimentation, and self-responsibility?

An experiment in repopulation has been tried out successfully in Italy. Riace and Camini are among the oldest settlements in Calabria, Italy. The place has been inhabited since antiquity. The sea is not far away. For over two millennia, the inhabitants of the villages lived here, in the foothills of the Apennines, making a living from agriculture, olive growing and viticulture. But after the Second World War, many young people left in search of employment, migrating to the wealthier north of the country or Germany. Of over 1000 inhabitants, there were less than 250 left.

The shops and the school closed. The houses fell apart. The Ndrangheta, the Calabrian mafia, took over and provided the remaining youth with jobs. The village of Camini was dying. Then something unexpected happened. In 1998, a boat with Kurdish refugees was stranded on the shores of Riace Marina. At this moment, Domenico Lucano, a young professor and later the mayor of Riace, another dying village nearby, had an idea: He applied for money to renovate the derelict buildings and accomodate the refugees and offer them job training. All of a sudden, there was life again in the narrow alleys. The success of Riace inspired many other villlages. In Camini, Rosario Zurzulo and his wife Giusy Carnà founded a cooperative, called Jungi Mundi, financed with the aid of the Italian ministry of the interior. They created employment opportunities for refugees, but also for Italians. Some of the original villagers, themselves work migrants, returned from the north, from Germany. The village built itself up again.

Over 150 refugees, from Syria, Sudan, Etritrea, Cote d'Ivoire, Irak, Bangladesh, and Afghanistan, among other countries, helped rebuild the old houses. Rosario had made a promising deal with the owners–their houses would be renovated and in exchange let to the refugees, and later rented out.

The state grants 35 Euro per day to the co-op for the reception of an asylum seeker. It is split in Euro and the local currency, which the refugees can spend locally only. This has helped inject more than 1 million Euro into the local economy in recent years, and local shops reopened. So did the school, which went from eight children up to fifty.

The bar reopened and became a popular meeting point for locals and new arrivals. Workshops were initiated that renewed traditional arts and craft, as the refugees brought their knowledge and merged it with the traditions of the locals.

Syrian women started to produce Aleppo-style soap and cooked jam, while Eritrean potters merged their knowledge with Calabrian ceramicists; new forms of pottery emerged. A fashion designer from Nigeria created colorful dresses in support of an artist from London, who came to Camini to start a new life.

The experiment proved all gloomy predictions wrong that an existing society can only accomodate a certain number of migrants.

At its peak, about 800 migrants, refugees and asylum seekers from twenty countries populated Riace, whose population was down to 600. Criminality was still lower than in most parts of Italy. Ten years after the process of rebirth started, the village of Camini is, at the same time, something completely new—an African-Arabian village in the hills of southern Italy—and a rebirth of the all-Italian village, as it still haunts the memories of the Italians and the dreams of the tourists, with the smell of fresh pastries in the alleys and children playing in the village square. For many inhabitants, the village is not a thing of the past; it became a space of rediscovery of societal practises long submerged by the market economy and its demands, and in particular, a space of experimentation with alternative life models.

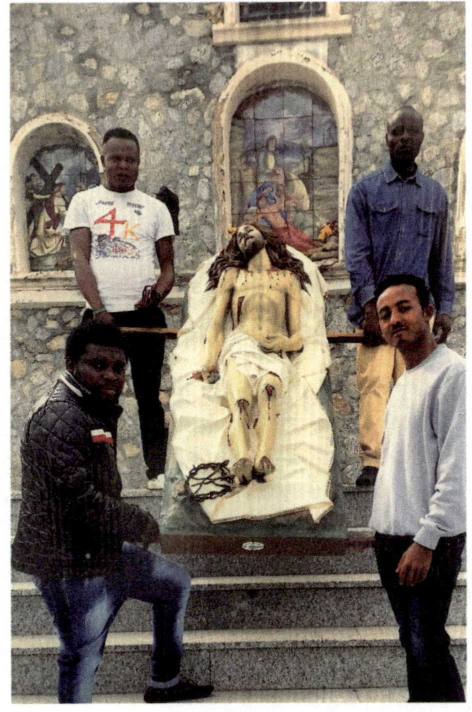

This might also attract dissatisfied urbanites who could work from there, and would only occasionally go "to town." A possible future takes shape, where the distinction of urban and countryside dwellers becomes obsolete: In some phases of your life, you might want to go out a lot in cities, in others, you might be happy to work and raise children near the mountains and the sea, or dwell with a circle of friends far away from the city's economic, technological and social restraints.

What is the countryside? It is an area full of mountains, fields, deserts, and savannahs—an area that is hard to control. The futuristic counter-model to the nostalgization of country living will be an open game with existing technologies, as they are by no means only in the hands of a few large corporate conglomerates. You can choose not to connect smart homes to the major data streams, or hook them up to a self-sufficient network that cannot be accessed by large groups like Google (see Tor Browser). You can use Facebook to exchange information without giving away too much personal data. Networks for sidestepping large data collectors could be one of the future's most important technological challenges.

After Work: A Future City

But city life might also drastically change—and not in the way Smart City developers advocate it.

It is almost too obvious to mention that the requirements and rituals of work have historically shaped the urban fabric of cities. The concentration of factories led to the growth of the modern metropolis, and the postwar market economy produced downtown office towers and endless commuter suburbs.

Today, almost every industrialized country in the world is facing a drastic shift: the accelerating development of the technological revolution and the streamlining of robotics is reshaping labor practices. Speculations in economic theory range from systemic optimism (some forms of labor will disappear, but digitalization will create even more highly qualified new jobs) to job apocalypse (digitalization and robotization will trigger a wave of mass unemployment). But these predictions are seldom mirrored in urbanism.

Even in far-fetched speculations about the future of the city, work is treated almost as an anthropological constant. The Stanford University report "Artificial Intelligence and Life in 2030" predicts that, "as cars become better drivers than people, city-dwellers will…live further from work, and spend time differently, leading to an entirely new urban organization."[1] The possibility of the massive disappearance of work and the subsequent decrease in the need for home-to-work transportation is not even mentioned as a hypothesis. While admitting that "AI will affect future labor demand, including the shift in skill demands," the study claims that this technology will "likely replace tasks rather than jobs in the near term, and will also create new kinds of jobs."[2]

In many future laboratories, we find a paradoxical technophoria—everything will change—paired with an assumption of a harmonious stability of the overall distribution of work. With an astonishingly intrinsic conservatism, many of the most daring smart city visions completely neglect any scenario in which wage labor and office jobs vanish in large parts from urban agglomerations. The axiomatic question is not addressed: If cities, their topography, their collective rituals, and their socio-psychological rhythms are built around and shaped by the idea of work and the concentration of human labor, then what would happen to the city if work as we know it disappeared? Where would these robot cars take us if not to work and back home? How would the disappearance of work affect our spaces and daily lives? What would the roles of a bedroom, a public space, a square, public transport, and city centers be?

According to the German information-technology association Bitkom, Germany alone will lose 3.4 million jobs to digitalization. That is one job out of ten. At the end of the 1990s, Germany had 200,000 jobs in the domain of communications technology; now there are only 20,000 left—a loss of 90 percent of all jobs in just twenty years.[3]

Sectors like banks, insurance companies, and car factories will be among the first to be affected. Self-driving cars—if they ever come—could make millions of jobs in the transportation industry obsolete. Robots, drones, and big data-driven algorithms will farm more efficiently. Tax advisors will vanish. The new field of "inverted mobility"—a term that refers to how everything, from goods (Amazon) to experiences (Oculus Rift), can be sent to your home—will rely on automated fulfillment centers and robotized delivery vans and drones. And it is by no means evident that all the people they replace will find other jobs in emergent sectors.

But what would happen if the majority—or at least a large number of citizens—stopped working? How would architecture react to this loss of a conceptual framework that has shaped the whole profession of urbanism and limited its imagination? While this change and the possible consequences have been widely discussed in the field of economic theory, three groups have remained conspicuously silent: social democrats (who still cling anxiously to the idea of full employment as the ultimate goal of a working-class party), Smart City planners, and architects.

This discussion is not taking place in the field of urbanism or architectural theory but in economics. Its focal point is the current debate about universal basic income (UBI).[4]

Given the fact that the nature of work will change drastically, a fundamental question has to be discussed: What kinds of spaces would a society need if it shifted its main goals from full employment and accelerated economic growth at any price to new forms of occupation, education, communication, and reproductive work? How would the city—its spaces, its rhythm, and its collective rituals (lunch breaks, after-hours drinks, holidays)—change if work as we know it vanished?

If the nature of work changed, everything would change: how we organize our days (with the kids at day care and long commutes to office buildings), how we prioritize our inter-human relationships (we spend most of our time with colleagues rather than with friends and family members), and how we dwell (now ideally near work). This axiomatic shift would open up new possibilities for architects. The much-hailed Smart City would not handle these changes adequately. Its incapacity to imagine new spaces for new demands makes it just a more efficient version of the existing urban model. With the changes in work, changes in demographics, technology, and social rituals would require new urbanistic strategies and architectural typologies beyond today's factories, office buildings, apartments, and houses. New spaces that encourage different ways of spending time together, bringing up children, taking care of loved ones, and living with friends outside the confines of the nuclear family could emerge. Small workshops could foster individual activity, and lives not restricted to a nine-to-five rhythm could take place in large, open, inhabitable landscapes, where education, loving, communication, the production of knowledge, and research could be organized differently. But where would these spaces be found?

Architecture Without Building: Reusing the Ruins of Late Capitalism

The answer is easy: They do not even have to be built, they are already there. Streets and parking spaces, mainly designed to organize individual traffic from home to office and back, could be reimagined and used for public parks with pools, table tennis, and theaters, in addition to new sites for small-scale local production, education, research, and caretaking.

In a study for a group of activists in San Francisco who want to educate children from less affluent families, we proposed to use the garages that had been built into the Victorian houses after the Second World War twice a week as schoolrooms; cars would be driven out and parked in the driveway, wooden benches and tables put into the empty space, and the private garage would thus temporarily become a part of the public space: a hundred garages could form a 5000 sqm school, meandering as an educational band through private houses, creating a new form of public space, an architecture without building.

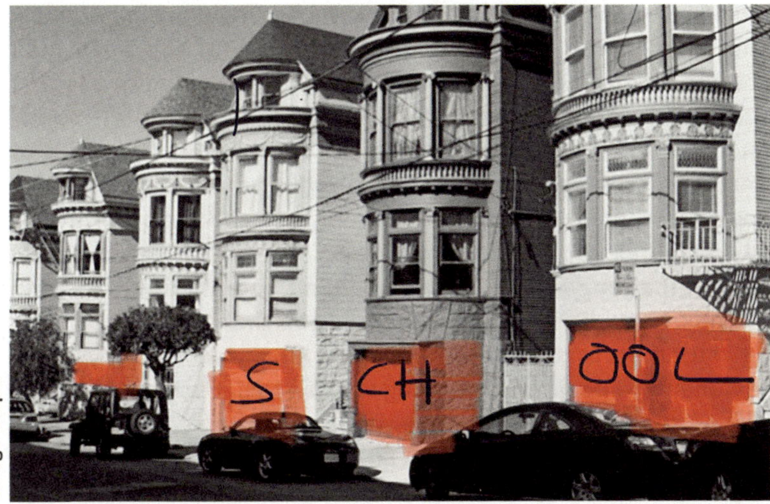

Garage Utopia

Many building typologies of late modernism will soon look like ancient ruins. The success of online retail and inverted mobility has triggered a rising number of dead malls and big-box stores, the success of online retail and digital communication has killed a remarkable number of post offices, and the disappearance of human labor from the service sector has led to the evisceration of office parks and towers. It will be one of architects' grand challenges to think about how to reuse these now-dysfunctional megastructures after the end of work as we know it.

Take the dead malls. Since the seventies, the mall was heavily criticized as a capitalist surrogate of urbanism, as a building typology that mimicked what it actually destroyed–the "real" town centers with their alleys, their central "piazza" and little "streets" with shops. But with the emergence of online retail, the mall, that once commodified everyday life, becomes an endangered species, killed by a new and even more comfortable and effective form of shopping. Today, there are already hundreds of "dead malls"–giant, deserted structures, placed strategically near or between towns. So, what to do with them? They are costly to destroy, and given the fact that building is a very Co2-intense practice, there are better solutions as to how to reuse dead malls. Actually, if you take out capitalist expectation, you have a very usable architectural frame for a new urban experience: A dead mall could be easily turned into a collective housing complex with a shared jungle in the former main arcade, small shops becoming units for families and larger stores spaces for co-housing, communes, co-working spaces, and other forms of collective, communal life. The dead mall could be turned into a twenty-first-century version of utopian socialist Charles Fourier's Phalanstery, a "grand hotel" apartment complex with four levels for 1620 residents, a kind of Versailles-for-everybody that inspired a whole movement of intentional communities.[5] The Phalanstery consisted of two lateral wings and a central part, dedicated to communication and education, with communal dining rooms, libraries, and studies, as well as a giant winter garden that guaranteed eternal summer to the commune. Cooking and laundry were remunerated positions, allowing women to participate in public life. As many of the repetitive, tedious, or unpleasant jobs as possible were to be eliminated using automation; working days were to be shortened; and a right not to work, as well as a "necessary minimum of aliments, clothes, and housing," were to be guaranteed to everybody.[6]

The Phalanstery was a counter-model to the nuclear family home and its moral foundations–monogamy, repression, and the isolation of women. According to Herbert Marcuse, the central idea of Fourier's giant socialist utopia was the "transformation of labor into pleasure."[7] Additionally, Hakim Bey argues, "In Fourier's system of Harmony all creative activity including industry, craft, agriculture, etc. will arise from liberated passion—this is the famous theory of 'attractive labor.'"[8]

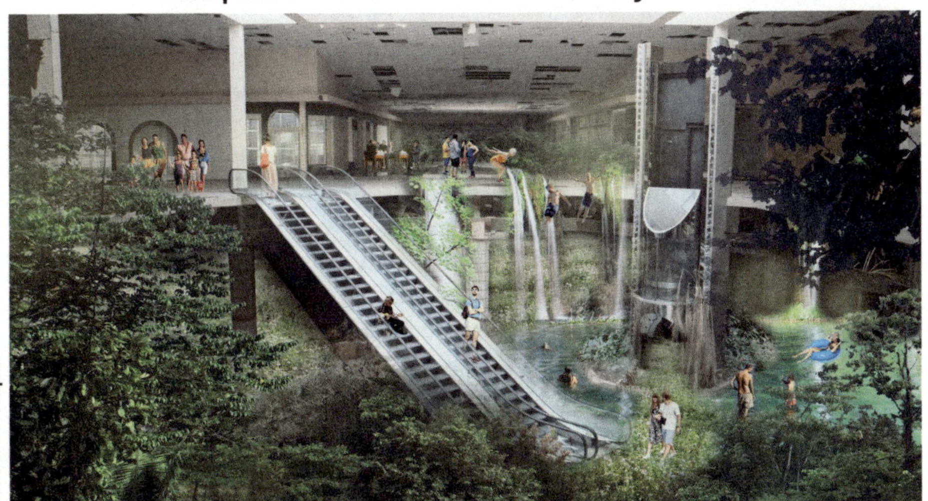

For Fourier, the Phalanstery was a form of spatial encouragement, a built frame that would enable people to experiment with and question the predominant social constructions, role models, power structures, and definitions of race and gender, turning depressed and exploited workers into "lovers & wild enthusiasts."[9] Today, for the first time, the technology required to realize this utopia is within reach. What started as a speculation 200 years ago, with Fourier's assumptions about post-nuclear family constellations, may become a reality: Unpleasant work will be robotized, and if the gain is not privatized but at least partly shared, former low-wage employees will benefit from this job loss by qualifying for other, more pleasant work or by dedicating themselves to other occupations in the field of previously unpaid reproductive labor, as Fourier predicted. His Phalanstery provided these workers with radically new spaces, like an artificial jungle where kids could play, a library for education, and even, in its first successful realization by Jean-Baptiste André Godin in Guise, in northern France, a public swimming pool.

All of these spaces are desirable models for a new architecture of the collective in a post-work world. A new form of Phalanstery, for example, could offer more urban residential options for families and non-workers. The Phalanstery could serve as a thinking model for an architecture that fosters community, experimentation, new role models, new gender relations, post-familial constellations, and new forms of love, education, and production.

Could a drastic reevaluation of what "work" could mean, beyond the fake amalgamation of wage labor with "fun" and "hanging out" in the creative industries, lead to a model that counters the overly controlled, labor-obsessed, exploitative, socially and aesthetically immobilized city? And could architects, who seem to be outpaced by tech companies in the design of Smart Cities, develop a new narrative that goes much further than a depressively blunt, only mildly smarter nine-to-five urbanism, with some sustainability ornaments and pleasurable work-life-balance hippie looks, that is sold to us as the future of the city?

1 Peter Stone et al., "Artificial Intelligence and Life in 2030," September 2016, p. 18, https://ai100.stanford.edu/2016-report.

2 Ibid., p. 38.

3 "Studie sieht Millionen Jobs durch Digitalisierung gefährdet," *Die Zeit*, February 2, 2018, https://www.zeit.de/wirtschaft/2018–02/arbeitsmarkt-digitalisierung-roboter-arbeitnehmer-stellenverlust.

4 On the question of UBI, see Niklas Maak, "Worlds without Work: From Homo Ludens to UBI Urbanism," *Harvard Magazine* (Fall–Winter 2018).

5 See Charles Fourier, *Theory of Social Organization* (New York: C. P. Somerby, 1876). On Charles Fourier and UBI, see Jack Cunliffe and Guido Erreygers, "The Enigmatic Legacy of Charles Fourier: Joseph Charlier and Basic Income," *History of Political Economy* 33, no. 3 (Fall 2001): p. 461.

6 Käthe Asch, *Die Lehre Charles Fouriers* (Jena, 1914), p. 128; my translation. On Charles Fourier's idea of automation, see Charles Beecher, *Charles Fourier: The Visionary and His World* (Berkeley: University of California Press, 1990), p. 295.

7 Herbert Marcuse, Eros and Civilization (Boston: Beacon Press, 1955), p. 217.

8 Hakim Bey, "The Lemonade Ocean & Modern Times," *Anarchist Library*, April 7, 1991, http://theanarchistlibrary.org/library/hakim-bey-the-lemonade-ocean-modern-times.

9 Ibid.

Exhibition at the Guggenheim, New York
Countryside, The Future

According to architect and urbanist Rem Koolhaas, the fact that 50 percent of the global population now lives in cities has become an excuse to ignore the other 98 percent of the world's surface: the countryside. The Solomon R. Guggenheim Museum has invited Koolhaas and AMO, the think tank of the Office for Metropolitan Architecture (OMA), to collaborate on a project that explores the radical changes occurring in the countryside, extending work underway by AMO/Koolhaas and students at the Harvard Graduate School of Design. On view through the summer of 2020, the rotunda exhibition *Countryside, The Future* will present speculations about tomorrow through insights into the countryside today. (More than any city, the vast non-urban territories of the countryside have become the frontier of transformation.) The exhibition will explore artificial intelligence and automation, the effects of genetic experimentation, political radicalization, mass and micro migration, large-scale territorial management, human-animal ecosystems, subsidies and tax incentives, the impact of the digital on the physical world, and other developments that are altering landscapes across the globe.

Not Vital

Me on Myself

On your right is Not Vital, reading. He is reading a book that was printed in 1560. It's written in Romansh. Next to him is his mother, Maria Vital Fontana Manzoni. She is also reading. It's a book about 7 dwarfs who lived in a side valley of the Engadin called Samnaun. She reads this book over and over again. Without using eyeglasses. Both Not Vital and his mother were born in the twentieth century, and she grew very old. There were two artists, Fontana and Manzoni, who had the same last names and also lived in the twentieth century. When asked if she liked Fontana, the mother said that she preferred Marc Rothko, and about Manzoni that she kind of liked his work, specially the Merda d'artista. Her son also did some works in shit. He bronzed cow dung and sold it to built a hospital in Nepal and a school in Africa. Maybe that's why she liked Manzoni. She was not into shit, I think. Not Vital was an artist who spoke Romansh. I don't know if he also spoke other languages. Most probably, because he travelled a great deal. Clearly his mother spoke German, too, since she read the book about the dwarfs in German. Most probably there is no Romansh translation of it. Not went to Africa, to the desert, and built himself a house just to watch the sunset. Must have been a strange man. He also built a school for hundreds of children. What kind of an artist must he have been! While in Africa he put the entire remains of a sundried camel into 16 silver balls, after speaking to a silversmith who was wearing a silver ring with a sphere. Then he showed this sculpture in a gallery in New York and the sculpture was called Camel. But

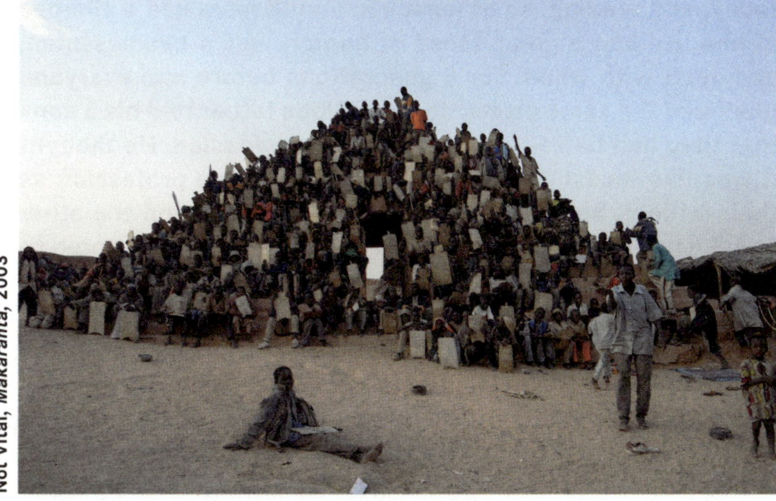

Not Vital, *Makaranta*, 2003

you couldn't see anything of the camel. Some people thought it was a joke but there was actually a camel inside. Not loved architecture and built many things. As a young boy, he had a 5-month vacation in the summer and he built huts in the woods. He spent time in these wooden houses and later when he read Italo Calvino's *Il barone rampante* (The Baron in the Trees) he felt he was part of that story. He adored, among others, Simon Rodia who built the Watts Towers in Los Angeles. Rodia was born in the nineteenth century. He came from Serino in Italy, went to California as an immigrant construction worker, collected all kinds of materials on the construction sites, and built 5 tall towers. The tallest was 40 meters. He worked at night and on weekends. When asked why he did all this he simply replied that he wanted to build something big. Rodia was not even 1.50 meters tall. Once they showed him photographs of works by a famous Catalan architect called Gaudi who also used broken ceramics in his work, and who, like Rodia, was born in the nineteenth century. Rodia asked if Gaudi built his buildings all by himself, without help. They were both very religious men. Not wasn't, and there is no record of his mother's beliefs. The mother of Not was a wonderful woman. She could focus when she met someone. She was modest but had great style. At one point in her life she wanted to become a singer and went to Winterthur to study singing. But the war broke out—I don't know which one exactly, must have been the Second World War—and she had to return to the Engadin. She married the father of Not. Sorry that he couldn't be here today, and reading, so at least you would have had a glimpse of him. He had a great sense of humor, was a businessman, and dealt with wood. For 5 generations before him everyone practiced the same profession, and Not's father told his 3 sons that they had better exercise another profession. He thought it was like incest if sons always did the same profession as their fathers. So one son became an architect, and the other one, I don't know. When Not told his father that he wanted to become an artist his father was kind of surprised and told him not to exaggerate. Another person Not very much admired was Gordon Matta Clark who died of pancreas cancer at the age of 35 in the second half of the twentieth century. He once met him in a restaurant in SoHo in New York that Gordon opened. Not liked the way he walked. This guy broke windows in the Bronx, cut holes in buildings to let the light come in, and once in New Jersey he removed the stones on either end of a house so the house split. A small slit opened in the middle of the house. Great. Buckminster Fuller was another person Not liked. He invented the geodesic dome, among other things. He couldn't realize much during his lifetime and he called himself the world's most famous failure. Not wanted to move in that direction. I don't know if he succeeded because he had freckles when he was a kid and lived in the mountains in Switzerland. Once he built a house that disappeared into the ground by pushing a button. The whole construction simply disappeared into the earth without leaving any trace, and animals like deer and foxes would walk over it without knowing that they were walking over a house. People came to see the house, including some architects, like one called Norman Foster who flew his own plane and his eyes lit up. He was born in the first half of the twentieth century. He called himself Lord, I don't know why. Not once asked his mother if she wanted to be called Lady

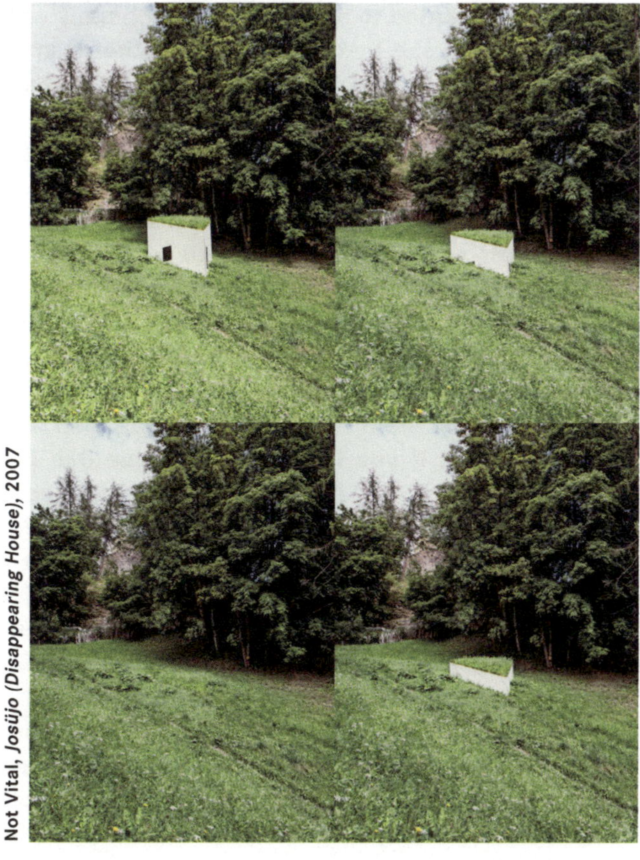

Not Vital, *Josüjo (Disappearing House)*, 2007

and she said no way. The constructions Not built in different parts of the world required some engineering skills. He was lucky to be a good friend of an engineer from his village in Sent. His name was Jürg Buchli. He helped Not make a house in Vienna that would go to sleep at night and get up in the morning. Jürg died in 2010 at the age of 66. Young for that time. He also worked for another architect called Zumthor. When Not went to school in Zurich he was in the same class as Bice Curiger. Bice was also born in the twentieth century, and rode a black Velosolex to school. She rode very fast and once did a drawing that she gave to Not which was a big foot that was pushed into a machine and on the other end many small feet were dropping out. Not was walking to school with a cane and she thought that he was a dandy. How funny. Maybe because Not was gay or something and maybe he was, I don't know. I can also stop. But Not and his mother don't seem to stop reading. His mother, as I told you, always reads. Probably because she wanted to hang on to something, since she didn't remember what she had for lunch. Why the dwarfs? Here is a picture of one of them. They found out later that the cause was the Laron Syndrome Type II. It is quite rare. Can you imagine being a dwarf and coming here to Zuoz and being seen by all these people? No way. People would ask questions about their height and their sex lives, wanted them maybe even to dance on the table, and never asked what flowers they liked or if they liked Brancusi. Who is also here is Hans Ulrich Obrist. He went to see Not when he was still in high school in St. Gallen. Not liked him, he told me, because he was able to retain so much information in his brain and he was fast. He liked fast people, he liked speed. Not was also fast and once he told me that if you lived twice, maybe like in the James Bond movie *You Only Live Twice*, then in the second life you can slow down. What a strange thought. That would mean that all slow people had already lived once. HUO, as he was called, was also born in the twentieth century. Most of the people mentioned here were born in the twentieth century. Let's move on to the next century. Well, most people lived on into the next century. Gordon Matta Clark didn't and neither did Simon Rodia and Buckminster Fuller. But the other people we've mentioned did, like Hans Ulrich and Not's mother, and Not did too. They never knew what happened to Not. He simply disappeared one day. Just like his house. Some people just disappear, like Saint-Exupéry who simply was gone one day. No traces were found of him. He also made a drawing with something inside that you couldn't see. An elephant in a boa. He flew planes like Norman Prince, but in the twentieth century there was a lot of flying around. I once read something by someone who made research about Not's life that in 2013, from January to August, for example, he took 48 plains. Insane. For what? It's as if swallows would have to travel 24 times to Africa and back in 8 months. One other person Not quite admired was this writer Xavier de Maître. He was born in the eighteenth century. Finally, someone from another century. He wrote 2 books. One is called *A Journey Around My Room* and 31 years later he wrote *A Nocturnal Expedition Around My Room.* Actually this is what these two people, Not and his mother, should read instead of what they are reading. Well, it seems that what they are actually doing is just that. They seem not to travel anymore. In one room. Not once told me that the reason he liked Xavier de Maître's idea was that it was exactly the opposite of what he did in his lifetime. Since I am not sure if they speak English, because Not spoke Romansh and his mother must have spoken some German, they won't take any questions and none will be answered and since they were supposed to speak for 20 minutes and take questions for 10 minutes, they will leave quite soon and we wish especially the mother of Not a happy birthday which is in 3 days. I just hope that the twenty-second century will be as pleasant as the twenty-first.

I am leaving and so are Not and his mother. They will go back to where they came from. It's not far. We always think that everything is so far, but life and death are quite near indeed.

Anna Gritz

Dead Horse Bay:
Lena Henke

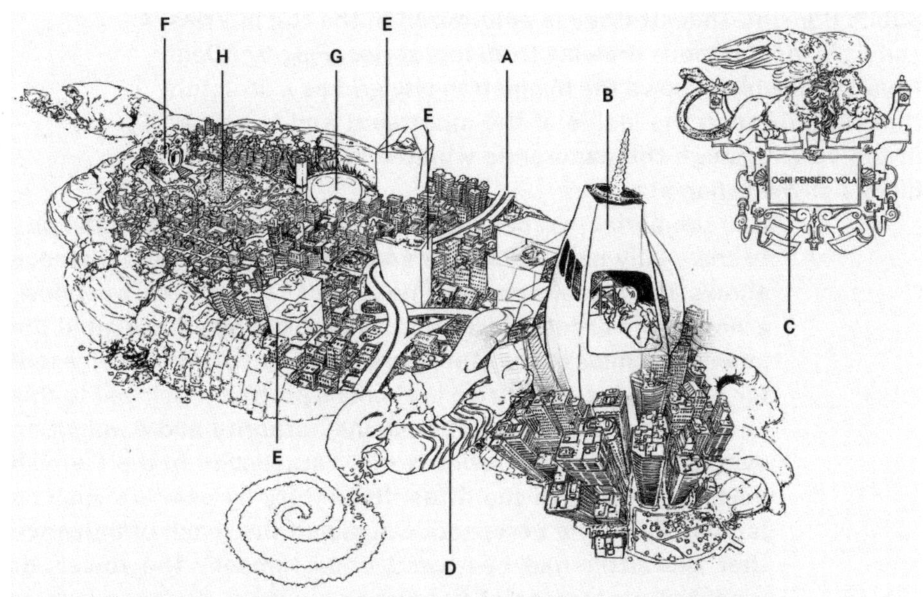

Slowly and with purpose the head of the Empire State and the Chrysler building bob up and down, fellating each other in a steady rhythm. Through a panoramic window their lovemaking is witnessed by a legion of anonymous, anthropomorphized Manhattan buildings deeply entrenched in the scene unfolding in front of them. The amputated arm of the Statue of Liberty makes a Cocteauish appearance in form of the table lamp on the bedside dresser, moodlighting a scene that is harshly interrupted by the spotlight that the Rockefeller Center casts in the bed upon entering and catching the couple inflagranti. This scene is taken from a short animation storyboarded by the artist Madelon Vriesendorp with Teri Wehn-Damisch and developed from a body of work that Vriesendorp had created in the early 1970s after she moved to Ithaca, NY with her husband Rem Koolhaas.[1] Her drawings would later become part of Koolhaas's influential text *Delirious New York* from 1978. In addition to the bizarre and surreal subject matter, it is the treatment of the city of New York as a pulsating, sweating, screwing mass of buildings, that is both stage and protagonist, that is so relevant to the work of Lena Henke. For *Dead Horse Bay* Henke also chose the urban fabric of New York City as a matrix, clouding her intimate sensation of the city with its public façade. In both women's artworks the interior and exterior becomes transposable, the city both interior setting and public domain. This strategy is epitomized in the rug in Vries-endorp's most famous drawing from this series, *Flagrant Delit,* from 1975, which shows the Manhattan city grid as a structure that runs through the inside of the apartment and is echoed in the view through the panoramic window in the geometric blocks of the urban structure.

It is the aerial perspective that reduces the chaos of the city to the easily navigable lines and channels of a map. Distance allows for the abstraction necessary to gain an overview, granting the order, which is so desirable when stuck amid the inner-city chaos below. The birds-eye view has long been a tool for mapmaking and is also in Henke's portrait employed to this end. It is a viewpoint that beckons authority and domination over the surveyed exterior world. Established in the Flemish portrait painting of the fifteenth century by painters such as Jan van Eyck, the perspective signaled the reach of influence that the sitter had bestowed upon himself. The tower, or tenanted vantage point becomes an optical device, a lens or camera as Beatriz Colomina calls it, consolidating inhabitation and the view onto the exterior word.[2] She recounts Le Cor-busier suggesting the possibility to inhabit the camera as a means of employing a system of classification.[3] One might take his point further and say that the mind can mimic a technolo-gy upon experiencing it. In a similar manner the perspective of a surveillance camera or the Google Earth zoom, once seen, can be called upon at will, allowing for a double entity–we can inhabit both the instrument glancing over a cityscape while being an active participant in it. It is as if, once observed, we carry this perspective within us, observing ourselves from the position of an elevated outsider, an internalized panopti-con of sorts, not dissimilar from Jeremy Bentham's and cer-tainly a perspective encouraged by much recent municipal city planning. And yet aside from suggesting an internal cor-rective this type of split perspective also allows for an incor-porated view onto our physical location. It is this incorporated view that Henke presents in this cityscape cum map. The gaze is multiplied and while we reside in her sight down on the city of her "Wahl Heimat" Manhattan, we also observe her through a window lying down on the top floor of the Freedom Tower, here displayed in the shape of a milk bottle that curiously re-sembles her own milk bottle sculptures. She is lying there playing with her sculptures as if they are dolls in a dollhouse, while surveying the ongoings of the city below through a massive window (B). Henke is employing a similar type of scale confusion here as practiced by Vriesendorp in her drawings. While some of Henke's sculptures appear as miniatures and others materialize in the cityscape blown up to the size of buildings, her detergent hoof dollhouses (D) can be found copulating not unlike Vriesendorp's skyscrapers on the shore of the Hudson River, spewing green water in the shape of a spiral (jetty), a nod to an another movement that was highly reliant on the aerial view. All the while specimens of her *Female Fatigue* series (2015)—New Museum, AT&T Building, Chelsea Hotel, and Flat Iron Building (all E)—are casually spread about the lower half of the island.

There is something easy about Henke's *Female Fatigues*, the way that the female bodies are slouching, cast from sand, on top of the sharp steel outlines of iconic architecture, constantly threatening to collapse, not made to last but to be rebuilt when needed. They are like inflatable rubber dolls, summoned into shape and existence through a mold, once desired and easily destroyed and stored away when not. The series developed out of a show entitled *DIE,* after Tony Smith. Amongst other works Henke showed large industrial size sand bags, the ones in which sand is delivered for construction sites. The sand was kept in the industrial bags, and moulded to resemble fragmented female bodies, an ass, a torso with head, a crotch with legs crossed as in *Lower Part (legs)* (2014). It is another self-portrait of sorts—Lena is assembling herself in fragments made of sand in the gallery. The shaped parts were then at times embellished with works from a series she calls *Chainmail* (2014), metallic chain nets cast in epoxy in FedEx boxes resembling medieval armour. The casual, almost sluggish body language of the sand sculptures can be seen in conversation with a type of feminist illustration common in '70s and '80s magazine culture with Claire Bretécher as one of the most famous protagonists. The lazy, lascivious poses appear borrowed from sources such as Bretécher's serial publication *Frustration* (1975–1980) which presents women slouched on couches, not wearing any bra, casually carrying a fag or breastfeeding a baby, habitually not poised or composed but instead perpetually irritated about the pitfalls of modern living (generally the pains of living with the other sex).[4]

This overly human, unapologetic, unpolished attitude is present in both Henke's sculpture and Vriesendorp's skyscrapers. Vriesendorp speaks of the drawings as "the result of an indepth analysis of the possibilities provided by architecture, marking a time in which the ridged corset of modernism had been thoroughly exhausted."[5] The physical manner displayed by the buildings, flaunting arousal, strain and physical exhaustion, opens up a perspective on architecture that suggests an unconscious double life. Their constitution as erotic beings is correspondent to Lena's treatment of architecture and sculpture as both not only hosting each other but as being emotionally and physically affecting. Her 2014 comic book *Yes, I Am Pregnant* was produced in reaction to the invitation to create a new work for the collection of the Sculpture Museum in Marl, Germany. Inspired by the richness in public sculpture in the city, a place that she experienced otherwise as desolate and without much public life, Henke decided to cast the sculptures in the public realm as the protagonists of a photo love story, a common subgenre in German teenage literature. The comic reframes and subtitles shots of the sculptures in the city tell the story of Marina and Paul, two pubescent sculptures in love, one a work by Marino Marini and the other by Paul Derkes. Their love story is told as a drama, unfolding through an unplanned pregnancy and the resulting quarrels with family and friends, and is illustrated through the sculptures shot in situ alongside a cast of auxiliary sculptures by Hans Arp, Joseph Jäckel and Hans Bucher. Inspired by the works in Ignazio Danti's famous Gallery of Maps in the Vatican Museums, Lena Henke deploys the aerial view not simply as an attempt to map a city, but as a portrayal of her life, yet herself in the very city. Not dissimilar from Saul Steinberg's iconic vistas of the New York City of the 1970s, the work presents a very personal vision of the skyline of the city, stretching and shrinking buildings and avenues at her leisure, going so far to transfigure the outline of Manhattan Island to match the famous anatomical drawing of the head of a horse by Théodore Géricault (G). The skin pulled away to reveal the underlying muscle strands evocative of highways and the infrastructure of the city grid. The reference to the horse goes far back for Henke, recalling her upbringing next to a horse riding stable in rural Germany, blurring her pastoral origins with her new urban home. The horse motive is picked up frequently in the work, from her saddles and horse blankets in works such as *Freeze Frame* (2014) and *Laundry Day* (2015), the detergent and milk bottle sculptures nestled in ceramic hoofs which are grotesquely distorted to the point that they begin to resemble vaginas, tenderly holding quarter coins between their lips–laundry money, one might assume.

The saying heralded on the emblem floating above the island (C) is taken from Dante Aligheri's inscription on the opening of a cave that bears the features of a monster with a wide-open mouth as its entrance in the Sacro Bosco Park in Bomarzo, in central Italy. The saying states "Ogni pensiero vola," meaning "Every thought flies away," advocating a letting go of reason upon entering the park with its cast of grotesque monstrosities. The gardens, which were built in the sixteenth century according to the vision of Pier Francesco Orsini, lay forgotten and overgrown for centuries until they were rediscovered and treasured by amongst others Jean Cocteau and Salvador Dalí. One of the creatures has also found its way into Henke's map (F), guarding the north entrance to Frederick Law Olmsted's Central Park, reminding us that as much as we would like to see our cities as places of communal decision-making, they were for the most part planned according to the visions and whimsies of individual men, Olmsted being just one of these, Robert Moses another. Henke makes nods to both men here, tracing the impact that the ideas of these two had for the city of New York: Frederick Law Olmsted through his concept of a central park (H) that embedded handmade nature as a democratic and civilizing force into the urban fabric and Robert Moses by restructuring the city's infrastructure with his curving park and expressways (A), extensive bridges and endless rows of red brick tower blocks punctuated only by the occasional asphalt playground. It is the ability to restructure on a massive scale to build a system that will order and shape the way people navigate a place and relate to each other that draws Henke to these men.

ANNA GRITZ is curator at KW Institute for Contemporary Art in Berlin.

1 The film entitled *Flagrant Délit* was produced for French television and premiered in 1980.

2 Beatriz Colomina (ed.), *Sexuality & Space* (New York: Princeton Architectural Press, 1992), p. 121.

3 Ibid.

4 Claire Bretécher, *Les frustrés* (5 albums, 1975–1980).

5 Madelon Vriesendorp in Klaus Leuschel, "Sex and the City? In architecture!", http://www.architonic.com/ntsht/sex-and-the-city-inarchitecture/7000243

Pacôme Thiellement

Looking For The Sphinx

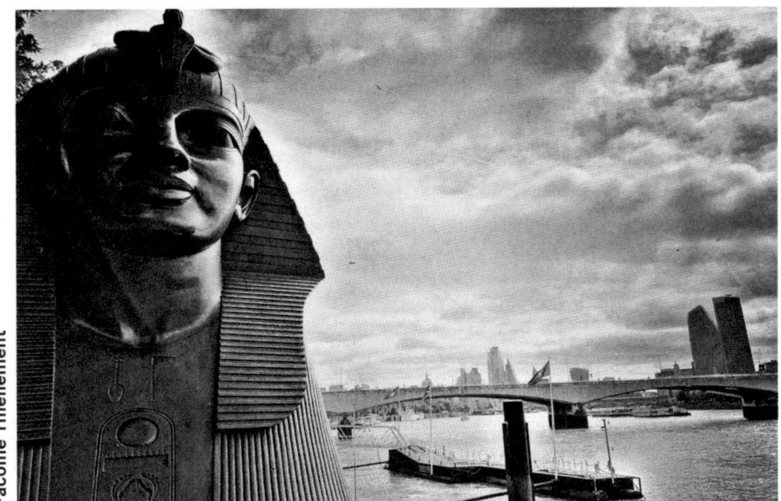

We still don't know what the Sphinx is. Standing in front of the Pyramids in Giza, the tallest statue in the world is a mystery weighing around 20,000 tons. It's been carved in a natural, 40-meters-high limestone bedrock. Its head has been extracted from a peak of hard, gray limestone and its body sculpted in a lower layer of softer limestone. Its whole being is facing the Levant. Archaeologists estimate that a million hours were necessary to carve Mister Mystery with burins, copper chisels, and wooden mallets.

The body could be a reclining lion's unless the flanks belong to an ox or a bull. Some suggest that initially it was a dog carved in stone during the Old Kingdom whose face was altered to represent Pharaoh Amenemhat II during the Middle Kingdom. The problem with this theory is that the Sphinx doesn't look like Amenemhat II at all and its body hardly looks like a dog's. Its head has also been identified as the one of Pharaoh Khafra who was reigning when the Sphinx was supposedly built, around 2500 BC. It looks more like it, indeed, but not that much. Some others suggest that its face doesn't belong to an Egyptian, but a Nubian, a Sudanese, or an Ethiopian. Recent theories—based on humidity traces that could only have appeared several thousands of years before—suggest that it may be much older.

Was it the guardian of the site? Arabs don't call it the Sphinx but *Abū al Hūl*, The Terrifying One. *Sphinx* is the name the Greeks gave the statue. We don't know if it comes from the Greek word that means "strangler," if it's been borrowed from *sthag*, a Sanskrit term meaning "hidden," or from Ancient Egyptian *shesepankh*—"living statue" or "living image." A stele describing the dream that inspired Thutmose IV to dig the statue out of the sand (in this dream, the Sphinx is named Horemakhet-Khepri-Ra-Atum and calls Thutmose "my son") was probably added around 1,400 BC. Beside that, we don't have any document that could unveil the meaning of this statue. Furiously mute in the Giza desert, Mister Mystery embodies the unknown always sparkling like a star in the night of our existences. And in our daily lives, all the strange encounters, all the unexpected coincidences, all the elusive things that yet guide our lives can be seen as the Sphinx getting closer.

> The Greeks brought the Sphinx to the stage in the Theban Cycle. But they turned Mister Mystery into Miss Enigma. Just as destructive as the Sphinx is protective, sporting the breasts of a pin-up or a femme fatale, the Sphinge destroyed crops and terrified people. She said that she would only leave Thebes when someone answered her riddle: *"What walks on four legs in the morning, on two legs at noon, and three legs in the evening?"* Creon, regent and brother of the widowed queen Jocasta, promised he would give the throne of Thebes and his sister's hand in marriage to anyone who would rid Boeotia from this plague. Came in Oedipus, with the solution: *"Man—who crawls on all fours as a baby, then walks on two feet as an adult, and then uses a walking stick in old age."* The Sphinge then killed herself by jumping from her rock. Oedipus became Jocasta's husband and the king of Thebes.

Performed between 430 and 420 BC, Sophocles' *Oedipus the King* shows Oedipus discovering his dire destiny. The play starts with Oedipus, already king of Thebes, husband of Jocasta, and father of the four children, granting a priest a meeting. In the name of the people, the priest begs him to find the source of the plague devastating the town. After triumphing over the Sphinge, Oedipus is some kind of a superhero for the Theban people. They think he's the only one who could shed some light on the plague destroying their beautiful land: *"Didn't you free us from the tribute we were paying to the riddle monster?"* Back from Delphi where he went to consult the oracle, Creon explains that the source of the plague is the unsolved murder of Laius. Oedipus starts protesting: Why didn't they start the investigation already? What was he supposed to do with such a brother-in-law? *"It was the Sphinx—she sang her enigmatic song and thus forced us to put aside something we found obscure to look into the urgent problem we now faced,"* answers Creon sheepishly. Complaining he has to do everything in this town, Oedipus starts the investigation. He meets prophet Teiresias and when he doesn't want to answer, Oedipus brutalizes him like a cop to get him to talk. *"The plague contaminating this land comes from you,"* Teiresias finally blurts out. *"You are the murderer you're looking for."* Paranoid, Oedipus suspects the prophet of plotting against him with Creon. He questions Jocasta, but all that she can say she got from the survivor of the attack that killed Laius. An old man comes in to say that Polybus, king of Corinth and supposedly father of Oedipus, has died. He also tells Oedipus that Polybus and his wife Merope aren't his real parents. He himself entrusted the newborn Oedipus to the king and queen of Corinth. The abandoned baby had been given to him by one of Laius' servants who happened to be the survivor mentioned by Jocasta. Jocasta, having already understood, hangs herself. Oedipus stabs his own eyes so he can't see the light of day anymore and asks Creon to ban him from the city.

> Since *The Interpretation of Dreams* in 1900, the character of Oedipus has had a universal function: he has become the "complex" of all human beings, supposedly both attracted to their mothers and rival of their fathers. By focusing on the murder of the father and the intercourse with the mother, Sigmund Freud, in his theory, concealed what initially made Oedipus unique: his talent for solving riddles, his victory over the Sphinge. Jean Baudrillard went as far as saying that it's by suppressing the presence of the Sphinge that psychoanalysis was built as a technique to fight the seductive power of enigma. The tragedy of Oedipus is the tragedy of the Western world: after changing mystery into enigma and the Egyptian Sphinx into the Greek Sphinge, the West hid the Sphinge behind the mother and swapped the enigma for the *"dirty little secret"*.

This was to reckon without the strange capacity of people to act under the dictation of form. Just when their image was vanishing from our reading of Oedipus, sphinxes started to invade cities, especially Paris. It shouldn't be a surprise for a city whose name literally means *"the house of Isis"* or *"the boat of Isis"*. The first mention of Paris as a "city similar to Isis" appeared in the writings of the monk Abbo Cernuus in the tenth century. The same idea can be found in the writings of Gilles Corrozet in the fourteenth century: he explains that a statue of the Goddess Isis was standing in the Place Michel Debré, where César's Le Centaure is now standing: *"Skinny, tall, straight, black because ancient, naked at the exception of some kind of cloth piled around her limbs, it was removed by a certain Monseigneur Briçonnet, bishop of Meaux et abbot of the place around the year 1514."*

Napoleon's 1798 expedition brought Egyptianity back to Paris. In 1806, the Egyptian Fountain was built at 42 Rue de Sèvres and in 1828, the Place du Caire was covered with hieroglyphic frescoes, columns, and heads of the Hathor Goddess. There were Sphinxes on the Fontaine du Palmier, and Sphinges at the Museum of the Legion of Honor, at the Picasso Museum, and at the Hôtel de Sully. At the Sphinx-Hotel, 106 Boulevard Magenta, two Sphinx heads are still visible to this day.

It's at the Sphinx-Hotel that Léona Delcourt settled when she arrived in Paris. She had people call her Nadja, contraction of the Russian word Nadjena, *"because in Russian it's the beginning of the word hope, and because it's only the beginning."* Born near Lille, she met André Breton on October 4, 1926. The poet is thirty years old, Nadja is twenty-four, and Surrealism just two. In the book that Breton wrote about their encounter, the first part is a succession of cryptic signs of her arrival as the birth of surrealism, from Victor Hugo and Juliette Drouet repeating *"Bridle gate"* and *"Pedestrian gate"* every day (the two doors opening *Nadja* echo the doors of horn and ivory opening Gérard de Nerval's *Aurélia:* they're the two uneven doors of love, implying, maybe unconsciously, how the woman will end up devoured) to the blood (Nadja's?) among the feathers of the dovecote of the mansion where Breton worked on the book.

Breton stumbled upon Nadja in the Place Franz-Liszt. They wandered and talked together in the Gare du Nord district, unable to stop, until Breton excused himself: he had to go home, his wife was waiting for him. *"That's too bad,"* says Nadja, *"But… and this great idea of yours? I was just beginning to understand it so well. It was really a star, a star you were heading toward. You can't fail to reach it. […] It's like the heart of a heartless flower."* "Who are you?" asks Breton, mesmerized. *"I am the soul in limbo,"* answers Nadja.

For eight days, Breton and Nadja saw each other every day and felt the "signs" multiplying around them. Nadja was relating to the character of Hélène in *Soluble Fish* while Madame Sacco, clairvoyant, had told Breton that he would soon encounter a woman named Hélène. Nadja could guess the color change—from black to red—of a window in the Place Dauphine and lines just read by Breton came to her via telepathy when she described the scenery. She was often overcome by panic. *"André?... You will write a novel about me. I'm sure you will. Don't say you won't. Be careful: everything fades, everything vanishes. Something must remain of us..."* In Breton's *The Lost Steps*, Nadja discovered "The New Spirit." It describes the striking vision of a young woman in the Rue Bonaparte. This woman approaches men with an *"extraordinarily lost"* bearing, to such an extent that Breton wonders if she is under the effect of a narcotic (what he understands about the woman of the story he apparently isn't willing to understand about Nadja). What does "The New Spirit" mean? That people will from now on be under the spell of a new way of life guided by encounters with strangers? Or the search for a geographical route announcing we broke out from jail?

> The woman of "The New Spirit" is compared to a Sphinx: *"This true Sphinx in the shape of a charming young woman going from one sidewalk to another to question the passersby, this Sphinx that spared us one after the other and, to look for her, to run along all the lines that, even very capriciously, can join these points."* When they walked along the quays to the Conciergerie, Nadja told Breton: *"I've been in jail too."*

Manuel Herz

The Test Façade School
Or: Serendipity in Tambacounda

In 2017 I was commissioned by the Josef and Anni Albers Foundation to design the new maternity and pediatric hospital in Tambacounda, in eastern Senegal. The Albers Foundation has been supporting the arts and medical facilities in Senegal for the past twenty years, and the Tambacounda hospital is their biggest project to date. The city being the regional capital for eastern Senegal, it receives patients from as far away as Mali. What had convinced the Albers Foundation to commission me was my suggestion that the whole architectural design process should be one based on research and local collaboration, rather than imposing a ready-made hospital design from the outside.

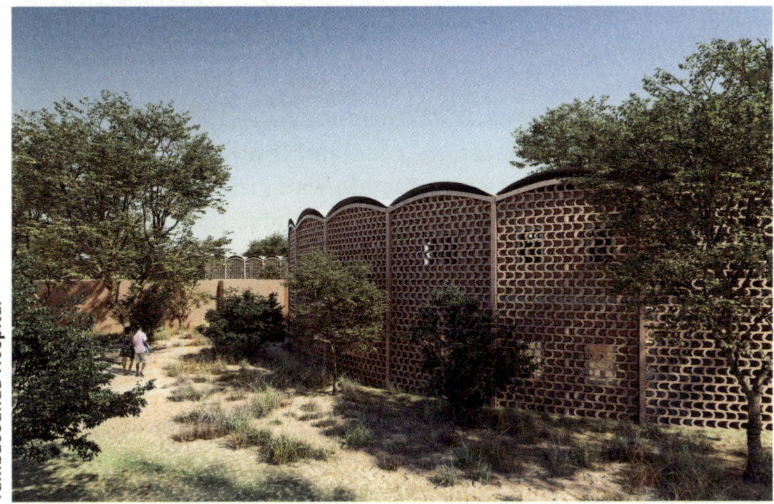

During the process it became clear that we needed to test the façade of the hospital. Based on the local climate, construction material, and local building methods, we had developed the façade as a brise-soleil to ventilate the building. Being one of the most important elements of the design, and crucial to the climatic performance of the building, we needed to find out if the bricks could be molded efficiently, what geometry of bricks we should choose, if openings in the perforated bricks were of the correct size, how much sunlight would be screened, if the flow of air would work, and what the visual effect of the bricks would be. We proposed something very typical for construction projects in the Western world: we asked the contractor, Magueye Ba, to build a test façade. The test façade, or façade mockup, would take a typical section of the façade of the hospital building. We suggested to Magueye Ba that it should be built in the back of the existing hospital compound.

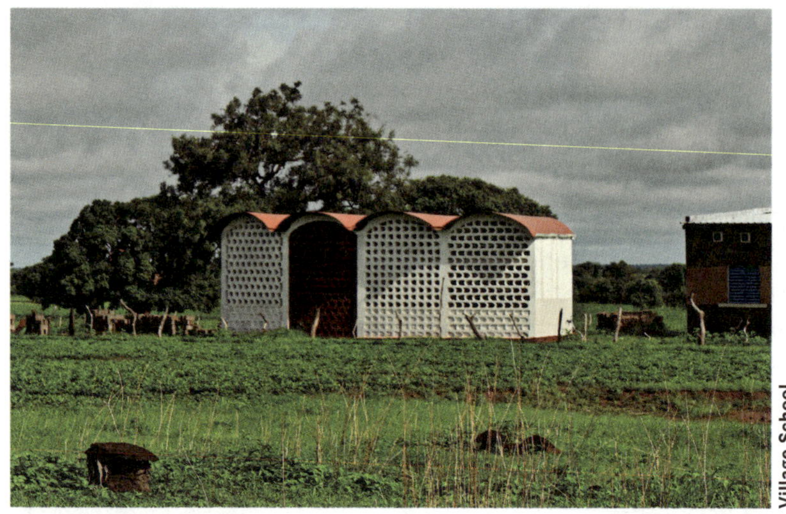

Two or three weeks later we received the first photos of the first bricks and how the test façade was growing. Subsequent photos showed more of the façade, but also left us wondering where Magueye Ba was building the wall, as we did not recognize the site. Our questions hereto were left unanswered. Eventually we received the photos of the finished wall, and were startled, or even stunned: Not only was it clear from the photos that the test façade was built somewhere in the rural regions of eastern Senegal, outside of Tambacounda. It was also not just a wall! Magueye Ba had extended the façade by three additional walls and a vaulted roof, to create a small building: it had become a village school in rural Senegal. Knowing that the small village of Makabing Sidi, approximately one hour south of Tambacounda, needed a school, Magueye Ba had decided to build the test façade in that village and to extend it into a school. He had taken my "Western" logic of erecting test facades–that are usually torn down after having looked at them for a short while–and translated it into his logic of thinking about the needs of the local community. This hybrid test façade/school was also a hybrid in terms of design: my façade design with slightly changed proportions and extended according to the design of Magueye Ba. The meeting of different minds, interests and logics had produced a completely new outcome that is characterized by hybridity and somehow due to serendipity, and in a certain way is much more beautiful than if it had been a pure object. The test façade became much more meaningful by gaining the program of a village school and an otherwise standard village school gained comfort and quality of climate and light through the use of the perforated bricks and the vaulted roof. Magueye Ba and myself can now claim joint authorship of a small school in Makabing Sidi.

These notions of hybridity and serendipity are very important to my architectural practice. Trusting chance encounters, appreciating combinations and synthesis rather than monadic purity, weaving different ideas together, and including collaborative approaches in the development of design and realization, this test façade school can stand pars pro toto for much of my architectural practice, whether it is taking place in Tambacounda, in the desert of southern Algeria, or in Zurich and Lyon.

Daniel Baumann and Marianna Simnett

Interminably Forever

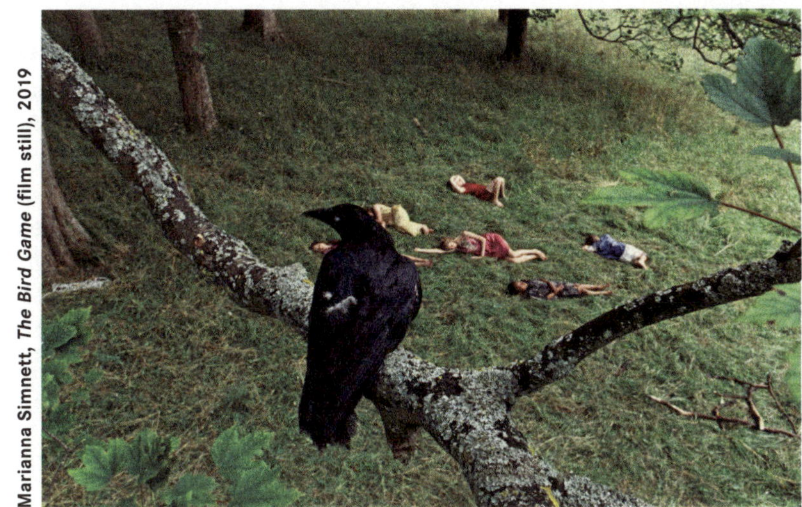

Marianna Simnett, *The Bird Game* (film still), 2019

Daniel Baumann   *The Bird Game* is a twenty-minute film about seduction and abuse. At the center of the story is a female crow who approaches a group of children playing in the grass under a big tree. She seduces them to play a game, drags them into a sumptuous castle where she kills one after the other to get access to the one girl of the group she wants to abuse. Why this intense story? Is it linked to the commission of *The Bird Game* to celebrate the 150th anniversary of the opening in 1869 of the Evelina Children's Hospital by Baron Ferdinand de Rothschild?

Marianna Simnett   I didn't start with the idea of abuse. I started by thinking about how to respond to this hospital which was founded during the Victorian era. And by questioning what sickness is today. It isn't necessarily a physical ailment but also a psychological one. So I wanted to build all of these mental worlds that were taking place architecturally and in physical space but that manifest on psychological levels inside the brain. Since the story takes place in the realm of artifice and make-believe it could be made up by the kids. The entire thing could be someone's fabrication or inner world. We see it in real space and in real time, but it takes on... like it digs into your own psychological world. So this is where it takes place, and this is why the crow can shapeshift and be kind and be cruel, even talk. It has a dream logic. I researched how crows have entered our myths and stories. They are almost always depicted as male. There's Ted Hughes's crow, and there's the raven in Noah's ark, the figure of quest, who searched for the first signs of life after the flood; there is the crow of discovery and manipulation. To feminize it was funny to me, because no one has ever done an old sexy female crow before. She has the voice of the amazing actress Joanne Whalley. So yes there is seduction, but it is not patriarchal or misogynistic because her true love is this young girl, so what we have is a lesbian avian love affair! All this confuses the politics of how you read the story as it unfolds in relation to abuse. It perverts the figure of the mother and the carer. So it is all very strange.

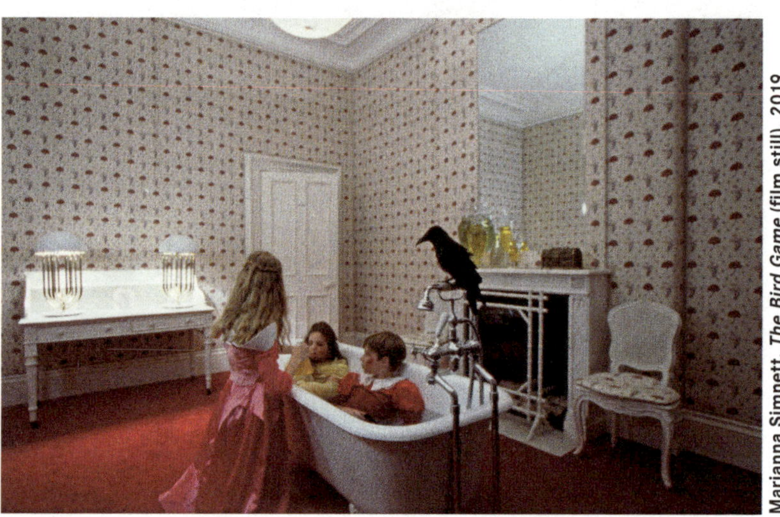

Marianna Simnett, *The Bird Game* (film still), 2019

Daniel   So within all this intense and loaded story unfolding in front of our eyes, I was struck by the strong presence of color. It's a rather gloomy story, so why is it so colorful?

Marianna   Right, since we are talking about art. Well, it's Disney, isn't it? The costume designer Kate Forbes picked Disney costumes for the children to wear in this completely oversaturated world. And the exotic colorful songbirds are referenced as jewels. They are the bait for the kids. You can't not be seduced by these gorgeous creatures. I wanted to use these Disney costumes but then destroy and vandalize them. It starts with them all dirty and covered in mud from playing and by the time they die they are in their full bling. Pristine. They even get an extra tiara or hat when they die, like power-ups in a video game. They become more and more Disneyfied as they approach their demise. Death in *The Bird Game* is blinding, bright and colorful.

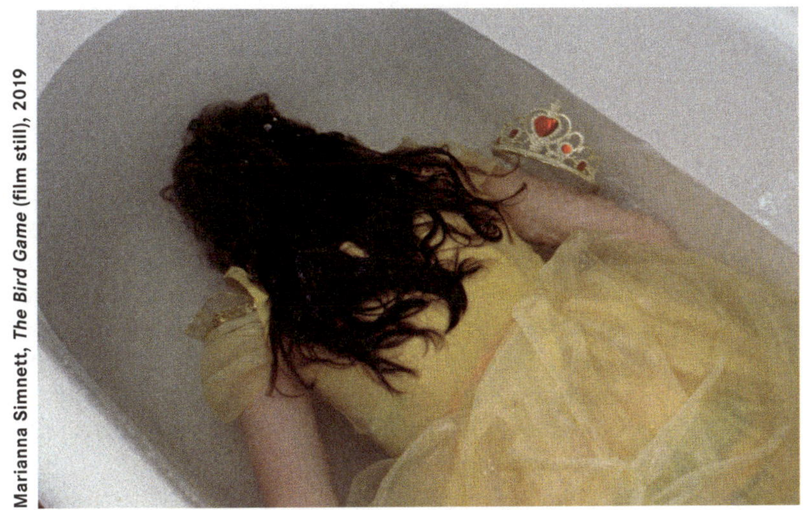

Daniel   The bright colors and the Disney reference add the twentieth century into the mix of references, from Ovid, to the Bible, to Disney. The twentieth century's fairy tale is Disney.

Marianna   The problem with Disney is they mostly have stupid endings. Why does the beast turn into a man again in *Beauty and the Beast*? Charlie Fox, co-writer of the film and author of *This Young Monster,* would puke at the thought of a perfect human. The fairy tales of today keep the beast as a beast. So in *The Bird Game* when the young Prince Philip should kiss the princess to wake her, he chokes on his own blood and dies at the point of the kiss. He was the obvious first child to kill. So I'm just taking the endings of these stories and flipping them.

Daniel   The color brings abstraction into the intense narrative. It has its own dynamic, it sometimes seems to split off and become its own thing, pretending or maybe achieving a certain autonomy from the story.

Marianna   Yes, to exist as a visual world as well. Take for example the ballroom scene. There are moments where I was thinking about Stan Brakhage and 1970s abstract experimental film. Robbie Ryan, BSC, who shot the film, used a slow frame rate when the crow was attacking to get this fast frenetic flapping. You get moments where the film could be a techno dance video, or something else entirely. With the music being so brutal, grungy, and nasty, you kind of forget about the story. You get taken in a different direction through color and sound. The composer, Oliver Coates, an extraordinary musician, didn't want to watch the film. He was blinded to it. It was two artists, me and him, working in parallel, but not looking at each other's work. We didn't want that awful thing where the music is supposed to feel sad, all that horribly manipulative music which just tugs on your emotional strings and ends up insulting the viewer because you're being told what to think. But you don't think what's prescribed because the viewer is always cleverer. We purposefully allowed for moments of disjunct in the very fabric of how we made it. We would do everything through communication, signs, signals, moods, colors, talking to each other, but not looking at each other.

Daniel   How exactly would you do this?

Marianna   I would say like: We need like a drone that sounds a bit like a brain squelch. Or I sent tracks like *The Shining* ballroom track—"Midnight, the Stars and You," by Al Bowlly & Ray Noble—or let's make this sound like dementia, and he would send me stuff by The Caretaker, who manipulates pre-existing recordings and turns them into something completely different. So much more in the realm of a feeling or the description of a mental disease which then would trigger certain sounds. I would give him a rough length, and sometimes he would send it back too long but it was so good I'd have to change things my end! He does his thing well, and I think I do too. So it was a bit like two artists having a fight, but with a lot of respect for each other.

Daniel   Do you still talk to each other?

Marianna   Just about.

Daniel   Obviously, *The Bird Game* is packed with a lot of ideas and references. We can't list and discuss them all here, but there is another motive I wanted you to ask about: sleep. It has a strong presence in the film and works like the colors: it comes in, fades away, comes back, as if it has a life of its own.

Marianna   Sleep is woven into this film. I think I was asked to do this film because of my previous work involving children, hospitals, and all things medical. I wasn't interested in making a work depicting hospitals. It was much more about the mental space they represent. You can pour into the film whatever you want about current-day anxieties people have, which is a real and growing problem. A couple of years ago I made a work called *Wing-sleepers,* commissioned by Art on the Underground, about birds that sleep on the wing while they migrate. I painted these birds, like sandpipers or swifts or frigates, who have hemispheric sleep. They can close down half of their brain and keep the other one alert for predators and flight. I started to get really into it and contacted the Max Planck Institut in Germany. They were really supportive and shared their research with me on sleeping pigeons. Military scientists are getting a hold of the fact that birds can stay awake for long periods of time and they are trying to implement this ability into soldiers on the battlefield so they can stay awake for longer. So there is a darker side to the research. It is not explicitly in the film, but it's the background research. Sleep is an important mythological theme as well: sleep associated with rape, specifically. With inertness, passivity, a lot can happen to people when they are sleeping. A lot of really interesting stuff happens in the half states, the subconscious. So sleep is really interesting, but is sometimes disregarded as silly or whimsical, or doesn't really count as real life. One of the things I got from the Max Planck Institut was EEG data from bird brains recording their brain waves when they are asleep. There is also a fascinating correlation between birds and bipolar patients because they display similarly manic slow and fast sleep waves. So now birds are helping us to understand mental health as well. There are major crossovers between birds and humans. They are also the only non mammalian species to have REM sleep. So there has been a whole cauldron of research that has fed into the film. The data recorded from the sleeping pigeons looks like a column of numbers. Pretty boring. But if you plot those coordinates into a score it would make music that sounded a bit like very jittery erratic waves. You can trace the numerical wave patterns. There are anomalies where the numbers don't fit the model. That's why the music in the brain data was really interesting to me. You can take the data and turn it into a musical score. We didn't do it, but we were looking at it.

Daniel   Are you going to use all this for new works?

Marianna   With sleep and data, I would like to do something live. A performance. With *The Bird Game*, I wanted to make a film without forcing all this information into it. I wanted people to just enjoy it.

Daniel   Interesting. The other question I had was about play. At the beginning of the film, the kids stay outside and play, they are invited to a game by the crow, to *The Bird Game*, and continue to play in the castle. Ultimately, play turns into death. Play is innocent and not. What is your take on play?

Marianna   James Bridle's book and work on the Internet is important in this context. Before writing *New Dark Age: Technology and the End of the Future*, he wrote the widely read text online called *Something Is Wrong With the Internet*. He talks about video farms where algorithms are self-producing content and how something like an apparently innocent Aladdin kids animation will suddenly show Aladdin having his head chopped off and all these violent things happening. Because an algorithm has produced it, and YouTube plays the next one automatically. Once you watch one video another one appears straight away, a variation of the one before. The parents have no idea, they just stick their kids in front of it, assuming all is okay. So you go through these permutations and all these children are being surreptitiously abused and traumatized by content that isn't really supposed to be for them because a computer is deciding what to make. I was thinking about that gaming and algorithmic decision-making and the responsibilities behind that. An older version of the film had the songbirds' heads popping off, and things that suddenly turn nasty, but completely accidentally.

Daniel   It is still there in the film though. For instance when the young prince comes to give the kiss, and then instead he chokes and spits blood. As if the algorithm had changed the narrative.

Marianna   Or when his friend says: "Wake up, stop playing." He doesn't wake up because he is dead. We shot it in this elaborate, gorgeous, baroque style, like they are in a fantasy castle in a game. I have licence to kill them because they can get up again, they are ghosts in a world of avatars. And shooting it on 16 mm made it extra exciting and complicated. Imagine shooting birds and kids on 16 mm. It's a recipe for disaster! These are the challenges I wanted to take on in this highly digital and technologized era.

Daniel   The technique forced you into a contrast to what you wanted to film, uncontrollable birds and volatile children, creating a contradiction. With the game as being an analogue activity, but nowadays is a very digital thing. Basically, you were always too late with your camera, or even wrong.

Marianna   Exactly. In video you can just shoot again and again forever. 16 mm had really extreme limits imposed on us and we couldn't shoot past a certain amount, because we didn't have the stock. It's expensive, and you just have to be very precise and enjoy the ride.

Daniel   I like the part when the film takes off into a different direction as in the scene with the blue bed. It is awkward, the acting, the colors, the sound, as if the film abandoned itself. There is a distancing moment in there, which I find intriguing, before you get dragged back into the narrative. So in the end, the girl who is left after all the others have died, jumps out of the window.

Marianna   Yes, the winner of the game.

Daniel   Exactly, the one the crow wants. She jumps out of the window and flies away as a crow. Why?

Marianna   Because she wins the game, and the winner transforms into a bird that never sleeps. They are the same character the whole way through, the old and the young crow. The old crow tells her story of how she transformed into a bird when she was twelve or thirteen. The young girl adopts the same story, sees her hands turn into wings, so there is a mirroring.

Daniel   So the victim becomes the predator and the other way around.

Marianna   Interminably forever.

Daniel   Not a very optimistic outlook.

Marianna   Well, how do you hold in your head the idea of a child suicide, which is what that scene is. If you look at it more bleakly, it's a young girl jumping out of the window and being coerced into doing so by a bird, which also could happen. But I wanted the lasting image to be one of transformation. We see a bird flying at the end, not death. It changes the story completely.

Daniel   Which brings us to transformation, the power of transformation. How big is that power? What is its potential? Is it illusionary? Is it just a tool for some hope, a man-made device for survival? Or is it real?

Marianna   No, I think it is real. And I think the world is wrong to think that this isn't actually the natural state of things. The idea of an identity or body being fixed is an illusion. So my mantra around transformation, which I am never tired of talking about because it just carries through all of my work, is that we are in transformative states all the time. It is optimistic, but it also feels very real. I am not the same body from one day to the next, I feel completely mutable and transformative in so many ways. It's not false optimism, it is a realistic position.

Daniel   Is it restless?

Marianna   Yes, it's restless.

Daniel   Would it not be nice to have a break?

Marianna   The point for me is that it is a continuous transformation. It's not about what you become. You keep transforming again, like a caterpillar, and you are constantly in a state of expending energy.

Daniel   Yet the film goes in both directions. There is the loop, or the circle in the way the girl becomes crow becomes girl. On the other hand you have the narrative and a narrative is always about transformation, it is at the very core of narration:

one thing happens after another, things change and lead to
another thing. The loop is contrary to this, it always gets back
to the start again. In *The Bird Game,* transformation loops
start over and over again. These two movements are obviously
very human, and natural: the days, months, seasons, years,
24/7 and then our lives from birth to death.

Marianna   It is true, the film is linear and a loop at the same
time. But the loop is loaded! Through the simplest repetition,
our little nymphet is now our predator.

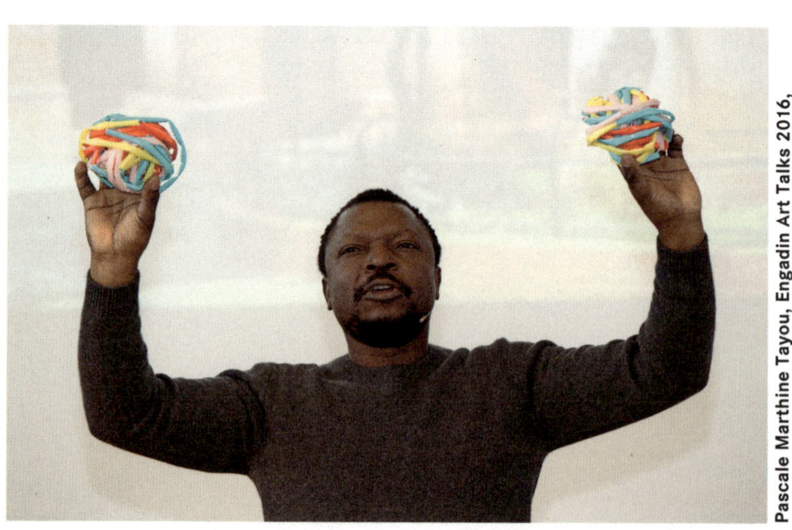

Pascale Marthine Tayou, Engadin Art Talks 2016,
Traces & Fragments

Postcard
Zvi Hecker

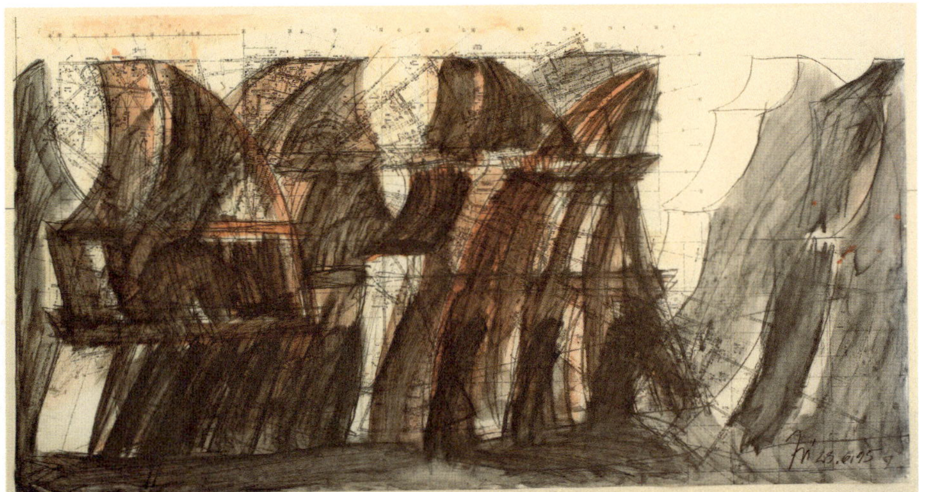

I Draw Because I Have to Think

Computer drawings are a necessary means of communication between the architect and his or her collaborators, and eventually with the construction people on site.

Sketches and hand drawings are less in demand these days, though their importance and usefulness have lost none of their validity. The significance and uniqueness of hand drawings lies not in the clarity of their message but in their inherent imperfection. They communicate with no one but their creator.

As our mind is never in complete control of our hand, it is free to create signs, left open for interpretation. Not once was I surprised at how hand drawing can evoke possibilities that most probably I would not have been able to imagine consciously.

As arguably the most complex of all arts, architecture has had to address many contradictory demands and conflicting interests within its overall design. No successful solution can be reached by sequential analysis but rather by intuitive synthesis.

In this respect, hand drawings help to channel the vague ponderings of the mind into visual images of a germinating concept. It is then up to the eyes to trace and decode its meaning.

The architect's way of thinking is through his eyes.

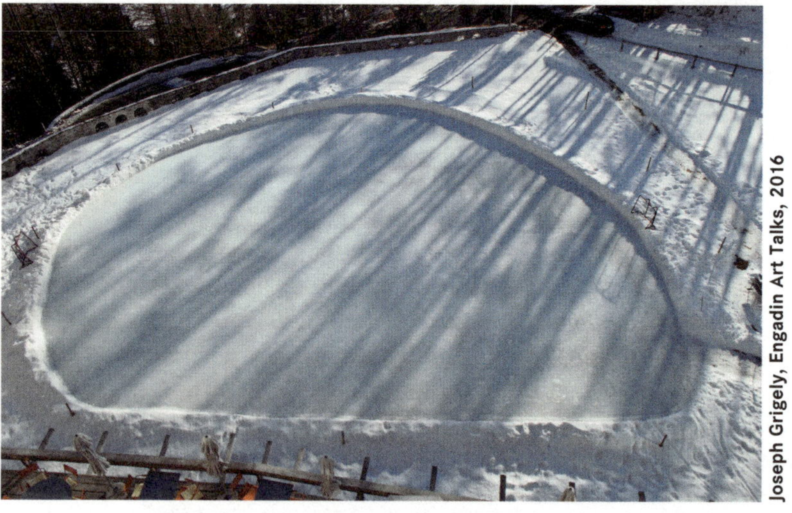

Joseph Grigely, Engadin Art Talks, 2016

One day in 1920, Robert Musil wrote in his diary a curious fragment: "construct a person from nothing but quotations." Everyday conversations tend to be evanescent and fleeting, so how can one collect these quotations? In my case, it comes from being deaf, and asking people to write down what they are saying—and the scraps of paper onto which people have written their daily conversations become a record of their voices and a construction of who they are, not only in words, but also in marks, smudges and lines.

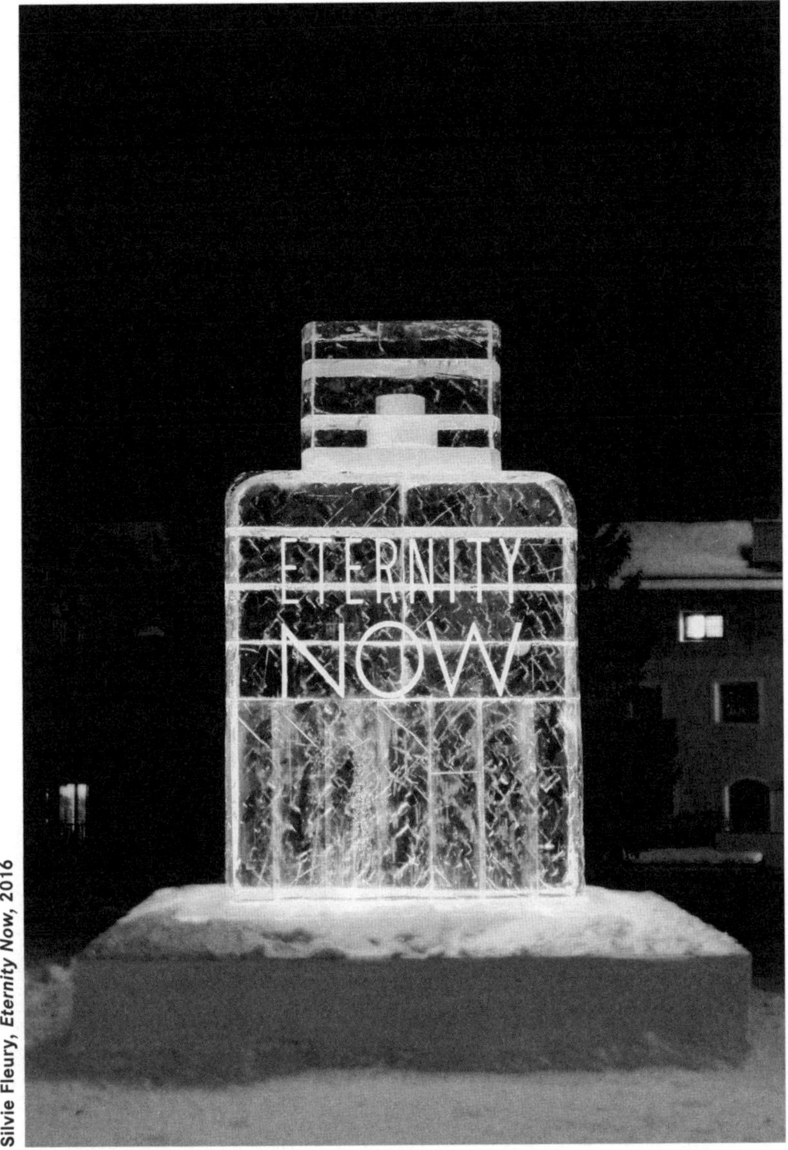

Silvie Fleury, *Eternity Now*, 2016

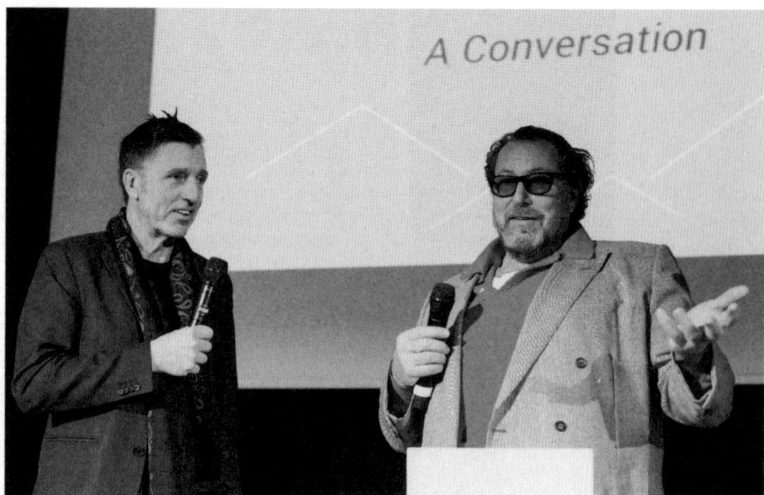

Albert Oehlen and Julian Schnabel, Engadin Art Talks
2016, Traces & Fragments

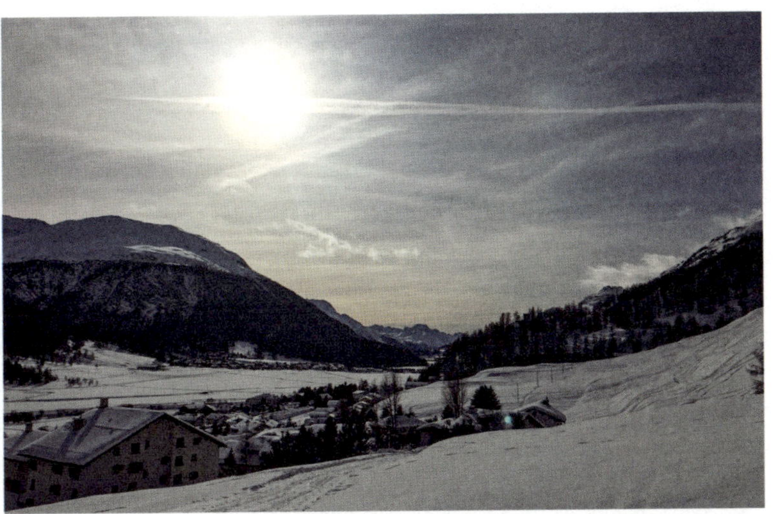

Ravit Helled, Engadin Art Talks 2019

It was my first time in Zuoz, and I was overwhelmed by the beauty of the place. In particular, it was amazing to look at the sky at night, as so many stars could be seen; it felt like the ideal place for an astrophysicist. Nor did I know what to expect from the talks, which also turned out to be a very positive surprise: there was an excellent overall atmosphere and I could feel the good energy of the participants. I felt as if I had landed on a different planet, and by pure luck. Hearing talks about art by the diverse speakers was very refreshing, and it definitely opened my mind.

Overall, it was a wonderful experience, and it made me a little bit envious of the artistic community, while at the same time motivated me to try to be a part of it. I hope I will reconnect with some of the interesting people I met there, and I deeply thank the organizers for inviting me as a speaker.

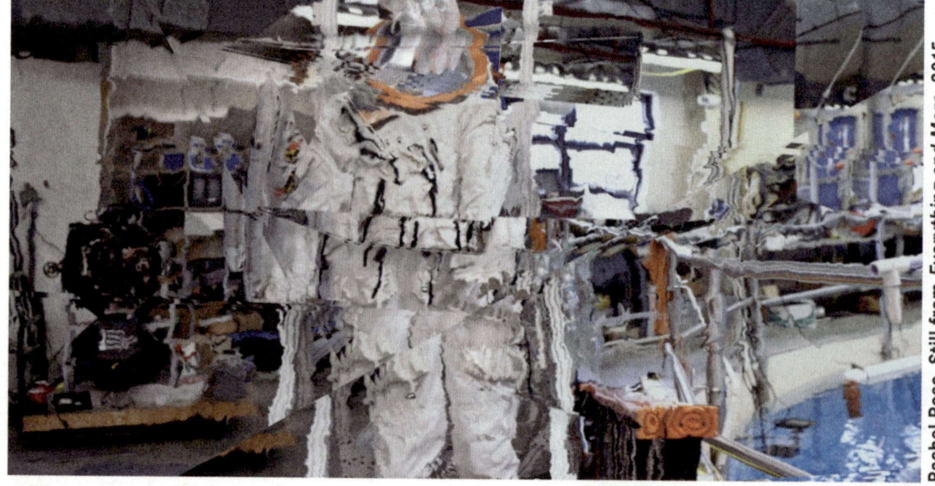

Rachel Rose, Still from *Everything and More*, 2015

Postcard — Joanna Leśnierowska

On an autumn afternoon in 1960, Yves Klein put on a suit, jumped from a roof and hung in mid-air. With his arms confidently outstretched and a look of elation on his face, he defied the laws of gravity and "proved" that he could fly. With his act, executed six months before Gagarin's historic escapade, he claimed to denounce the moon race. "A man in space! The painter of space leaps into the void!" was how he captioned the photograph of the leap, and with this he landed, forever, in the history of the avant-garde. The photographic "record" was, of course, a photomontage, and the courageously leaping Klein was awaited not by a void but by his unrestricted faith in the power of art and the necessity of questioning the obvious. That, and the outstretched arms of a circle of people holding a safety net.

> Symbolically initiated by Klein, the "practice of leaping into," as an act of both protest and affirmation, has made its way into broadly defined contemporary culture, and has become one of the constitutive elements of contemporary choreography.

So did I spread my wings on a January afternoon in 2019 to introduce to an E.A.T. audience Muzeum Susch's ACZIUN—the choreographic program within which we wish to engage in many many "leaps into"

> to express our frenetic faith in the body

acting, thinking, experiencing, vibrating, the body-object and the body-process, the dreaming body, the becoming-body and the (self-)transforming body, which is fluid, material and fictional, kaleidoscopic, autonomous, social and political, radically stripped down and exposing

> the body which is involved, multivocal, resonating, dialogic and dialectic, defying and embracing laws of gravity, balancing on the edge of a jittery world in an act of survival

the body in (constant) movement the dancing body
leaping bravely into the unknown
and landing safely in a community

> just as I could land with grace in the so generously supportive community of Engadin on a January afternoon in 2019.

Together we will leap, jump, hop, sway, and pulsate; we will rock, bounce, levitate, fly and fall, and jump up all over again

> until the Alps shake.
> And we hope we will never stop!

DOUG AITKEN, born in California in 1968, lives and works in Los Angeles and New York. He is widely known for his innovative fine art installations; his body of work ranges from photography, sculpture, and architectural interventions to films, sound, single- and multi-channel video works, and installations. His eye leads us into a world where time, space, and memory are fluid concepts.

NAIRY BAGHRAMIAN lives and works in Berlin. She predominantly works with sculpture, photography, and text. Her art has been widely exhibited, including at the Skulptur Projekten 07 in Münster (2007); at the Kunsthalle Basel (2006) and the Kunsthalle Baden-Baden (2008), both solo exhibitions; and together with Phyllida Barlow at the Serpentine Gallery London (2010). In 2011 her work was shown at the 54th Venice Biennale.

CECILIA BENGOLEA is a performance artist with a particular interest in dance anthropologies. Since 2005 she has collaborated with François Chaignaud, with companies including Lyon Opera Ballet and Tanztheater Wuppertal Pina Bausch, recruiting them to challenge their usual repertoires and style with a fresh and experimental edge.

MATTHIAS BRUNNER began his career as movie buff, critic, film producer and film curator for arthouse movies in Switzerland. He has collaborated with many film festivals including Filmex and the American Cinematheque in Los Angeles, the Locarno Film Festival, and the Zürich Film Festival. In 1992 he became a film curator for Art Basel and a member of the European Film Academy.

ISO CAMARTIN is a Swiss essayist and journalist. He was Professor of Rhaeto-Romanic Literature and Culture at the Swiss Federal Institute of Technology (ETH) and at the University of Zurich from 1985 to 1997. In this capacity he taught and researched on linguistic and cultural minorities, and the cultural history of the Alpine region.

JULIAN CHARRIÈRE is a French-Swiss artist whose work bridges the realms of environmental science and cultural history. Marshalling performance, sculpture, and photography, his projects often stem from fieldwork in remote locations with acute geophysical identities such as volcanoes, ice-fields, and radioactive sites.

CLAUDIA COMTE is a Swiss artist whose work is defined by her interest in the memory of materials and by careful observation of how the hand relates to different technologies. Her artistic output, of which her playful site-specific installations are best-known, is guided by a distinct rule-measurement system of her own creation, wherein each artwork specifically relates to one another.

HANS DANUSER is one of the pioneers of contemporary photography in Switzerland. In addition to photography, since the 1990s,

Danuser has also been exploring a range of issues associated with "art in and with architecture" in various media and materials. His works have been shown in important exhibitions both in Switzerland and abroad, and he has participated in international events such as the Venice and Lyon Biennales.

ANDREA DEPLAZES is an architect who lives and works in Chur and Zurich. In 1988 he finished his studies at the ETH Zurich under Professor Fabio Reinhardt. In the same year, together with Valentin Bearth, he founded the architectural office Bearth & Deplazes AG in Chur, which they now run together with Daniel Ladner. The bureau's best-known project is the new Monte Rosa SAC-hut (2009).

ELIZABETH DILLER is a founding partner of Diller Scofidio + Renfro (DS+R), a New York-based design studio whose practice spans the fields of architecture, urban design, installation art, multi-media performance, digital media, and print. She is a fellow of the American Academy of Arts and Letters and the American Academy of Arts and Sciences, and an International Fellow of the Royal Institute of British Architects, as well as Professor of Architecture at Princeton University.

CERITH WYN EVAN'S conceptual practice incorporates a wide range of media, including installation works, sculptures, photography, film, and text. He has participated in numerous group exhibitions internationally, including the Venice Biennale (1995, 2003 and 2009) and the Venice Architecture Biennale (2010), the International Istanbul Biennial (2005), and documenta 11 (2002).

SYLVIE FLEURY is a Swiss artist known for her mises-en-scène of glamor, fashion, and luxury products. Her artwork, which has been compared to Andy Warhol's Pop Art and Duchamp's ready-mades, aims to critique and comment on the superficiality of consumer society and its behavior. Through recontextualizing something superficial, she aims to add intrinsic value to the presented object.

HAMISH FULTON is a "walking artist" who lives and works in Canterbury, UK. Studying sculpture at the Central Saint Martins College of Art and the Royal College of Art in London in the 1960s, he started to explore his travels as fundaments of his artwork. This practice brought him to various mountains worldwide, including the Engadin.

GIORGIO GRIFFA is an Italian abstract painter best known for his images painted on raw materials such as un-stretched canvas, linen, and burlap. Although Griffa never received a formal art education, he immediately showed an exclusive interest in painting and joined the art world working as an assistant to painter Filippo Scropp. In the early 1970s, the painter left his practice of figurative painting to explore abstraction, that still characterizes his unique artistic style.

JOSEPH GRIGELY creates work that is fundamentally about conversations. As he is profoundly deaf, his works are based on daily life experiences and the scraps of paper on which people communicate with him. Through his work, a combination of notes and sounds, he examines the themes of communication, language, and perception.

ZVI HECKER is a Polish-born Israeli architect whose work is known for being asymmetrical and metabolist in style. Hecker is a poet of form; he has also worked in painting and sculpture. He is often referred to as an artist whose profession is that of an architect, and his output has been compared to that of Antonio Gaudí for its expressiveness and expansion of architectural ideas.

RAVIT HELLED is an Israeli planetary scientist and a professor for Theoretical Astrophysics at the Institute for Computational Science, Center for Theoretical Astrophysics & Cosmology, University of Zurich. Her scientific work concentrates on planet formation, planetary interiors, and extra-solar planets. She is also strongly involved in space exploration and is a science team member of various ESA and NASA space missions.

LENA HENKE is a German artist. She has developed a diverse body of sculptural works, often arranged in comprehensive spatial installations. Henke's work references urban planning, Land Art, human relationships, sexuality, and fetishism, consistently infiltrating the patriarchal structure of art history with an intelligent and humorous tone. Her formal language and use of materials often allude to Minimal Art, vividly combined with Surrealist imagery, to examine the structures of street life and the ideas of city planners and urban theorists such as Jane Jacobs, Roberto Burle Marx, and Robert Moses.

MANUEL HERZ is an architect based in Basel, Switzerland. His projects include the Synagogue of Mainz, housing projects in Germany, Switzerland, and France, and a museum extension in Ashdod (Israel). He has taught at the ETH Zürich and Harvard GSD, and is currently Professor of Urban and Territorial Design at the University of Basel. His research focuses on the relationship between migration, architecture, nation building, and spaces of refuge.

THOMAS HIRSCHHORN is a Swiss artist known for his immersive environments, which challenge the viewer to navigate spaces that have been inundated by the artifacts of consumption. Combining found imagery and texts, bound up in low-tech constructions of cardboard, foil, and packing tape, he stages imagistic assaults in a DIY fashion that overwhelm our senses and defy our expectations.

BETHAN HUWS is a Welsh artist. Language is at the center of her conceptual work. She explores this topic in a range of media, spatial interventions, objects, and textual works. Her delicate, often filigree works are always mysterious and mystical at heart. They often connect with the beginnings of Modern Art, in particular Marcel Duchamp, whose work Huws refers to in several of her creations.

KOO JEONG A is a South Korean visual artist known for her minimal installation art. She uses diverse types of media, such as drawings and photographs; however, she works primarily on the invention of spaces. The major aim of her interventions is to place the soul in that space, by organizing everyday objects in an extremely precise manner, through which new spatial structures and perspectives arise.

ERLING KAGGE is a Norwegian polar explorer and was the first in history to reach the "three poles"–North, South, and the summit of Mt Everest–on foot. In 1993 he became the first person ever to walk alone to the South Pole. Kagge has written eight books on exploration, philosophy, art collecting, and silence. His books have been published in thirty-nine languages. Based in Norway, Erling searches for moments of peace amidst a life with three noisy daughters, and works as a writer and publisher.

JOANNA LEŚNIROWSKA is a Polish dance curator and writer, dramaturge, and performance-maker. She has published in major Polish professional papers as well as abroad (in Germany, Israel, and the Czech Republic, amongst others), has lectured at the Universities of Poznan and Cracow, and has given many speeches abroad on Polish dance and contemporary choreography. In 2004 she created the first official dance space / choreographic development center within the Art Stations Foundation in Poland.

NIKLAS MAAK is an architecture theoretician who has undertaken continuous research on the history of mass housing, and models to re-engage with communal dwelling and collective housing. He has pursued parallel careers as a writer, educator, newspaper editor, architect, and visiting professor. For his essays, Maak has been awarded the George F. Kennan Award (2009), the prestigious Henri Nannen Prize in Germany (2012), and the COR Prize for architectural critique (2014).

SARAH MORRIS is an American artist. She has produced a large body of work using both painting and film, which create a new language of place and politics. Morris' paintings and films contain elements that complement and connect to one another, generating a constant back-and-forth play between the two. Within the framework, Morris' work plays with social and bureaucratic typologies to implicate occluded systems of control.

EILEEN MYLES is an American poet and writer who has worked in fiction, non-fiction, and theater. She is considered one of the savviest and most restless intellects in contemporary literature. Her audacious and singular poems relay thoughts and experiences in a genuine lyrical language.

ERNESTO NETO studied sculpture at the renowned Escola de Artes Visuais do Parque Lage in Rio de Janeiro. A large proportion of his artworks take the form of expansive biomorphic sculptures, which are always conceived for specific exhibition settings. They are made of elastic fabrics and can be entered, stroked, and caressed by viewers.

ISABEL NOLAN is a Dublin-based artist. Her multi-disciplinary artistic output, which encompasses sculpture, textiles, paintings, drawings, photography, and writing, explores notions of reality and identity, and the human compulsion to understand and define our situations and relationships with others.

ALBERT OEHLEN was born in 1954, in Krefeld, and lives near Zurich in the eastern part of Switzerland. He remains among the most innovative and controversially discussed artists of today. In his work, traditional painterly expression is infused with a steely reference to technology. His art offers a raw confrontation with the deficiencies of visual language.

GIANNI PETTENA is an Italian architect, artist, and critic, as well as being Professor of History of Contemporary Architecture at the University of Florence, and Professor of Design at California State University. Along with Archizoom, Super-studio, and Ufo, he belongs to the original nucleus of the Italian radical architecture movement. Pettena has exhibited at the Venice Biennale, the Barbican Center in London, the Centre Pompidou in Paris, and the FRAC Center in Orléans.

PHILIPPE RAHM is a Swiss architect, and the principal of the firm Philippe Rahm architectes, based in Paris. His work, which extends the field of architecture from the physiological to the meteorological, has received an international audience in the context of sustainability.

TOBIAS REHBERGER is a German artist. With his various forms of artistic output, including sculptures, industrial objects, and handcrafted articles, he explores the wider sphere of structural design and architecture, thriving on chance connections and unexpected encounters. Rehberger undermines artistic ideals such as genius and authenticity, and questions forms of presentation, functionality, and perception. In 2009, he was awarded the Golden Lion at the Venice Biennale.

RACHEL ROSE is an American visual artist known for dreamlike video and installation works that address how we define mortality. Her subjects range from zoos and a robotics perception lab, to Philip Johnson's Glass House, the American Revolutionary War and nineteenth-century park design. She anchors these sites in a range of perspectives on death—from our vulnerability to catastrophe to the impact of history on our lifespan.

HANS JOERG RUCH is a Swiss architect. In 1989, he set up his own practice in St. Moritz. Besides architectural work in farmhouses and patricia houses in the Engadin, his main projects have included the extension of Hotel Saratz, Pontresina, and the renovation of the Segantini Museum in St. Moritz.

ROLF SACHS is a conceptual artists and designer whose work never fails to intrigue and surprise audiences, pushing them to question preconceptions. His multidisciplinary approach is playful and inventive, and encourages human interaction, as well as provoking emotional and sensory reactions.

TOMÁS SARACENO is an Argentinian artist known for his floating sculptures, community projects, and interactive installations that propose and explore new, sustainable ways of inhabiting and sensing the environment. His oeuvre could be seen as an ongoing research, informed by the worlds of art, architecture, natural sciences, astrophysics, and engineering.

MICHAEL SCHINDHELM is a writer, filmmaker, performing arts expert, and cultural advisor for international organizations. Previously, he worked as a director and cultural advisor in Basel, Berlin, Dubai, Hong Kong, Moscow, and Zurich.

JULIAN SCHNABEL is an American painter and filmmaker. In the 1980s, Schnabel received international media attention for his "plate paintings"—large-scale paintings set on broken ceramic plates. Schnabel directed *Before Night Falls,* which became Javier Bardem's breakthrough Academy Award-nominated role, and *The Diving Bell and the Butterfly,* which was nominated for four Academy Awards.

MARIANNA SIMNETT lives and works in London. Through performance, video, watercolor, and installation, she challenges how bodies are perceived and imagined. Uncanny narratives display the body as a site of dispute, performing surgical interventions and gestures of collapse and ecstasy.

PASCALE MARTHINE TAYOU is a Cameroonian artist. His work is deliberately mobile, elusive of pre-established schema, and heterogeneous. Tayou's objects, sculptures, installations, drawings, and videos have a recurrent feature in common: they dwell upon an individual moving through the world and exploring the issue of the global village.

JUERGEN TELLER is a German fine-art and fashion photographer. In his unique portraits of models intermingling their celebrity lifestyle with the everyday, Teller examines social constructions of beauty. His work is distinctive for its candid feel, regularly depicting his subjects in isolated surroundings with washed-out, overexposed light, often with unguarded expressions, and seemingly unposed.

PACÔME THIELLEMENT was born in 1975 in Paris to a French father and an Egyptian mother. He directs experimental films and writes essays, mostly on pop culture, art, poetry, and gnosis.

OSCAR TUAZON is an artist. His practice encompasses a wide diversity of large-scale sculptures and installations that cross the line between art and architecture, form and function. Inspired by what is called "outlaw-architecture" (a kind of extreme DIY architecture), his works explore the physical space and refer to minimalism. Tuazon's works, which are characterized by a combination of natural and industrial materials such as wood, concrete, and metal, are structures and installations that can be used, occupied, and engaged with by viewers.

ADRIÁN VILLAR ROJAS is an Argentinian artist. He has built his practice across numerous media to create immersive environments and experiences that seem to be in a state of perpetual space-time travel. Evolving over the years towards the design of topography-based, mutant, organic-inorganic systems, he invites viewers to explore an unpredictable microcosmos of his own creation.

NOT VITAL was born in 1948 in Sent in the Engadin. At the age of fourteen, he was sent to high school in Chur, and later studied art for two years at the Centre universitaire expérimental de Vincennes before spending two years in Rome where he had a small circus. Unable to make a living as a fire-eater and juggler, in 1974 he moved to New York, where he had a studio till 2012. Now he lives and tries to work in Sent, Beijing, and Rio de Janeiro.

NINA VON ALBERTINI lives in Paspels (Grisons, Switzerland). After working as a jewelry designer in Milano and New York, she studied agronomics and soil physics at the Swiss Federal Institute of Technology (ETH), Zurich, and conducted research at the ETH's Institute of Terrestrial Ecology. In 2001, she founded an office for environmental engineering and landscape architecture in Paspels. Her goal is for environmental issues to become a key factor in large-scale construction projects, especially if they are realized in vulnerable natural environments.

LAWRENCE WEINER creates sculptures in the medium of language. Weiner always publishes his language works in his publications first, and subsequently on billboards, on house fronts, in newspapers, or in exhibition spaces. In Zuoz he realized a work for Hotel Castell (1999/2004).

PETER ZUMTHOR is a Swiss architect known for his exploration of the tactile sensory qualities of spaces and materials. Zumthor trained as a cabinet maker in his father's shop, and as a designer and architect at the Kunstgewerbeschule Basel and at the Pratt Institute, New York. In 1979, he established his own practice in Haldenstein, Switzerland, where he still works. He won the Pritzker Architecture Prize laureate in 2009 and was awarded the RIBA Royal Medal in 2013.

A big thank you to Katharina de Vaivre for organizing the talks for many years and to Patricia Mosquera for her work on this publication. Last but not least many thanks to Finn Canonica, editor-in-chief of *Das Magazin,* and the mastermind behind this book. Cristina Bechtler

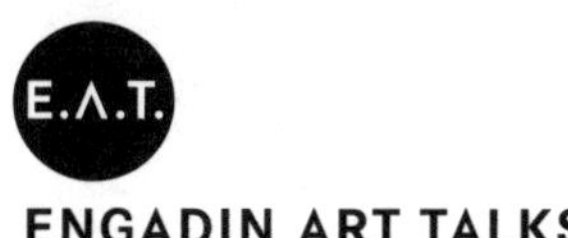

ENGADIN ART TALKS

For their generous support we thank:

GEORG UND BERTHA
SCHWYZER-WINIKER
STIFTUNG

ZUOZ

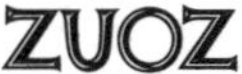

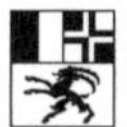
Kulturförderung Graubünden. Amt für Kultur
Promoziun da la cultura dal Grischun. Uffizi da cultura
Promozione della cultura dei Grigioni. Ufficio della cultura
SWISSLOS

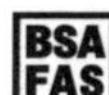
Bund Schweizer Architekten
Fédération des Architectes Suisses
Federazione Architetti Svizzeri
BSA Zürich

Thinking in Thin Air
An Anthology of a Decade: Engadin Art Talks
Edited by Finn Canonica for Engadin Art Talks

Editorial concept: Cristina Bechtler, Finn Canonica
Assistance: Patricia Mosquera
Design: Atelier Landolt Pfister
Coordination: Max Wild
Copyediting and proofreading: Sarah Quigley
Lithography, printing and binding: DZA Druckerei zu Altenburg
Paper: Munken Print White 18, 90 gsm

Lars Müller is supported by the Swiss Federal
Office of Culture with a structural contribution for
the years 2016–2020.

Lars Müller Publishers
Zürich, Switzerland
www.lars-mueller-publishers.com

ISBN 978-3-03778-624-6

Distributed in North America by ARTBOOK | D.A.P.
www.artbook.com

Printed in Germany